In TUNE with God

To order additional copies of *In Tune With God*, by Lilianne Doukhan, call 1-800-765-6955.

Visit us at **www.autumnhousepublishing.com** for information on other Autumn House® products.

In Tune with God

LILIANNE DOUKHAN

Published by Autumn House® Publishing, a division of Review and Herald® Publishing, Hagerstown, MD 21741-1119

Autumn House® titles may be purchased in bulk for educational, business, fund-raising, or sales promotional use. For information, please e-mail SpecialMarkets@reviewandherald.com.

Autumn House® Publishing publishes biblically based materials for spiritual, physical, and mental growth and Christian discipleship.

The author assumes full responsibility for the accuracy of all facts and quotations as cited in this book.

Unless otherwise noted, all Bible texts are from the *Holy Bible, New International Version.* Copyright © 1973, 1978, 1984, International Bible Society. Used by permission of Zondervan Bible Publishers.

Texts credited to NKJV are from the New King James Version. Copyright © 1979, 1980, 1982 by Thomas Nelson, Inc. Used by permission. All rights reserved.

This book was
Edited by Jan Schleifer
Cover designed by Ron J. Pride
Interior designed by Tina M. Ivany
Cover art by Jupiter Images
Typeset:Bembo 11/14

PRINTED IN U.S.A.

14 13 12 11 10   5 4 3 2 1

Library of Congress Cataloging-in-Publication Data
Doukhan, Lilianne.
  In tune with God : the challenge of music in worship / Lilianne Doukhan.
     p. cm.
  Includes bibliographical references and index.
1. Church music. 2. Music in churches. 3. Music—Religious aspects—Christianity. I. Title.
  ML3001.D68 2009
  264'.2—dc22
                                2009037334
ISBN 978-0-8127-0500-3

To My Students

Table of Contents

Prologue:
In Defense of Music

I am writing this book in defense of music. I am a music lover. My life has been filled with—and fulfilled by—music, starting with piano lessons at the age of 4 and continuing through my conservatory degree in piano performance, my studies in organ, and my Ph.D. in musicology. Awakened and nourished in my childhood by the sounds of eastern European folk music, my love for music took off to farther shores, embracing the strains of the simple church hymn and the wonders of the great classical works. Later, after having the privilege to live a number of years immersed in Hebrew, Arabic, African, Indian, and even Chinese cultures, I also developed a love for the sometimes strange but always intriguing resonances of various musics of the world. My activities as a church musician, beginning at an early age, have added practical insight to my work in church music, and, together with my academic background, today inform my contribution as chair of the Worship and Music Commission at Pioneer Memorial Church, on the campus of Andrews University in Michigan.

Much has been said about music during my journey through life so far, and much is still being said. Too much of what I have heard is vilifying, accusing, destroying. Fifteen years ago the Seventh-day Adventist Theological Seminary of Andrews University asked me to develop a course in the philosophy of church music and to consult with pastors, churches, and musicians all around the world who had a burden for worship music. These past 15 years of my teaching career have given me the opportunity to reflect about this subject, to research what really happened in history, to observe, analyze, share, and discuss experiences and thoughts about music with people from a great spectrum of cultures. Often, other people's reactions to music left me surprised or perplexed, and obliged me to learn to listen to others even more carefully and to open my mind to different and new understandings of music. I wrestled with questions and sought answers, but music always remained for me a wonderful companion and source of inspiration.

The time has come to speak up in defense of music. What was meant to be a most beautiful gift to humanity has often become a source of discord, disgust, hatred, and separation. It is time to come to the rescue of music and to give it back its innocence and dignity.

This book does not want to add to the interminable debate about music. While it does dissipate or correct some misconceptions along the way, its purpose is not to criticize, destroy, or prove wrong existing theories and opinions. Rather, it proposes to look outside personal opinions and preferences to find objective criteria that can transcend subjective approaches and help formulate a balanced and informed opinion about these important matters. I am a strong believer in the principle that one of the best ways to counteract error is to implant the truth.[1]

When dealing with religious matters such as music in worship, it seems only natural to turn to the Sacred Scriptures to find wisdom, counsel, and guidance. This is one of the major aims of this book. In addition, I will frequently refer to the writings of Ellen G. White, which are abundant on the topic, and filled with great insight and common sense. Further, I will look at history to draw lessons from the experiences of the church in the past and to see how problems similar to today's were dealt with in other times and places. Finally, practical lessons will be drawn to apply what has been learned to the reality of musical practice and discussion in the church.

Before any study about music can be undertaken, it is important to understand the process of music: what it is made of, how it functions, and what determines our reaction to it. Here, too, many misunderstandings and preconceptions need to be weeded out so that discussions and dialogue may rest on facts and reality rather than on imagination and perpetuated myths. In order to be convincing in one's argument, it is important to look for *truth* in matters of music.

I invite you to follow me on this journey through the intricacies of music and the musical experience, especially—but not exclusively—as they relate to practices in the church.[2]

At this point I would like to express my gratitude to a number of individuals who have accompanied me on my journey in music and in one way or another, though always significantly, have contributed to the present work. My first thought goes to my parents, who instilled in me at a very early age the love for music, together with the discipline needed to develop talent through assiduous and hard work. Then my gratitude goes to my husband,

Jacques Doukhan, and my daughter, Abigail, faithful but also challenging partners in dialogue and discussion, who encouraged me all along the way on this difficult task. A number of my teaching colleagues, musicians, theologians, and scientists contributed to a better and more correct understanding of the topic. Finally, I want to thank my many students who, by sharing their own experiences, have always been a source of inspiration and renewal, leading me constantly to reconsider and adjust my position on the vast and diverse reality of the musical experience.

---

[1] Ellen G. White, *Christ's Object Lessons* (Washington, D.C.: Review and Herald Publishing Assn., 1941), p. 77.

[2] While each of the chapters of this book present self-contained sections, the reader is encouraged to follow the proposed order of topics; indeed, the progressive acquisition of knowledge proposed in the outline will help in bringing about a more solid understanding of the subject under study.

PART ONE
The Musical Experience

CHAPTER 1

{ *The Nature of Music* }

One of the major reasons disagreement occurs in discussions or dialogues about music is the lack of information on the topic. The partners in dialogue may be ill-informed or not informed at all about the subject matter and may rely entirely on their personal feelings,[1] taste, opinion, or presuppositions. Instead of speaking to each other in an informed way, they might be speaking about two different things or about the same thing from a different perspective.

Music is first of all an objective phenomenon, related to multiple aspects of life. It is connected to physics through the laws of acoustics; to mathematics by way of the numerical proportions that define the intervals; to psychology because of its impact on human behavior; to history in the way it reflects the values and thought patterns of the various epochs; to culture, of which it functions as a mirror; to economics, which drive the business of music; to politics, which appropriate music as a means of propaganda; etc. This is not to say that anyone who wants to carry on a sensible conversation about music needs to be informed and proficient in all these subjects. It shows, however, that music is an objective subject matter that needs also to be approached in an objective way.

Before we can undertake a fruitful study or discussion of the topic of music or, more specifically, church music,[2] we must take care to devote some time to understanding how music functions and how it affects us: What is music, and what is the nature of the musical experience,[3] from the side of both the artist/performer and the listener? Obviously, we will be able to scan only the surface of this topic. It is much too broad for the scope of this book, and must therefore run the risk of appearing schematic, especially in the eyes of the professional musician. The following observations and elaborations should be taken for what they are intended, namely, a quick introduction, on behalf of the novice in musical matters, to the mechanisms of music, music writing, and music perception, with the purpose of creating a starting point and common ground for reflection and discussion.

The Nature of Music

"Music is a universal language." This statement can be heard again and again when dealing with music, particularly church music. It is certainly a true statement. Indeed, all human beings respond to music; they do so, however, in different ways. In order to better understand the extent to which this statement is true, we need first to explore what music is and how it functions and affects us. At first we will take a look at the three main elements that make up music: melody, harmony, and rhythm. Then we will consider general principles that make a piece of music work.

Contrary to popular myth, musical composition does not happen by chance. It is a conscious and willful act, during which the artist uses musical language—very much in the same way a writer uses letters, syllables, grammar, and syntax—to convey not only beautiful sound but meaning, thoughts, ideas, and ideals as well. The language of composers is always determined by cultural language, i.e., the language of their time and place. Through their works composers celebrate life, comment on life, express their view of life, draw attention to issues in society, protest, criticize, accuse, stir awareness and consciousness, or drive home a reality. They entertain and please, excite and move, challenge and liberate, or they simply create a musical background. Some of their works are meant to elevate thoughts and inspire hope, courage, and vision. True artists have something to say to society, and they say it in a language—art—that speaks to their culture.

Moreover, while music speaks to many people at the same time—in a *universal* manner—it also addresses each individual in a very personal way, according to his/her own experience, needs, and sensitivity—in a *particular* manner.

The interest in and longevity of a piece of music will depend on the way the essential components of music—melody, harmony, and rhythm—are put together and interact with one another. The more complex and subtle the relationships, echoes, variances, and allusions, the more satisfying, deep, and long lasting the listening experience will be. *Balance* is the key behind any durable musical work. There must be balance between the elements of music—melody, harmony, and rhythm—and balance between the principles of variety and repetition.

THE PRINCIPLE OF BALANCE
Balance Between Melody, Harmony, and Rhythm

It is the mutual interaction of the three basic elements of music that makes up a musical composition. Each composer uses these elements in his/her own creative ways and thus gives expression to the creative genius. This is the essence of style: through an infinite variety of possibilities in combining the elements of music, each composer develops his/her own style, distinct from that of other composers. The way melody, harmony, and rhythm and other elements of music interact, how they alternate, and the lesser or greater emphasis that is given to one or the other, in turn, makes a composition unique and at the same time creates what we call style. On a broader level style also applies to a type of music distinctive of a particular time in history (baroque, Romantic, jazz), society (folk), or group (country, hip-hop, etc.). This is how we distinguish between jazz (which itself created a number of substyles), bluegrass, country, rhythm and blues (R&B), gospel, Christian contemporary, and, in classical music, between baroque, Romantic, and a multiplicity of twentieth-century styles.

The concept of style, however, goes beyond an artist's particular approach to composition. Style is also determined by a society or culture and its values. Music is at its very core a cultural phenomenon, a mirror of society. As the composer is part of his/her culture, his/her music and style will always happen within the context of a society, dependent on its understanding of art and the beautiful, the purpose of art and the artist, the source of inspiration, etc. The composer will make use of a particular musical language that is produced, understood, and assumed by people living in that culture.[4]

Balance Between Variety and Repetition

The richness of the musical experience is governed by yet another basic principle verified in life and nature, namely, that of variety and repetition, the equivalent of tension and relaxation. Tension is essential to create direction and forward movement. But tension must be relieved by moments of repose in order to retain its dramatic character. Too much tension sustained for too long a time creates confusion and chaos, even illness. Judicious use of variety creates interest, as it adds an element of surprise and unexpectedness. Lack of variety, on the other hand, or too much repetition, brings about dullness, shallowness, boredom, and lack of interest. The appropriate use of repetition, however, is a vital element in the musical experience. It creates satisfaction through familiarity and pleasure through recognition.

A purposeful alternation between repetition and variety is also an important factor in creating form and direction. Direction imparts and sustains meaning. As in good storytelling, it keeps the attention span going and engages the listener to the very end of the experience. A musical piece lacking form and direction is like an engine idling: while it produces some sound, it will not be able to fulfill its purpose to convey meaning and to touch the listener's heart and mind. In order to produce a satisfying and meaningful musical experience, it is essential to observe a healthy balance between variety and repetition, which is guaranteed by a judicious and proportioned use of all the elements of music.

It is essential to keep in mind these basic components of the craft of musical composition in order to arrive at a healthy evaluation of the musical process. To do so, one does not need to be a trained or professional musician—one needs only to develop good observation skills and an informed understanding of what makes up music and how music functions. The following section, as it looks into the three main elements that constitute music, aims at helping the reader reach that goal.

THE ELEMENTS OF MUSIC

Music is basically made of melody, harmony (in Western culture), and rhythm. There are additional elements that shape music, such as timbre (the particular quality of sound of an instrument), tempo (how fast or slowly a piece of music is performed), volume (the loudness), texture (how many various parts and how they interact with one another), and more. For the purpose of our study we will consider here only the three basic constituents of music: melody, harmony, and rhythm.

Melody

Melody is the way sound is organized in space in a horizontal manner. It is a succession of tones of different heights (pitches)—we speak of high notes and low notes. In order to qualify as a melody, this succession of pitches must be organized and perceived as happening in an orderly relationship with one another. Melodic organization happens on the level of form and rhythm. A single-standing melody is a very versatile entity; indeed, it can easily be accommodated to any style, from opera to church—and even to rock. Because of the flexible character of a melody, the same tune has often been used for different settings, from secular to sacred or vice versa.[5] Melodies have a strong cultural flavor and are shaped according to the scale patterns used in a given setting. While Western melodies use the diatonic scale built on 12 equidistant semitones, Arabic and Asian tunes use scales made of five or six tones within the octave (pentatonic and whole tone) and may accommodate intervals smaller than the semitone.[6] This gives them their characteristic flavor that is sometimes difficult for ears not attuned to those sounds to appreciate.

The way notes are organized into a meaningful and beautiful continuous line—a melody—is one of the most difficult challenges for the composer. Great composers often distinguished themselves by their gift of melody. Josquin, Palestrina, Bach, Mozart, Puccini, Brahms, Gershwin, Hammerstein, the Beatles, etc., are among the greatest writers of melodies. Andrew Lloyd Webber, the English composer who wrote a number of immortal melodies for his musicals (*Cats, The Phantom of the Opera, Joseph and the Amazing Technicolor Dreamcoat*), mentioned how he would struggle for weeks with small details that would make the melody sound *just right*. All these composers mastered the difficult art of writing effective melodies, melodies that touch the heart and remain forever in the memory of the listener, melodies perpetuated throughout the ages.

It is a general assumption that the emotional impact of music resides in the particular qualities of the melody. In reality, harmony and rhythm, the other two components of music, play a much more important role when it comes to touching our emotions.

Harmony

Harmony is another way music is organized in space—this time in a vertical manner. As two or more voices blend together, they form a musical fabric very much like the texture of a woven cloth. When several voices sound simultaneously, we speak of polyphonic texture. We distinguish between horizontal and vertical structures of polyphony. In horizontal arrangements, called linear counterpoint, several melodies run simultaneously, but the distinct voices move quite independently of one another, in separate rhythms. These structures were predominant in early medieval polyphony, throughout the Renaissance, and predominantly up to the seventeenth century.[7] Vertical structures of polyphonic music are made up of several pitches sounding simultaneously, called chords. Such structures, in which all voices move at a similar rhythm, create homophony. Chords are the foundation of harmony.

Chords are classified into consonances and dissonances. Consonances are often described as forming pleasant, agreeable sounds, whereas dissonances are said to produce unpleasant, distressing sounds. Consonances are generally associated with relaxation and closure; dissonances are associated with forward movement and tension. These descriptions are not absolute, universal values but rather subjective appreciations, matters of style. The appreciation of consonance/dissonance changes according to an individual's concept of pleasantness/unpleasantness or tension/relaxation. It also depends on the culture in which the music functions and the extent to which an individual is familiar with the prevailing musical style. The concept of consonance and dissonance has constantly changed through time. It is actually a process called the emancipation of the dissonance[8] that primarily contributed to changes in musical style. A style can indeed be defined by its harmony. Specific chords and harmonic patterns define jazz, blues, or country in the field of popular music, but also baroque, classical, late Romantic, and twentieth-century styles in classical music.

Several functions can be attributed to harmony. Within the field of sensations it creates interest and expectation (tension) and brings about feelings of pleasantness (relaxation) or unpleasantness. On the level of cognitive appreciation, harmony brings structure and organization to the music. The particular way of arranging chords in succession is called harmonic progression. These progressions are classified from strong to weak. Movement in music is achieved through appropriate use of harmonic progression. Harmony has the ability to impart a forward movement to the music, to have it stall, or to bring it to a close by a slowing down of its harmonic rhythm. Harmony also lends "color" to a piece, according to the types of intervals that make it up.

In the history of music, the more we advance in time toward the nineteenth century, the more composers play around with the concept of color. Composers of the Impressionistic school of music used chords predominantly to create colors rather than to produce structure and progression.

It took the Western musical world five centuries to develop its polyphonic language, which became the basis for its harmonic system.⁹ An extra two centuries of exploration of the harmonic language made music a powerful vehicle to convey emotions. As the harmonic language evolved throughout the centuries, composers were able to create impressions such as strength, tenderness, fright, awe, tragedy, seduction, contentment, etc.

Rhythm

Because of the complexity of the topic and the important place rhythm takes in discussions about music today, this section is given considerably more in-depth treatment than our discussion of melody and harmony. Rhythm is the element of music that inspires most heated debates. Out of misinformation, ignorance, or simply prejudice, most of rhythm's antagonists are quick to condemn it as the "evil" element in music. However, rhythm is not only a basic ingredient of music; it is essential to every aspect of our lives. We cannot live without rhythm. Therefore, to look down on rhythm as an invention of evil would be to deny a basic principle of Creation. Indeed, rhythm is the governing principle of life. Consider any gesture or activity that articulates human life. It will be rhythmically based: walking, talking, breathing, eating, working, our heartbeat, the cycles of day and night, etc. Nature also is ordered by rhythm: light and darkness, the lunar cycle of weeks, the four seasons, the movement of wind and waves, etc. In much the same way, rhythm is the basic element that governs music. It is the way music is organized in time, and it refers to the way sounds are ordered in time and to their relative durations. The following exercise will illustrate this principle. Take a simple scale (a succession of eight adjacent pitches) and sing it in a descending pattern. It will still be only a scale. Now animate it with a particular well-known rhythm, and it becomes music, a familiar song: "Joy to the World." There is no melody without a rhythmic component.

In music, as in nature and our daily lives, rhythm carries the function of organizing movement and sound into distinct groupings. This happens on several levels of the musical discourse. We distinguish between the concepts of beat or pulse, meter, accentuation, and melodic rhythm. Beat or pulse refers to the subdivision of the musical flow into regular basic pulsations or units of time. Meter concerns the organization of these pulses or beats into distinct groupings of 2, 3, or 4, but also into asymmetric or additive units. Accentuation is particular emphasis given to a specific tone within a rhythmic group that makes it sound more prominent than others (louder or longer, etc.), lending the tone higher hierarchical status, a quality that helps the listener recognize the articulation of the various rhythmic units. Finally, melodic rhythm involves patterns created by the flow and turns of the melody or the speech patterns inherent in the lyrics. These patterns are actually superimposed onto beat, meter, and accentuation.

Rhythmic perception is not solely an external physical phenomenon dictated by the properties of music. Rhythmic interpretation involves a factor of perception on the part of the listener, who mentally manipulates the various rhythmic components of a piece of music.[10] We seldom perceive the rhythmic structure of music as a series of single or separate beats or accents, but hear them rather as *resultant* structures, that is, in combination with each other. The more complex these structures—such as in genres using cross-rhythms in which several distinct layers of rhythmic patterns are sounded simultaneously—the more resultant is the listening experience. An example of this can be found in the perception of beat and counterbeat as a resultant phenomenon rather than a dichotomy.[11] There is, then, much more to rhythm than a rigid metric pattern; rhythm is quite a complex phenomenon whose interpretation is based on both external and internal criteria.[12]

There are two particular aspects of rhythm that create animated debate in churches and deserve to be given more attention, namely, beat and syncopation.

Beat

The concept of beat is generally associated with popular music, but it is actually a part of all musical performance. We have already seen that it belongs to the concept of pulse rather than meter. For the past century the word "beat" has generally come to be understood as a sustained or exaggerated accentuation of the basic pulse, generally produced by a prominent sound source, such as a foundational instrument (e.g., a double bass or bass guitar), percussion, or even hand clapping. Beat may be enhanced by a prominent counterbeat obtained through variably strong marking of the unaccented part of a pulse or measure. Musics that consistently emphasize a basic pulse featured together with predominantly repetitive rhythmic patterns distinguish themselves from the rhythmic practice found in Western music, mostly (but not exclusively) from before the twentieth century. This music basically featured an alternation of accented and unaccented beats or pulses animated by varying rhythmic patterns. Rhythmic practices based on the principle of repetitive pulse or beat are not exclusive to popular styles; they are also found in certain genres of twentieth-century classical music, e.g., primitivism and minimalism, represented by composers such as Igor Stravinsky, Aram Khachaturian, Béla Bartók, Carlos Chávez, Arvo Pärt, Philip Glass, etc.

Syncopation

According to the *Guinness Encyclopedia of Popular Music*,[13] syncopation involves "rhythmic displacement created by articulating weaker beats or metrical positions that do not fall on any of the main beats of the measure." If you hum or sing to yourself the song "Give Me Jesus,"[14] you will find an easy illustration of the concept of syncopation. In the first, second, and third phrases of the hymn, on the words "when I," the strong accent falls on the offbeat of the meter, as emphasis is given to the normally unaccented second half of the beat (traditionally considered the weak portion of the beat), on the word "I." This emphasis is achieved through a lengthening of the note on the word "I" and a corresponding shortening of the previous note (on the word "when"). In the last line of the hymn the technique is repeated on the words "have all this world," where the accent is put on the word "all" through a lengthening of the second beat in the measure, traditionally considered to be a weak or secondary beat in a 4/4 time.

Syncopation is generally explained as a musical feature that was first brought from Africa by slaves and later became a major ingredient of jazz and rock music. Because of this perspective syncopation has been understood as intricately tied to heathen/animistic practices and interpreted as an instrument of evil. For this reason it has often been shunned from church. An objective and historical study of the practice of syncopation, on one hand,

and the traditional rhythmic practices characteristic of African music, on the other hand, reveal that the situation is not this simplistic and that such an explanation of syncopation is outright erroneous.

The most characteristic element in African music is not syncopation, but its use of cross-rhythms. Ethnomusicologist Arthur Morris Jones comments appropriately on this fact. He says, "The very essence of African music is to *cross the rhythms*. This does not mean syncopation. On the whole African music is *not* based on syncopation."[15] The practice of cross rhythms can be likened to a kind of rhythmic counterpoint, similar to traditional Western melodic counterpoint, though done in a much more sophisticated manner. In cross rhythms several voices compete with one another through different, sometimes conflicting, meters and rhythmic patterns (2 against 3, 2 against 3 against 5, etc.). Similar techniques are used in classical music of India and the Middle East; both use a system of complex rhythmic modes, respectively called *t~la* and *§q~>*. Here again, it is the *resultant* effect of these compound rhythms that is perceived and analyzed by the listener rather than the separate rhythmic elements. The overall effect is one of great interest and complexity, challenging not only the various performers but also the minds and bodies of the listeners and dancers.

Syncopation, on the other hand, has been a basic rhythmic feature of Western (European) music since the dawn of polyphonic music in the Middle Ages. To come closer to our times, the rhythmic principle of sacred or secular Renaissance music from the fifteenth and sixteenth centuries—by composers such as Josquin des Prez, Heinrich Isaac, Orlande de Lassus, and Giovanni Pierluigi da Palestrina—is strongly governed by the practice of syncopation. Any sacred music written in those times, whether a motet (a polyphonic setting of a Latin text, for religious use) or mass, features abundant use of syncopation. Music was then composed according to a linear principle, and one way of setting the various voices off from one another, in order to create variety and diversity, was to animate them with different rhythmic patterns. This was mainly achieved by offsetting the accentuated parts in the different voices. This Renaissance principle of composition was carried into the baroque, where it became a staple of church style and has since then remained a basic technique in contrapuntal writing. We find a wealth of syncopation in the sacred works by composers such as Claudio Monteverdi,

J. S. Bach, and G. F. Handel. Often, the final sections of choral works of these great composers end with choral fugues, rhythmically animated polyphonic sections brimming with syncopation that create an effect of exhilaration and a triumphant climax to the whole work. In an eyewitness account of a rehearsal of Bach's "Cum sancto spiritu" section from the *St. John Passion,* the rector of St. Thomas Church at Leipzig, where the composer himself was conducting the choir, commented about how "the rhythm takes possession of all his [Bach's] limbs."[16]

The Western style of music making, including the technique of syncopation, was imported into the colony of Louisiana by early French settlers. By virtue of its particularly tolerant attitude toward local cultures and its fluid cultural boundaries, the colonial city of New Orleans, around the year 1800, was brimming with music bringing together European and African traditions.[17] It was then that the practice of syncopation mixed with African musical practices. The resultant combination later came to characterize the world of jazz.

In today's popular music styles, beat and syncopation are closely associated and thus given a much more prominent character. We saw earlier that the rhythmic component in music cannot be considered a freestanding entity. Instead, it must be placed within the larger context of the other musical elements. Syncopation and beat must therefore be looked at in this broader perspective rather than as isolated elements of the musical discourse. Are they the sole governing elements in the music? Do they alternate with rhythmically less pronounced but melodically more interesting moments? Are they heightened through intense harmonies, or do they stand out against uninteresting melodies and poor harmonies?

As we already noticed, the richer and greater the interplay between the elements of music, the deeper the musical meaning and the more satisfying and longer lasting the musical experience. This principle of balance has something to do with the way we perceive and receive music. It touches our hearts, minds, and bodies through emotional, physical, and intellectual stimulation. In other words, it affects us on a wholistic level. The same is true for the principle of alternation between tension and relaxation, i.e., between rhythmically or harmonically pronounced or heightened sections and rhythmically and harmonically more inactive or less colored sections. In a musical style in which one of the elements becomes domineering at the expense of the others through a monolithic, sustained, and pronounced presence, the principle of balance is destroyed, and the wholistic effect of music that should characterize our worship music, in particular, is lost.

The Effects of Rhythm

In order to appropriately use and evaluate the rhythmic element in music, we must be aware of how rhythm works and adapt it to a given cultural setting. This has been achieved by studies in the field of the psychology of music. To illustrate my point, I turn to an authority on the psychology of music, Carl E. Seashore,[18] recognized by his peers as a pioneer in matters of scientific study of the psychology of music.[19] I directed the choice of my source purposely to an objective and clinical study outside the field of religion and written before the advent of rock music to eliminate any religious agenda or stylistic prejudice on the part of the author. In reading these paragraphs, one can easily verify their validity in one's own musical experience, whatever style is under consideration. Seashore presents the effect of rhythm on three levels.

1. Rhythm creates emotions.

"Rhythm affects the circulation, respiration, and all the secretions of the body in such a way as to arouse agreeable feeling. Herein we find the *groundwork of emotion*; for rhythm, whether in perception or in action, is emotional when highly developed, and results in response of the whole organism to its pulsations. Such organic pulsations and secretions are the physical counterpart of emotion."[20]

A first observation that comes to mind in reading these lines is the relationship the author establishes between rhythm and the emotions. We generally connect rhythm with physical response, such as toe tapping, marching, swaying of the body, etc. But here we learn that rhythm affects our psychological response. It is rhythm, not necessarily melody or harmony as is generally assumed, that governs our emotions. And it does so through the stimulation of various physiological functions of the body.

Seashore also writes that in order to have such an impact, rhythm needs to be highly developed. This means that to achieve these effects, the rhythmic element needs to have a dominant or predominant character in the music.

It is important to be aware, then, that rhythm is a powerful agent of influence in our emotional lives. The impact is all the greater since it affects an aspect of our personalities, the emotions, that can easily get out of hand and beyond the control of our reasoning.

2. Rhythm empowers.

"Rhythm gives us a *feeling of power;* it carries. It is like a dream of flying; it is so easy to soar.... There is an assurance of ability to cope with the future. *This results in the disregard of the ear element and results in a motor attitude, or a projection of the self in action.*"[21]

One of my former students illustrated this process in a very graphic way. He told us the story of a time in his life when he was experiencing personal difficulties, because his parents were in the process of divorce. He had trouble coping with the situation and had taken to the habit, each day after he came home from school, of lying down on the floor, putting a pair of headphones in his ears, and listening for half an hour to rock music. The driving beat, enhanced by the high volume of sound, restored his psychological abilities and gave him the strength to cope with the future. He did this for a few weeks until he noticed that the effect of the experiment lasted little more than a few hours, after which he fell back into his depressive and desperate mood. He understood then that listening to music as a remedy for his troubles was, in fact, a deception, nothing more than a quick fix that would never bring him the lasting and enduring strength he was looking for. The feeling of power imparted by the music provided a way to avoid confronting a painful reality. Shortly after that time, he was encouraged to turn to prayer and was able to start the long and difficult process of healing—and ultimately to achieve it.

We all have experienced the energizing power of rhythm when, worn out from a day of work and still more to come, we get into our cars, turn on the engines, and hear lively rhythmic music streaming from the radio. We start tapping our feet (motor attitude)—or our fingers on the steering wheel for more security—and feel energized and ready to go on with our tasks (projection of self into action).

3. Rhythm stimulates and excites.

"Pronounced rhythm brings on a feeling of elation which not infrequently results in a mild form of ecstasy or absentmindedness, a *loss of consciousness of the environment.* It excites, and it makes us insensible to the excitation, giving the feeling of being lulled. . . . *One becomes oblivious to intellectual pursuits . . .* feels freedom of movement—action without any object other than the pleasure in the action itself. There comes a sort of autointoxication from the stimulating effect of the music and the successful self-expression in balanced movements sustained by that music and its associations."[22]

The words used in this paragraph remind us of another reality of today, namely, the use of stimulants in general and recreational drugs in particular. Expressions such as stimulation, elation, ecstasy, and loss of consciousness of the environment point to similar experiences. With any stimulant, the consumer progressively gets accustomed to and dependent on it, needing ever-increasing quantities or degrees of the stimulus to achieve satisfaction of his/her need. Anything with a lesser stimulating effect seems dull and uninteresting. A similar effect can easily be observed in our consumption of rhythm: the more we listen to rhythmically animated music, the more the need increases for stronger and more accented rhythms.

Notice that Seashore places these phenomena in a context of "pronounced rhythm," i.e., music that features rhythm prominently and on a continual basis. The effect of pronounced and sustained rhythm can lead the individual to become so absorbed in the actual engagement and enjoyment of the rhythmic activity that there is a progressive loss of interest in the rational or cognitive control of the situation. The capacity for control can diminish progressively and even be shut out and eliminated. This can easily be verified in some worship experiences of a charismatic type, where the musical element is very animated, prominent, and sustained, helping the believer to reach the desired stage of being touched by the spirit. The stimulating and autointoxicating effects of music with a highly pronounced and sustained rhythmic element may result in making us oblivious to the voice of reason or of the conscience. The situation is made even more complex by the fact that these responses happen without our even noticing them. We are so taken by the pleasurable experience that everything else is ruled out.

A number of examples from the secular, military, and religious worlds illustrate this mechanism. The first is found in dance. There was a good reason for the great swing dance bands in America to take off and become so popular precisely during the Great Depression years (1930s). It was the distinct need, in the midst of all the hardship, worrying, and despair, to find a way to "lose consciousness of the environment," to forget the harsh and often unbearable reality and get completely absorbed, at least for a few moments, in a pleasurable activity—"action without any object other than the pleasure in the action itself."

My second example is drawn from the military world. From the earliest times of humankind, war making has been accompanied by music and song. Even the Bible has its own examples of such practice: the trumpet blasts (from the ram's horn, or shofar) played a decisive role at the conquest of Jericho (Joshua 6) and contributed to the scattering of the enemy by Gideon's forces (Judges 7), etc. Soldiers are trained to march to war while singing. Why is this method so effective? According to Seashore,[23] as soldiers sing their marching songs or march to the sound of a military band, they reach a stage at which they are completely absorbed by the marching movement, which creates a sort of absentmindedness through its monotonous repetitiveness. The singing of songs of patriotism and victory in combination with the marching creates some feeling of elation or even ecstasy. The subjects become "oblivious" to the reality that they are actually marching off to kill or be killed.

One may similarly observe the ambiance in clubs to verify the impact of a sonic experience. Psychologist and author John Booth Davies has adequately described such a setting. The emotionally heightened ambiance in an environment of loud repetitive sound intensified with stroboscopic lighting affects the attitude of the dancers. They are apparently oblivious to anything that goes on around them, but they never completely lose consciousness—they are still able to discriminate between various sounds and to continue making automatic rhythmic responses.[24]

Illustrations taken from the popular religious scene, such as Pentecostal celebrations or scenes of possession, testify to the mechanism just described. In a first stage the dancing excites. Then the dancer becomes "insensible to the excitation" (getting entirely absorbed in and concentrating totally on the pursuit of the physical activity per se), "oblivious to intellectual pursuits" (giving up rational control), and ends up in a sort of ecstasy (receiving the Spirit/possession). Anybody watching a trance or possession dance can observe these different stages.

It is essential, however, to point out that this process does not happen in a mechanical or automatic way. Seashore himself took care to make this very clear. As he speaks about the gratifying experience of "auto-intoxication" and "successful self-expression," he explains how the two happen through the combined effects of both the music *and* its context and associations.[25] In other words, at the base of such experiences (be it dance, war, or religion), there lies a deliberate investment, an intent and readiness, in participation. Getting into a trance does not happen automatically, as a result of the effects of music, etc., but requires a voluntary letting go and surrender to the experience. This explains why musicians providing the music for events related to possession do not automatically enter the state of trance themselves.[26]

We now understand better why rhythm is such a basic ingredient in music: it is rhythm that makes music so interesting and powerful. But, as with anything else, this powerful tool can be misused or abused to the point that it carries us beyond the limits of our full control. When dealing with church music—but equally in our personal listening habits—it is especially important to realize how rhythm functions and how it affects us as individuals or as groups, so as to use it appropriately. We need to clarify in our own minds what we are looking for during our personal musical experiences and, particularly, during worship, and measure and adapt the level of the rhythmic activity of our music accordingly.

Here is a last reflection on rhythm. The foregoing explanations might suggest a possible answer to the question What makes the rhythmic element so prominent in today's society? In a world of stress, deadlines, insecurity, self-doubt, and disillusionment—in a time when the exploration of hitherto unknown regions of the personality and the pursuit of new sensations through a variety of stimulants is occupying so much time and money—one reason for the incessant pursuit of rhythm might be to fulfill a need for freedom, power, and expanse.[27] In that sense it becomes even more important for the church to present to its worshippers through its music something more than the world does, a music that is not content with merely covering up our needs, and that takes the searching mind and soul to the real and lasting solution for these human quests and needs.[28]

It is a fact that the single elements that make up music, such as a note, a chord, an instrument, etc., do not carry in themselves a meaning or message, just as a letter of the alphabet, a number, or a rhythmic pattern of the spoken language does not carry a meaning in itself. Both manifestations, the spoken language and the musical language, acquire their meaning only from the moment that their elements start being combined—and according to the interpretation that is made of them in a given cultural context. If I do not know the Spanish language, the word "*madre*" does not carry any meaning for me. It remains neutral, a mere juxtaposition of letters of the alphabet. If, on the contrary, I have learned this word from my earliest childhood, it not only carries the meaning of the person who gave birth to me; it is also ripe with a wealth of associations that come with the word "mother": provider, security, consolation, unlimited love, sacrifice, etc. It works the same way with music. A given melodic turn, a particular chord progression, a rhythmic pattern, or a specific instrument may evoke a number of different meanings. Where do those differences come from? What is it that makes us appreciate one type of music over another one or, on the contrary, leaves us indifferent to it? How is music a universal manifestation? These are questions we need to address.

---

[1] On the common tendency to build an ethical argument on personal feelings, see the following comment by Dagfinn Føllesdal, professor of philosophy at Stanford University: "The view that the strength of our feelings is a measure of the ethical rightness or wrongness of an act is characterized as the most widespread fallacy in . . . ethical discussion" (from "The Ethics of Stem Cell Research," *Jahrbuch für Wissenschaft und Ethik* 11 [2006]: 67).

[2] In speaking about church music, we will focus mainly on music made by the people, that is, congregational singing.

[3] A note to the reader is in order here: our discussion of music is specifically aimed at the phenomenon of music. Whenever we speak of music, it is always meant as music per se, independent of the meaning of the lyrics that might accompany a particular song or piece.

[4] Occasionally, some groundbreaking composers will transcend the rules of given conventions and create new styles, e.g., Debussy, Schoenberg, and, in the world of popular music, rock and roll.

[5] This phenomenon will be revisited in our discussion of *contrafacta* (see "The Practice of Contrafacta," pp. 166-173 of this book).

[6] The semitone is the smallest interval in Western musical tradition. It represents the distance between any two neighboring keys on the keyboard, white or black.

[7] While polyphonic writing was a predominant compositional technique during those times, it lost its primary character during the late eighteenth and the nineteenth centuries. However, it never disappeared totally from musical composition and became again a pre-

dominant element in twentieth century music, especially during the first half of the century (cf. atonality and neoclassicism).

[8] For a description of this concept, see Jim Samson, *Music in Transition: A Study of Tonal Expansion and Atonality, 1900-1920* (New York: W. W. Norton, 1977), pp. 146, 147.

[9] Even though the practice of harmony as found in the Western world is not part of many a musical system around the world, the same complexity of structure can be observed in musical languages that use predominantly rhythm and melody only. Thus, for example, Indian and African vocal and/or instrumental music demonstrate a very complex interaction of rhythmic patterns that can be compared to the complex interaction of melodic lines found in Western polyphony under the term *counterpoint*.

[10] A similar process of rhythmic manipulation is also applied by the performer and is at the origin of the concept of *groove* in popular music. Groove refers to a characteristic rhythmic pattern of the music used in a repeated manner, producing a distinctive rhythmic feel within a repetitive context. In classical music the same concept is found in terms of stretching or compressing a given tempo during performance (rubato).

[11] Cf. Maury Yeston, *The Stratification of Musical Rhythm* (New Haven, Conn.: Yale University Press, 1976), p. 77: "The rhythm of a musical work is first considered to be the summation of its attacks: a resultant rhythm."

[12] For an in-depth discussion of the mechanism of rhythm, see John Booth Davies, *The Psychology of Music* (Stanford, Calif.: Stanford University Press, 1978), chapter 12: "Rhythm: Tonality's Poor Relation."

[13] *Guinness Encyclopedia of Popular Music*, 2nd ed., Colin Larkin (New York: Stockton Press, 1995), s.v. "Syncopation."

[14] Hymn No. 305 in *The Seventh-day Adventist Hymnal*; musical arrangement by Alma Blackmon (1984). The same rhythmic displacement can be found in hymn No. 580, "This Little Light of Mine," (musical arrangement by Alma Blackmon), on the phrase "I'm going to let it shine," in which, through rhythmic displacement, emphasis is given to the word "it" by lengthening the weak (second) part of the second beat.

[15] Arthur Morris Jones, "African Music," *African Affairs* 48 (1949): 294. Jones spent many years in Africa as a missionary and specialized in the study of African rhythm.

[16] Quoted by Wilfrid Mellers, *Bach and the Dance of God* (New York: Oxford University Press, 1981), pp. 209, 10.

[17] The African tradition contributed musical techniques such as call and response (improvisation) and polyrhythms.

[18] Carl E. Seashore, *Psychology of Music* (New York: McGraw-Hill Book Co., 1938).

[19] Cf. Robert W. Lundin, *An Objective Psychology of Music*, 3rd ed. (Malabar, Fla.: Robert E. Krieger Publishing Company, 1985), p. 115.

[20] Seashore, pp. 143, 144. (Italics mine.)

[21] *Ibid.*, p. 142. (Italics mine.)

[22] *Ibid.*, pp. 142, 143.

[23] *Ibid.*, p. 143.

[24] John Booth Davies, p. 195.

[25] Seashore, p. 143.

[26] For a more detailed discussion of this phenomenon, see "How Does Music Convey Meaning?" pp. 57, 58 of this book.

[27] See Seashore, p. 142.

[28] This principle should also become a concern within cultural settings that feature a high threshold of rhythmic tolerance, and needs to be considered accordingly.

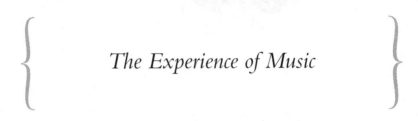

CHAPTER 2

The Experience of Music

In the movie *Out of Africa* there is a halting scene in which the sounds of the second movement of Mozart's Clarinet Concerto in A Major stream out of a strange black box, an early phonograph, striking us almost as anachronistic in the given context. The strange sounds attract a crowd of Kikuyu people, who listen with smiling faces to the music.

Incidents such as these are readily picked up to prove the point that classical music can be appreciated immediately by anyone, even the least educated. The problem with such affirmations is whether the intrigued reaction of these individuals should be interpreted as a real aesthetic appreciation or as curiosity, surprise, or even bewilderment.

What is really the character of the musical experience? Is it, indeed, universal in the sense that all individuals around the world are able to experience the same aesthetic experience at their first hearing of, say, Bach, Mozart, Bob Dylan, or U2?

A basic step in learning about the musical experience is to understand that each person's response to music happens simultaneously on all levels of his/her personality—the physical, emotional, intellectual, and spiritual levels. The musical experience is an integrated human process, involving cognition (especially sequencing and memory), the emotions (pleasure and expectation), and the body (motor coordination).[1] Some scholars speak of three dimensions of music:[2] the symbolic dimension of music that creates an intellectual or spiritual response, the rhetorical dimension that creates an emotional response, and the ecstatic dimension that creates a physical response. A fulfilling and artistically valuable experience encompasses all three aspects of the human being.

In regard to worship music, the wholistic character of the musical experience becomes even more important. The biblical perspective of worship addresses the human being in his/her wholeness: the body (our senses), the emotions, and the mind.[3] All three are included in the spiritual experience. Putting a preferred emphasis on one of these elements at the expense of the others impoverishes and adulterates an authentic worship experience.

MUSIC AS A UNIVERSAL EXPERIENCE

We have all heard it said that "music is a universal language—everybody can understand it." Such words are often used to impose a certain style of music upon a congregation to convince it to worship in this particular style. The statement may be true—but only to a limited extent. Ethnomusicologist Bruno Nettl noted that while "music is a cultural universal, it is not a universal language." There are a number of universals in the way music functions in society, i.e., as a religious ritual or as an emblem of identity. But, continues Nettl, "humans speak many mutually unintelligible languages.... The world of music consists of musics that are not mutually compatible."[4]

We all react to music in some way or other. We respond physically to animated music by tapping our feet or toes, swaying our bodies, or outright dancing. We are filled with joy, sadness, triumph, anger, or inspiration and wonder. Our response to music on the universal level could be qualified by this phrase from Iris Yob, assistant professor of education, State University of New York at Genesco: "Music describes without circumscribing."[5] This means that we do all respond to the musical stimulus but in a very general and nonspecific way. Sometimes reactions to a single piece of music can be drastically different from one individual to another. French music scholar Jules Combarieu, in his book *Music and Magic*, expresses this in a very pertinent way. He writes, "Which is the degree of exactitude which musical expression can attain? Musical images must not be applied to one single object only; they can be interpreted in different ways. Their interest and poetry probably lies in this very fact."[6]

Because of this broad range of understandings of a single piece of music, there seems, then, to be more to the quality and degree of the musical experience than an innate human response to music. Indeed, beyond its universal character the musical experience is foremost an acquired experience.

MUSIC AS AN ACQUIRED EXPERIENCE

I make it a habit to introduce my courses on church music with a listening exercise meant to demonstrate how we react to music. My class is generally made up of individuals from countries all over the world. This gives a particular flavor to the experiment and makes it even more relevant and interesting. This part of the course has become a favorite moment for the students, not only because they can participate actively in the experiment but also because the exercise is an incredible eye-opener that makes them understand, firsthand and almost instantly, the intricacies of the musical experience.

There are two sections of music in this experiment: a group of selections taken from secular music covering a wide range of styles and periods, and a number of selections taken from various types of sacred music chosen from an equally wide range of religions. The secular selections are all instrumental, i.e., they do not contain any words. This avoids any associations with a particular situation.

As I play the various excerpts of music, the students all react in some way to the music, but they do so in very *different* ways. Their interpretations may vary considerably, according to the basic mood of the music, or the students may not be sensitive to or touched by the music at all. What for some feels invigorating or transcendent, comes across as boring or uninspiring to others.[7]

The ensuing class discussions are quite animated because each student often feels offended by other individuals' lack of appreciation for his or her preferred style. As we examine together the deeper reasons behind these divergences in opinion, we learn that an individual's reaction to music is determined by a certain number of acquired or learned factors. These factors include one's familiarity with the style, formal or informal education in matters of music, cultural setting and environment, and particular values and beliefs. Associations that come spontaneously with the hearing—such as the remembrance of a mood, event, or situation, or certain gestures and actions that accompanied the first or subsequent hearings of this type of music— may also need to be taken into consideration. The combination of value systems and/or associations determines, in the listener's mind, whether a style is acceptable or not, and results in value judgments about the music.

The classroom experiment reveals that music does not happen in a vacuum but is intimately tied with, and carried by, a given culture or society. Robert

W. Lundin, author of *An Objective Psychology of Music,* concurs that musical responses are "acquired through one's life history....A large part of anyone's responses are culturally determined." The way we judge a particular musical style or event, he continues, "will depend on the conditions under which we build up our musical behavior. These conditions refer, not only to one's intimate musical surroundings, but in general to his whole musical culture. We, therefore, include not only the general Western musical culture but also our own family, school, and other intimate sources of musical stimulation."[8]

Based on where we come from, the kind of music that nourished our childhood, and the kind of musical education we received or the values that were attached to certain styles, we react in different ways to certain types of music. We may not even react at all to styles that are unfamiliar to us. Music acquires meaning only through context and education.

A particular style of music must, then, be understood within the context of the community or cultural group that gives it its meaning. It is also the community or cultural group that determines when an earlier established meaning changes or becomes obsolete. Musical meaning "ceases to be effective when the relationship between a group and the symbol (musical language) changes in space and time."[9] The history of many a hymn bears witness to this principle.[10]

A good understanding of these realities is important to any reflection or discussion on church music. There is no universal way music is appreciated in different cultural settings. In one setting it can be very well received, even applauded. In another setting it may be perceived as inappropriate. Therefore, it is important to learn to decode or understand the meaning of a style within a particular cultural setting. On the other hand, it is just as important not to fall into the trap of quick judgments on value and statements as to the implicit "good" or "evil" nature of a style, chord, melody, rhythm, or instrument. Some people speak of "good" instruments for worship (piano, organ, violin, flute) and of "evil" instruments (saxophone, guitar, synthesizer, etc.). They forget that it is the *context* generally associated with these instruments, chords, or rhythms that determines their meaning and evaluation.

One would be very hard-pressed to demonstrate that a given chord (e.g., a ninth chord or jazz chord), rhythmic pattern (syncopation), or instrument (saxophone) is evil or inappropriate in and of itself. This would be the equivalent of lending the power of good or evil to a letter of the alphabet, a syllable, or even a word without its context. Good or evil connotations are given to a specific word within a particular linguistic setting, which is just the product of social conventions. If someone addresses me with a four-letter word in Chinese, it will not have any effect on me—I might even interpret it as a compliment if it is said with a smile! Musical language is not much different from verbal language. The isolated components of a language—letters, syllables, even words—do not carry any moral weight in themselves. They acquire meaning as they are put together into phrases, sentences, and paragraphs, and then they are given significance within a cultural language group. The interpretation of those meanings must be learned, and the learning process happens within a given cultural setting, determined by the value system of that culture.

It is exactly the same for the musical language. When melodies, chords, rhythms, and harmonies are combined together, they are given a specific meaning within a particular cultural setting; they are then interpreted as happy or sad, elevating or debasing. Every society or subculture develops a concept of what is sacred and what is entertaining, and what is tasteful or vulgar. Expressions of respect, veneration, adoration, and solidarity—sacred or religious attitudes basic to the human race—are shaped according to established value systems. Every society develops its own verbal and musical languages to translate these concepts. The interpretation of musical content does not primarily happen on the basis of the innate nature and quality of the musical sounds produced,[11] but according to the context in which this type of music is created and performed, i.e., the circumstances the music is associated with.[12] The meaning of a vocabulary of words or music is reached through cultural consensus or convention. It becomes difficult, therefore, to judge the content or meaning of a style of music if we are not familiar with its function and meaning within that given society—if we have not learned to understand its meaning in its original context.

---

[1] The social dimension of music holds an equally important place in the musical experience. This dimension will be dealt with in depth in a separate section.

[2] See Andrew Wilson-Dickson, *The Story of Christian Music: From Gregorian Chant to Black Gospel: An Authoritative Illustrated Guide to All the Major Traditions of Music for Worship* (Oxford, U.K.: A Lion Book, 1992), p. 11.

[3] See the worship models presented in Isaiah 6:1-8 and Revelation 4 and 5.

[4] Bruno Nettl, *Excursions in World Music*, 5th ed. (Upper Saddle River, N.J.: Pearson, Prentice Hall, 2008), p. 13.

[5] Iris M.Yob, "The Arts as Ways of Understanding: Reflections on the Ideas of Paul Tillich," in *Philosopher, Teacher, Musicians: Perspectives on Music Education*, Estelle R. Jorgensen, ed. (Chicago: University of Illinois Press, 1993), p. 14.

[6] Jules Combarieu, *La musique et la magie: Étude sur les origines populaires de l'art musical, son influence et sa fonction dans les sociétés* (Paris: Alphonse Picard, 1909; reprint Geneva: Minkoff Reprints, 1978), p. 360.

[7] Elizabeth Brown and William Hendee, in their clinical study of reactions to music, came to the same conclusion: "Quite simply, music can mean different things to different people at different times. Music is a very individual and complex experience" (from "Adolescents and Their Music," *Journal of the American Medical Association* 262 [September 1989]: 1662).

[8] Lundin, pp. 100, 101.

[9] Yob, p. 16.

[10] For example, in *The Seventh-day Adventist Hymnal* (1985 ed.), hymn nos. 8, 101, 141, 255, etc., are all based on original folk melodies. See also the hymn "Land of Light" in James Nix's, *Early Advent Singing* (No. 22), based on "Old Folks at Home," by Stephen Foster, which was included in the supplement to the 1855 SDA hymnal, with a text by Uriah Smith (rev. ed., [Hagerstown, Md.: Review and Herald Publishing. Assn., 1994]).

[11] An erroneous popular myth, for instance, interprets music in the minor mode as being associated with sadness, and music in the major mode as being expressive of happiness. In reality, the majority of folk music uses the minor mode (which actually belongs to modal language) both for happy songs or dances, as well as to depict sad situations.

[12] This brings up the case of rock music, which will be discussed later (see "Excursus: The Case of Rock Music," pp. 195-200). This type of music needs to be dealt with separately since it falls more under the category of a music *culture* than a musical *style*.

CHAPTER 3

{ *The Meaning of Music* }

There are several assumptions about music and its capacity to convey meaning. Misunderstandings and misconceptions about the issue, lack of information, and oversimplification of the matter have contributed to spread a number of beliefs and convictions, which are then perpetuated from generation to generation, bringing about endless discussion and debate. The purpose of the following reflection is to demystify and clarify some of these misunderstandings and misconceptions. First, we will take a look at the concept of sacred music and investigate what makes a style of music sacred. Then we will look at the issue of aesthetics versus ethics. A number of questions will articulate that section: Is aesthetics equivalent to ethics? Is there good music and evil music? How does music convey meaning? Where does the real power of music lie? How can we use music responsibly?

SACRED MUSIC

Is there a sacred style of music? What makes a musical style sacred? A good way to provide answers to these questions is to listen to different types of sacred music. I have my students listen to and react to selections of music from different religions, music such as Tibetan Buddhist chanting, Jewish synagogue chanting, religious rap, a South American folk mass, Gregorian and Orthodox chanting, Black spirituals and Black gospel, traditional Protestant hymns, classical sacred selections, etc. Every selection played was written with the specific intent to convey a religious message—or is at least understood, in popular imagination, to have been so. The sacred character of the music is indicated either explicitly by the words or implicitly by means of the ritual, liturgical, or religious setting in which the music is generally performed.

In my class the listeners' reactions were interesting to observe, especially since they provided clues to the answers we were looking for. Selections in familiar styles were acclaimed with great enthusiasm, pleasure, and personal—sometimes even physical—investment in the experience. In general, the music played in these excerpts was perceived as conveying some quality more or less related to the concepts of transcendence, grandeur, or majesty. However, a more detailed analysis of these impressions revealed considerable differences in appreciation. The various reactions covered such diverse and opposite moods as wonder and fright, elevation and boredom, spirituality and entertainment. Settings evoked by the playing of J. S. Bach's Toccata in D Minor, for example, ranged from a lofty cathedral to haunted houses, horror movies, and cartoons. It is because of this *uncircumscribed* character of the musical experience that the works of J. S. Bach are used indifferently both in Christian worship and satanic worship.[1] As shocking as this may sound, both these worship styles are looking for an atmosphere of transcendence and magnificence, and they do indeed find these qualities in the music of J. S. Bach.

Unfamiliar selections, on the other hand, such as Tibetan chants, for instance, were met with bewilderment, incomprehension, or outright laughter. Less familiar selections, such as Orthodox chants, were often received with indifference. This demonstrates how music loses its sacred character if not perceived as such. It also confirms what was pointed out earlier, namely, that when the music is taken out of its context, it loses its meaning, which, in this case, is its sacred character. It would be difficult to sustain a plea in favor of the sacred character of music inherent in a given musical style. For music to be understood as sacred, it needs to be accompanied by extramusical elements that lend it its sacred character. It is the religious cultural context, the learned experience, that creates this understanding.

On the other hand, compositions that were originally not meant as sacred works have over time become associated with a sacred context. Handel's oratorio *The Messiah* had originally been written as a fund-raiser for an orphanage and was initially performed in theaters and by opera singers.[2] Massenet's "Meditation" from *Thaïs* comes straight out of an opera dealing with the seductions of a courtesan at the time of Alexander the Great, interweaving themes of worldly temptation and spiritual quest. Similarly, the saraband, originally a sensual dance imported from Cuba via Spain, had become a slow stylized dance at the time of J. S. Bach, and in our time is typically played in churches on the organ as a meditative piece for worship. These are just a few examples of how religious culture can transform a secular piece into a sacred one.

These few examples illustrate how difficult it is to determine whether a musical selection has a sacred character or not, especially when there are no words at all or words in a language that is not understood. The same forces that shape our musical understanding of secular music also shape our understanding of sacred music. The importance of a learned or acquired experience in the understanding of music is again verified. Our religious culture and environment, our beliefs and value systems, and the associations we have formed in regard to certain categories of music all influence our interpretations of musical selections as sacred. The sacred character of music does not reside in a particular style per se but in artificial conventions that were one day established (and/or changed) on the basis of a set of criteria or traditions within a societal group. These conventions determine the way music is understood and registered as sacred in the mind of a group of listeners. This understanding, in turn, influences the attitudes and manners in which the music is performed. There is no such thing as inherently sacred music, neither by the use of a particular instrument or genre nor by a given musical style. Our interpretation of music as sacred is also a learned experience.

Maybe the answer to the question "Is there a sacred style of music?" needs to be explored from a different perspective, through the question "Is there a purpose to be fulfilled by sacred music that will qualify a musical selection as sacred music?"

The Purpose and Role of Sacred Music

As one listens to various types of sacred or church music, that is, music connected to a religious event, one discovers a similar multiplicity of style differences as encountered in secular music. Within each tradition the musical style featured in a religious setting is considered an adequate expression of the religious or liturgical truth and sensitivity. What unites them all in their great diversity is that, within their respective settings, they fulfill the basic purposes and functions of sacred music. Some of these functions and attributes of sacred music are to convey a theology, to serve as a vehicle for expression and communication, to be defined within a cultural setting, and to delight God.

Sacred Music Conveys a Theology

This can probably be considered as the main purpose of sacred music, and it should happen in a threefold manner:

1. The music must reflect the character of the god worshipped. Traditions of sacred music reveal the face or character of their deity or higher power. Within their respective languages the musics will evoke transcendence or immanence, distance or closeness, punishment or love. The God of the Judeo-Christian faiths is a God of beauty, holiness, sovereignty, goodness, righteousness, and truth, but also of love, compassion, and mercy. Such are the attributes that sacred music within the Judeo-Christian tradition strives to translate into sound.

2. The music must speak about the nature of the relationship that exists between the believers and their god. In our listening in class, we discovered relationships of a fearful, trustful, respectful, mysterious, and supernatural nature. The various musical selections spoke of relationships that involved ecstasy, meditation, blind ritual, emotional response, or cognitive participation through learning and understanding. The nature of our relationships with God in the light of the biblical tradition encourages attitudes such as adoration, trust, love, repentance, obedience, and submission.

3. The music must tell about the values and beliefs of a particular group. The biblical account teaches us values that affirm Creation and uphold and enhance our relationships with God, our neighbor, and nature.

These are the values that must be conveyed or conveyable by a musical style in order for the music to qualify as sacred music. But the role of sacred music goes beyond carrying truths and values. It also implies a factor of communication.

Sacred Music Is a Vehicle for Expression and Communication

Music is able to communicate above and beyond verbal expression and to touch the realms of the unutterable. When words are insufficient expression, music still speaks and touches the heart and mind. Herein lies one of the primary purposes of art in worship. Whether in a secular or sacred setting, music functions as a vehicle for expression and communication, both on the vertical level, that is, our relationships with God, and on the horizontal level, our relationships with fellow worshippers. A sacred experience not only consists of receiving truths and blessings; it also implies the possibility of a response on the part of the believer, a channel to verbalize the heart's desire. The musical experience creates avenues for wholistic or emotional responses. It engages the believer with his or her whole being and enhances the sacred event. It provides a channel to communicate simultaneously as a community and as an individual.

Sacred Music Is Defined Within a Cultural Setting

In the face of so much musical variety, it appears that sacred music styles are also defined by conventions. A religious community needs to determine which musical language belongs to *its own cultural setting* and which is appropriate to express the values attached to the sacred and supernatural as they are understood within that given culture or subculture. In order to preserve true worship values, it is essential to understand that any discussion of musical style must take place *within* the framework of a given style category, not *among* different styles.[3] We have already understood that there is no such thing as a *sacred music style* per se—it varies from one cultural setting to another, from one musical language to another. What is important, however, is to determine whether a particular choice *within* a given style is appropriate for a worship experience. The prerogative of the choice of a musical style for worship is not simply a right and privilege for a group or community; it is first and foremost a responsibility.

Sacred Music Is God's Delight

God delights in music. Too often we think of music as a human pursuit for enjoyment, but music was already part of the heavenly experience before the creation of the human universe. The book of Job tells us that the Creation process was accompanied by the song of angels (Job 38:4, 7). As the Redeemer was born, the angels rejoiced with singing (Luke 2:13, 14), and God Himself will rejoice with singing over the saved sinner (Zephaniah 3:17). It was God Himself who dictated a song to Moses and commanded him to teach the Israelites to *sing* the law (Deuteronomy 31:19), and who gave instructions to David for the setting up of a musical liturgy in the Temple (1 Chronicles 23 and 25).

When we speak about sacred music or worship music, another dimension is added to the musical experience, namely, the sacred, or divine. There are two partners in worship: God and humanity. In worship, music is performed for God by human beings. The holy is approached in a human language. This creates a constant tension, a healthy tension, between the vertical and the horizontal. As is true for every component in worship, music also partakes of the tension between the vertical and the horizontal.

Any discussion about music, sacred or secular, that happens from a religious perspective, that is, assuming a life in relationship with God, will naturally lead to ethical considerations. The way this relationship between ethics and aesthetics is commonly understood has given rise to a number of misunderstandings that need to be sorted out in order to facilitate healthy discussion and exchange.

AESTHETICS VERSUS ETHICS: DOES MUSIC HAVE GOOD AND EVIL IN IT?

Many people will affirm that as they listen to "good" (secular or sacred) music, they feel elevated in their minds and souls, and it helps them become better and more spiritual people. There is a tendency to "intertwine and even fuse moral and aesthetic judgment,"[4] that is, to identify an aesthetic experience with an ethical experience. Such a perspective assumes that beautiful music is necessarily good music and vice versa, and that the contemplation of something beautiful and artistic (or ugly and vulgar) has a moral effect on us, i.e., makes us become better (or worse) people. Music that elevates our minds is not necessarily sacred because of that quality, and music that comes across as cheap or that is performed poorly has nothing to do with religion or morality, but simply with bad taste. It is important to clarify and understand the particular nature of the aesthetic and the ethical experiences and to distinguish between the two.

Consulting an encyclopedia definition of the aesthetic experience reveals the following meaning: "In the very act of concentrating our energies upon an aesthetic object, our spiritual state is improved; there is a release from tension and a kind of inner clarification that was not present before. The effect includes a heightening of our sensibilities, a refining of our capacities for perceptual and emotional discrimination, and a capacity to respond more sensitively to the world around us."[5]

It is essential at this point to find out what the author means by "spiritual state." He indeed refers to it in terms of "a release from tension," an "inner clarification," "a heightening of our sensibilities," "perceptual and emotional discrimination," and a more sensitive response "to the world around us." Such characterizations partake primarily of the aesthetic rather than the religious. Even though such activities and exercises deal with the realm of the human spirit in their reference to the mind and the senses, and are thus connected with a "spiritual" experience, they do not refer to a religious experience in the etymological sense of the word, namely, as a life connected to God.

It is important to distinguish between an aesthetic (spiritual) experience and a religious experience; they are not equivalent. Harold Best brings out the difference between the two experiences quite clearly in the following statements: "The beauty of God is not aesthetic beauty but moral and ethical beauty. The beauty of the creation is not moral beauty; it is aesthetic beauty, artifactual beauty. Aesthetic beauty lies in the *way* and the quality with which something is made or said. Truth lies in *what* is said. . . . Being emotionally moved by music is not the same as being spiritually or morally shaped by it."[6]

While on the level of God, aesthetic and moral beauty (excellence and goodness) are one and the same, on the human level, because of sin, aesthetic beauty is not necessarily synonymous with goodness. The question comes up immediately, then, is it possible that an object, a created thing in itself, can carry good or evil? Can a tree or a rock convey moral power, a power to change us for good or evil? Likewise, can a sound, a melody, a rhythm, or a given level of volume carry and convey good or evil? When we listen to music—to what we commonly call beautiful music, art music—or contemplate some artwork, does this imply that we become better persons? If that is the case, music would have the power to carry moral meaning, i.e., to implant good and evil in the human soul. Some people have advocated this theory and still do so. It grew out of a legitimate concern for the well-being of the human soul and its preservation from evil, and was then carried and perpetuated through the ages. These theories reach all the way back to the church fathers and, ultimately, to the ancient Greek philosophers.

Indeed, in studying the writings of the early church fathers and the earliest music theorists of the Christian era, as well as some comments on music made by theologians who lived much closer to our time, one is surprised to find a vast correspondence of opinions about the nature and power of music. Together with other concepts taken from Hellenistic thinking, the Greek theories about the power of music strongly infiltrated and permeated Christian theology and philosophy. There was a common thread of belief in the power of music to affect and change the character, all the way back from John Calvin (sixteenth century A.D.)[7] to Justin Martyr (second century A.D.).[8] Clement of Alexandria,[9] Basil the Great,[10] Saint John Chrysostom,[11] Saint Augustine,[12] Boethius,[13] Cassiodorus,[14] and Isidore of Seville[15] all were influenced by platonic ideas and considered the spiritual world as the only real world; material effects are only signs of spiritual reality. In this sense, music, as a sign of spiritual reality, is able to exert spiritual power in the lives of the believers.[16]

When being confronted with such strongly defended theories, it is one's duty to search and find out where they come from and to what extent they are right and in keeping with the biblical views. In the next pages, we are taking a quick look[17] at the ideas that lie at the basis of this theory, namely, the Greek theory of aesthetics, and how it relates to ethics.

The Greek Theory of Ethos

The belief in the moral power of art is illustrated by the famous saying of Plato that "rhythm and *harmonia*[18] [in the arts] permeate the inner part of the soul, bring graciousness to it, and make the strongest impression, making a man gracious if he has the right kind of upbringing."[19] For a number of Greek philosophers aesthetics and ethics were intimately interconnected.[20] Both attributes belonged to the ideal world of forms and ideas, which was made up of perfect truth, beauty, and goodness, which in turn formed the highest principle, unity, the one. Perfect beauty and goodness could exist only in the ideal world, and the highest endeavor of a human being was to pursue good, beauty, and truth.[21] According to Plato's analogy of the cave,[22] manifestations of human achievement could only be mere reflections of the invisible forms. Art, on the contrary, was understood to be one way to embody—and lead to—this ideal world. Indeed, artworks were not merely seen as the product of inspiration, applying to the world of senses. They were first of all understood to be expressions of rational, numerical relationships,[23] obeying the same mathematical rules that governed the whole universe. It was, incidentally, Pythagoras' discovery of the mathematical ratios of musical intervals that gave rise to the idea that the universe was founded on rational and harmonious principles. Thus art, and especially music, became a mirror of the cosmic, enabling the human being to participate in the ideal world.

Aesthetics (beauty) and ethics (virtue) shared not only a similar nature[24] but also a common function, namely, to regulate, order, and moderate excessive (irrational) passions of the human soul. The human soul (the microcosm of the universe) had been created as a mirror of the universal soul (the macrocosm of the universe) and partook of the same laws and properties as the universe.[25] The philosopher was responsible for the education of the rational part of the soul by teaching virtues through the exercise of the intellect. The musician dealt with the irrational (emotional) part of the soul, allowing it to receive virtue by means of particular modes *(harmoniai)* or rhythms. To Plato, the philosopher and the musician shared a common source of inspiration: "The wise man is similar to the musician, since he has his soul organized by harmonia."[26]

Beauty and virtue were, indeed, identified and measured by the same criteria. In Greek thinking, the universe and all of its manifestations were understood as forming harmonious relationships. These were governed by mathematical laws that demonstrated order, measure, and balance. In the same way, beauty was also defined in terms of mathematical rules, as can be seen in the principle of the golden mean or the mathematical proportions found at the core of the theoretical system of music.[27] As fifth-century B.C. Greek sculptor Polyclitus said, "The beautiful comes about, little by little, through many numbers."[28] In keeping with Plato's analogy of the cave, the theoretical study of the numerical relationships that governed music was advocated over and against the actual practice of music because "it compels the soul to look upward and leads it from things here to things yonder," [29] thus helping the soul toward the apprehension of the beautiful and the good.

Both Plato and Aristotle understood virtue as harmony, balance, and measure, that is, an absence of excessiveness.[30] For example, bravery (fortitude)[31]—the virtue most often associated with proper music education in ancient Greece[32]—was situated somewhere in the middle between cowardice and foolhardiness, which were seen as excessive emotions. Bravery was defined as the "capacity to preserve through everything the right and lawful belief as to what is to be feared and what is not"[33] and represented the mean (middle, average) between the two extreme emotions. In that sense, bravery denoted a harmonious and balanced attitude.[34] The idea of the average, indeed, represented the guideline to ideal human behavior. Sadness and melancholy, even compassion, were considered as lying outside of the accepted norms of "equity" in regard to discretion or temperance. Thus, musical scales that were understood to incline the soul toward these emotions (e.g., the Lydian and Mixolydian modes) were banned.

The function of music was to organize "harmoniously" all things.[35] For the ancient Greeks, the moral value of art resided precisely in this teaching of the rational principles of balance and harmony (equity). Behavior that did not feature harmony, balance, and measure was considered to be evil. Vice versa, a virtuous action was considered to be beautiful because it demonstrated harmony and balance. Beauty, i.e., harmony and proportion, embodied the very structure of the good. Virtue was intimately tied to aesthetics.

But how was it possible to arrive at this aesthetic/ethical experience? What was the process that enabled music, the arts, to have an impact on the human soul? An essential step in reaching the aesthetic—and therefore ethical—experience in Greek antiquity was through contemplation. According to Plato, during contemplation of works of art (architecture, sculpture, paintings, music, drama, etc.), the individual would "take delight in [beautiful things] and receive them into his soul to foster its growth and become himself beautiful and good."[36] Through the intellectual exercise of contemplating works of art, the human soul would be able to obtain knowledge and to identify with eternal virtue, truth, goodness, and beauty. Greek philosophers believed that the physical object in itself stood for the spiritual power. Contemplating the object would then automatically affect the spiritual dimension within the contemplator.

The contemplation of works of art such as the statues, which typically represented gods, was primarily meant to elevate the human soul and become a model for it—as we "dwell amid fair sights and sounds, and receive the good in everything, beauty shall flow into the eye and ear . . . and insensibly draw the soul . . . into likeness and sympathy with the beauty of reason."[37] The oversized dimension of these statues referred the human being to the ideal and metaphysical nature of the contemplation in which beauty transcended virtue. In a similar manner the contemplation of music, while passing through the sensory aspect of the soul, was able to lift the human soul out of the transitory and accidental character typical of the musical experience onto the permanent and essential level of the universal experience. It achieved this goal by means of the rich mathematical relationships embedded in its melodies, and the principle of unity embodied in its rhythms. In Greek thinking, music served as an avenue to gain a better understanding of the ideal forms of the virtues of beauty and goodness, thus bringing the individual closer to the ultimate goal of existence, the contemplation of the eternal. In this perspective, harmony and balance (proportion) represented the very structure of good.

As one considers the Greek approach to music, one might feel very much in agreement with such a perspective. Is it not true that we are affected by the music we are listening to? But how does music affect us? Are we helplessly at the mercy of musical influences? Does music indeed have the capacity to change our characters into the image of the contemplated emotion?

At the very beginning of our study we learned that music affects us on the levels of our bodies, minds, and feelings. We speak of music as cheering us up, energizing us, and elevating us, but also as making us sad or nostalgic. We need to remember, however, that to the Greeks, the impact of certain melodies, rhythms, and instruments went beyond a mere effect on the emotions. These musical elements indeed were understood to act directly on the very character of the person and to have power to shape, change, and transform it. Art, in Greek thinking, involves a process of identification: "Mele [melodies[38]] do actually contain in themselves imitations of ethoses; . . . people when hearing them are affected."[39] This would mean that when we listen to music representing anger, mildness, courage, temperance, etc., it would change our soul to these various states. Such transformations were possible because of a "certain affinity of the soul with the harmoniai and rhythms.[40] The soul becomes the harmonia; i.e., the character is changed to express the emotion contained in the music: "Music has the power of producing a certain effect on the ethos (character) of the soul."[41]

The Biblical Perspective

The belief that a physical component of music has the power to determine an ethical or a spiritual condition—leading into evil or good behavior or thinking—belongs, then, to a pagan way of thinking that leads to a spirit of idolatry. In idolatry the object in itself is granted a magic power. In the case of music such power would be attributed to a melody or scale pattern (e.g., blues, folk), a particular chord structure (seventh chord, ninth chord, major triad), a rhythmic pattern (syncopation, marching rhythm), or the sound of a particular instrument (guitar, drum, saxophone, piano, organ). The Word of God teaches us, though, that the transforming power does not result from the contemplation of human work, whatever it is. Instead, it belongs only to the divine action—it is the work of the Holy Spirit. "We all . . . beholding . . . the glory of the Lord, are being transformed into the same image . . . just as by the Spirit of the Lord" (2 Corinthians 3:18, NKJV). The good resides in God alone, and it is only as we look to Jesus that "by beholding we become changed."[42] It is interesting to observe how Paul uses Greek philosophy's concept of contemplation to introduce an entirely new truth of a completely different order. He speaks of contemplation but refers to the transforming power that belongs to the contemplation of "the glory of the Lord."

Moreover, in biblical thought the transforming power does not reside in the passive act of contemplation, but in the active response of hearing and obeying the divine voice of revelation.[43] As the great Jewish commentator S. R. Hirsch put it so eloquently, "Human excellence does not consist in lifting our eyes towards God in the hope to contemplate Him, but rather in being elevated by Him . . . so that we may see the world according to His point of view."[44] This elevation toward transformation happens only by the power of the Divine Spirit and cannot be obtained by the contemplation of human objects of creation, such as works of art. When our wills are aligned with the will of God, when we see the world from the perspective of God, then character excellence and highest ethical behavior will be achieved. Biblical ethics are not arrived at and developed by means of contemplation, but by the responsible acts of listening and submitting in willful obedience. Biblical ethics imply active collaboration: the Holy Spirit convinces us of sin, and we respond by hearing and obeying. It is not a human object that acts upon me but rather the Spirit and the Word of divine revelation.

There appears, then, to be a fundamental difference between the Greek view of good and evil and the biblical understanding of what is right and wrong. The Greeks conceived good and evil in terms of harmony and disharmony. Good music was music whose language reflected the mathematical principles of balance and harmony. Moreover, it was not the concrete things on earth that were important for them, but rather what pointed to a higher level, in order to come closer to the perfect understanding of the good. Nearer to our time, modernism, an art movement of the late nineteenth century, adopted a larger view of ethics, insofar as the good was also very conceivable as disharmonious or ugly, such as an act of sacrifice or renunciation. Translated into music, this means that excessively emotional music, dissonance or clashing sounds, would also qualify as art, especially as a representation of reality. On the other hand, evil could present itself as very harmonious, logical, and well structured, such as the Nazi machine during World War II. Against these secular approaches, the biblical point of view of good and evil situates itself on a totally different level, namely, that of obedience or disobedience to the law of God. It is no more an abstract principle, but places the individual actions on the level of a relationship with God and fellow humans. It becomes, then, essential to make a use of music that is in harmony with the laws of God.

If we want to place our discussion of music into a biblical perspective, we must be aware of the differences between these various concepts of ethics and be careful not to apply a Greek concept of ethics to a modern approach, or even more so, to a biblical one.

Through the voice of church fathers and modern theologians, this Greek understanding of the relationship between ethics and aesthetics reached all the way down to our times and can be recognized in the terminology that still characterizes our conversations about music, that is, our use of "good" and "bad" to characterize music.[45] Words such as "good" and "bad" belong to the realm of ethics and can therefore become very equivocal and misleading. This is true especially when people use these terms indiscriminately, applying them when speaking about music in aesthetic terms: good music, that is, artistic and well crafted, versus bad music, that is, simplistic and poorly crafted. In terms of ethics, the qualifiers "good" and "bad" refer to ethical/unethical or moral/immoral actions or thoughts. In terms of aesthetics, the same words refer to external qualities of things (how something looks or sounds).

As we strive to foster better understanding and to create fruitful dialogue, we must carefully choose our vocabulary when speaking about music, and limit ourselves to exact and precise terminology. We need to make sure there is no ambiguity in the way we use these terms. In any genre of music, whether classical, religious, or popular, there are pieces/songs that belong—from an aesthetic standpoint—to the domain of the profound or sublime (art music); and then there are those that partake of the superficial, the intellectually and artistically cheap (commercial music). There is music that is complex, refined in its internal relationships and allusions, and well crafted. And there is also music that is simplistic or mediocre, in bad taste or even outright vulgar, and poorly crafted.[46] These are characterizations that remain on the level of an aesthetic appreciation and are more adequate for discussions of musical quality.

While these dichotomies of musical appreciation belong to every age of musical composition, they seem to resonate much stronger regarding music from the past century. The beginnings of this phenomenon must be traced back to the early nineteenth century, when, under the democratic impulse of the French Revolution, and with reference to the ancient Greek model, music was understood as a powerful tool to teach and entertain the masses. During the twentieth century the great flowering of commercial music that took off around the 1950s widened the rift between what we may call cultivated, or serious, music (rather than classical music) and popular music (light music). Cultivated, serious music is understood to provide spiritual meaning and aesthetic fulfillment by challenging the listener to participate in the process of interpretation. To an increasing degree during the recent past decades, music came to be considered primarily as entertainment and merchandise, catering to the collective taste and imagination and to a consumer culture. In such a culture there is little time for the decoding and understanding of a musical language. Rather, there is the desire for immediate use and gratification, accelerated emotional stimulation (pleasure generation), and the spectacular. In following this path, music has become an adequate picture of its culture: art and music have become consumer products.[47] One should take care, however, not to fall into a simplistic appreciation of art music versus popular music. As church music scholar Donald Hustad discussed so appropriately, there is not much relevancy in discussing the "relative worth" of serious music and popular music. Both genres give pleasure and communicate meaning. While art music might be "more profound in its delineation of meaning," popular music "gets to the meaning more directly."[48] There is, then, obviously a place and function for both serious and popular music, and this place may very well include the event of worship—as long as the right meaning is conveyed in a tasteful and appropriate manner.

APPROPRIATE VERSUS INAPPROPRIATE

Beyond the aesthetic appreciation, there is another dimension that needs to be introduced as we speak of music in the context of worship, namely, the dimension of *appropriateness* and *inappropriateness*. A song or piece of music, whichever style it is representing (classical, traditional, popular), can feature the highest artistic characteristics and still not be *appropriate* for a given occasion. What is appropriate for rejoicing is not appropriate for mourning. What is appropriate for protest or entertainment or for recreation or leisure may not be appropriate for a sacred setting. What is appropriate in one culture for worship may not be appropriate in another culture. What might have been appropriate for worship in a given time in the past may not be appropriate for today's worship.

The decision in favor of the appropriateness or inappropriateness of music must be made based on a set of values and criteria that define a given event. In the case of worship music, it is the values attached to worship that define appropriate or inappropriate worship music. The problem with worship music comes not so much from a wrong understanding of music, but rather from a lack of understanding what worship is or from very personal and subjective opinions with regard to worship. If we want to tackle the matter of appropriate versus inappropriate music, we first need to remedy our ignorance or misconceptions about the very source and foundation of worship music.[49]

The above discussion on aesthetics versus ethics has taught us that it is, indeed, suspicious to attribute to musical elements (melody, harmony, rhythm, chords, instruments) any power of good or evil. But what about a musical discourse conveying meaning? Does a musical experience speak to us in a specific way? How do we capture the meaning as we are listening to music? Why do people have different understandings while listening to the same music?

How Does Music Convey Meaning?

What characterizes art, and music in particular, is that while it has the ability to speak to everybody in general, it speaks differently to each individual. Compare how you were touched by a sermon to the way a friend was (or was not) moved by it. You might find different applications, and this is in the explicit context of spoken words. When referring to the ability of music to "open up levels of reality that otherwise are closed to us," professor Iris Yob observes that "the symbols of art and music are most effective pointers simply because they suggest without delineating and describe without circumscribing."[50] We need to keep this distinction in mind when we speak about the messages that music conveys. On the universal level these messages remain very general and undefinable. It is on the level of the individual experience that we attribute specific meaning to a work of art. A number of statements about music, made by authorities in the field of music and aesthetics, will help to further clarify this point.

In an October 1951 presentation for the Elson Lectures under the auspices of the Library of Congress, Jacques Barzun, professor of history at Columbia University, made the following statement on the ability of music to communicate meaning: "Music communicates something beyond the relation of its audible parts. It conveys a meaning which some people catch and others not; a meaning which is not *in* the notes, since these can be played correctly and yet meaninglessly; a meaning which is not universally intelligible, since listeners vary in their judgment of composers, of works, of performances; a meaning which like verbal meaning depends on a mass of previous knowledge and feeling. This last truth is not merely one of common observation, it has also been the subject of experiment."[51]

French scholar Jules Combarieu, who did an extensive study on the relationship between music and society, noticed moreover that the quality of music (its vocabulary) and the mode of performance (its context) are only one side to the effects of music. He points out that one also needs to consider "the ideas which are in the mind of the listener and which associate with the listening experience."[52]

This insight was corroborated by John Milson, commenting in the *BBC Music Magazine* about how extramusical elements affect our understanding of music: "Often when we speak of 'understanding' a work, what we have in fact done is aligned its sounds with our own emotional and narrative and pictorial agendas. The music remains, at best, richly suggestive and essentially ambiguous: powerless (Stravinsky famously said) to express anything, even if well able to imply a great deal." [53]

Finally, Harold Best addressed the same issue in a religious context: "Music has no interior beacon that guarantees permanent meaning. Unlike truth, which is transcultural, absolute, and unchangeable, music can shift in meaning from place to place and time to time. . . . The more a piece of music is repeated in the same context, the more it will begin to 'mean' that context."[54]

What we learn from all these statements is that, contrary to popular belief, music does not convey in itself, in its vocabulary (scales, chords, instruments, styles, etc.), specific meaning. For this reason a particular kind of music is not universally understood in the exact same way. It will take on different meanings according to time and place. What lends the music its meaning is the context in which it is performed, the nature and degree of knowledge of the listener about this particular music, and the ideas or associations in the listener's mind at the time of the listening experience.

These realities, indeed, are not foreign or unknown to us; we can verify them very easily in our personal experiences with music. As we saw earlier, they were made very plain during our class listening exercises with both secular and sacred music. We had identified at that point several cofactors in the musical experience. The musical vocabulary and the context of the performance certainly play their role in the degree of understanding, or lack of understanding, of the music. However, appreciation and meaning in music are predominantly the result of the listener's personal imagination, expectations, and willful intention. Daniel Levitin, neuroscientist and professor of psychology and music at McGill University, comments extensively on the essential role of anticipation and expectation in the musical experience: "The setting up and the manipulation of expectations is the heart of music. . . . Music communicates to us emotionally through systematic violations of expectations."[55] This means, then, that we hear in music what we expect to hear, what we want to hear, and what we invest personally into the listening experience, in terms of our personalities and based on the memories of previous musical experiences.

Let me illustrate this point with an example taken from a video tape on African drumming, "Listening to the Silence."[56] At a given point in the video recording, we see an excerpt of a possession scene accompanied by drumming. Four or five drummers provide the rhythms that accompany the event. We see the dancer whirling and jumping until he reaches the state of trance and is carried off by two assistants. During the whole scene, we can observe the drummers, who go about their business, talking, laughing, and joking. While one person was affected by the rhythm to the extent that he fell into a trance, the others—those who actually produced the desired effect—were not affected at all.

This example demonstrates that the musical experience per se does not have power over us to induce us to certain behaviors or actions. The effect of music depends on how willfully we invest ourselves personally into the listening experience, bringing with us our imaginations and expectations, etc. This is what happened to the individual who entered into a trance. Any such experience comes with a thorough personal preparation and a willful investment of one's personality at the moment of the happening. The drummers were just doing their job and were not interested in entering into a spiritual experience; therefore, they were not affected by the music in the same way.

When I was a missionary on the island of Mauritius, in the Indian Ocean, I had a chance to observe the rituals of the Hindu festival *Thaipoosam Cavadee*. I watched people walk over beds of hot coals, an act performed as a spiritual exercise. Before they could achieve such a feat, the candidates had undergone a thorough spiritual preparation for several weeks, including a vegetarian diet and/or fasting, and other spiritual exercises. Both the physical and spiritual preparation, as well as their willful investment in the experience, made it possible for them to go through the exercise unscathed. The accompanying music, played on an oboelike instrument and a small drum, was a mere accessory. The successful performance of this act was not induced by a particular type of music, but was instead the result of a thorough physical and spiritual conditioning.

We must, then, acknowledge that music has no magical power per se. We hear in music what we want and expect to hear in it. What we hear is a result of what we invest into our listening experience. The seventeenth-century philosopher Spinoza made the same point: good and evil are not present in things; it is the value we ascribe to the things that makes them good or evil. It is the relationship between the things and the mind that creates good and evil.[57]

Music does not belong in the pagan realm of deities and forces of nature that are believed to have power over human beings, and against which we apparently have no defense. It is true that such theories have been perpetuated through the ages and were adopted by religious and secular powers in turn. As Christians we do know, however, that we are called to take responsibility in regard to our thoughts and actions that are the result of the state of our hearts and not the inevitable influence of an exterior agent. The Gospel of Mark makes this very clear: "Nothing outside a man can make him 'unclean' by going into him. Rather, it is what comes out of a man that makes him 'unclean.' . . . For from within, out of men's hearts, come evil thoughts, sexual immorality, theft, murder, adultery, greed, malice, deceit, lewdness, envy, slander, arrogance and folly. All these evils come from inside and make a man 'unclean'" (Mark 7:15, 21-23).

Commenting on this passage, Harold Best observed, "It is not what music does to us, it is what we choose to do with music, by virtue of the condition of our heart. . . . It is up to each individual and within each person's power to decide what moral actions can be taken or refused when music is heard."[58]

How often have the evils listed in Mark 7 been ascribed to the effect of music on a listener? To throw the blame on music is to refuse one's moral responsibilities. It is time to rehabilitate the reputation of music and to recognize its real role. It is time to look deeply into our souls to find and eradicate those hidden evils that we like to blame on music. *The moral power of music does not reside in the music itself, but resides where music intersects with experience, that is, in an event.*

In the same way that music has no magical power to lure us into wrongdoing, music also has no power to make us better persons. Throughout history music has failed, indeed, to make us more ethical or moral persons. This was a recurring dream of more than one political power, namely, to use music to better humanity. In modern times it was picked up particularly by the theorists of the French Revolution (Marie-Joseph Chénier, etc.) and then by the great Romantics of the nineteenth century (Lamennais, Liszt, etc.). They invested music with the role of educator of humanity in order to create, as proposed by the Greek model, a better society. Once the church had been abolished by the French revolutionaries, the arts, and especially the musical arts, were meant to take its place and to fulfill the role of religion.[59]

History has repeatedly shown the failure of this undertaking. The biblical account of David playing the harp before Saul (see 1 Samuel 16:15-23) reveals the precarious character of this position. Saul had David come before him to play the harp to soothe his "evil" spirit. The Bible says, "David would take his harp and play. Then relief would come to Saul; he would feel better, and the evil spirit would leave him" (1 Samuel 16:23). It is significant, then, to observe that on a later occasion the same music had no calming effect: "But an evil spirit from the Lord came upon Saul as he was sitting in his house with his spear in his hand. While David was playing the harp, Saul tried to pin him to the wall with his spear, but David eluded him as Saul drove the spear into the wall" (1 Samuel 19:9, 10). It is significant that the Hebrew word *ra'*, which has been translated by the New International Version with the word "evil," has been translated by the New King James Version with the word "distressed," a translation that confirms our observation about the nonethical significance of music.

Another example that illustrates the failure of music to produce better people is related to the Nazi experience. It is a well-known fact that Nazi officers were very fond of classical music and, within the context of the concentration camps, made it a habit to listen to the music on a regular basis. The officers even arranged prisoner performances for their personal enjoyment. There is a stark contradiction between the brutal and inhumane behavior of these officers and the ennobling and civilizing effect classical music is declared to exert on the listener.[60] If there were a direct relationship between the music and the behavior of the listener, classical music, because of its high aesthetic standards, would lead the listeners to treat their fellow humans with the greatest respect and according to the highest moral standards. The Nazi example belies such a theory in a flagrant manner. Once a student of mine tried to salvage the theory by offering the following explanation: the effect of the music was not noticeable because the officers had not yet listened long enough to good music! Indeed, centuries of education and re-finement were not able to achieve one of the purposes that political and spiritual leaders have long attributed to music: to change people, making the world a better place.

These examples make us reconsider the theory of the moral power of music. Regular exposure to classical music may contribute to a certain intellectual refinement. It may foster structural qualities in our thinking. But it certainly does not have the power to make us better people in terms of ethics or morality. This is where the difference between the aesthetic and ethical experiences we discussed earlier becomes clear. We learn from our observations that while certain individuals are affected by a given type of music (e.g., led into ecstasy or possession), others remain completely untouched by it. What affects me in one sense does not necessarily affect my neighbor. In other words, there is more to the musical experience than the sound experience itself. My musical experience also depends on who I am, what my background is, and what I want or allow myself to put into it.

Nonetheless, we all have experienced that music does indeed affect us in one way or another. Where, then, does the real power of music reside?

THE REAL POWER OF MUSIC

We have seen that the positive or negative power of music cannot be found in the musical elements or a given musical style. The real power of music lies in its ability to *transform* a given situation, namely, to intensify, to beautify, to stimulate, to create associations, and to build community.

Intensification

While music does not create action, it does create intensification. When music accompanies words, events, or any given situation, it intensifies the experience by imparting emotional impact to the context and by causing strong emotional responses. It drives those experiences into the innermost regions of our souls and creates a deep-seated meaning that emerges in long-lasting memory.[61] The higher the level of tension, the greater the impact of the experience. A scientific explanation of this effect is that music increases our receptivity to other stimulations.

Willem Van de Wall, renowned music educator and a seminal figure in the early development of the discipline of music therapy, writes, "The varied uses of music increase people's receptivity to other stimuli and thus may indirectly strengthen the effect of the message whatever it may be."[62] We all have such examples to tell: the melody of a hymn reminds us of a deep spiritual commitment that took place as we were listening to that song; the sound of a children's song brings back dear memories of our childhood; listening to an oldie makes us feel younger as it transports us back to our teenage years and experiences, etc.

The intensifying impact of music should not leave us without concern. While intensification is a wonderful experience, it is not a selective process. Any experience will benefit from it, the desirable as well as the undesirable ones. Music will not only intensify positive and desirable experiences. It exercises the same power of intensification on immoral, disruptive, or alienating experiences, driving them deep into our souls and memories. This effect, however, is achieved not only with popular music (pop, rock, and their associated styles) as is generally assumed; it happens with any kind or style of music, including classical music.[63]

Beautification

Beyond its power of intensification, music also embellishes and beautifies an event, words, experiences, or actions. Music makes anything it accompanies appear more beautiful, more desirable, more seductive and alluring. Have you ever watched a television advertisement in mute mode? Most of the effect is lost. There is a reason that stores play music—to attract customers and keep them roaming around. The sound of music embellishes the shopping experience and entices customers to buy.[64] But this is also precisely how temptation works—and has been working since the beginning of time—namely, through *deception* and *delusion*. Evil is presented as desirable, attractive, or even good and beautiful. Such circumstances create ambiguity and often end in syncretism, the mixing of desirable and undesirable values. We must be aware that while immoral behavior is not originated by music, music can contribute to the legitimization of immoral behavior, making it feel all right to indulge in a certain attitude because it feels so good and is so beautiful.[65]

Stimulation and Empowerment

Earlier in this book we saw that music, and more particularly the rhythmic element, has a stimulating and empowering effect (see pp. 29-32). Music animates life and energizes us into action. It appears, however, that the result is an ever increasing need for higher levels of tension and a search for pleasure for its own sake and, in the wake of those, an increased chance for greater abandonment of control.

In terms of musical language, the stimulating effect of music is dependent on the degree of loudness and dissonance and on the complexity of rhythmic interrelationships. Interestingly, the history of the development of musical style over the centuries has shown a gradual increase in dissonance and loudness. This can be observed in the changes undergone by the harmonic language since the beginning of polyphonic music in the thirteenth century. Musical treatises from those times are filled with discussions about which intervals are recognized as a consonance or a dissonance. Furthermore, the history of instrument building since the 1600s has been marked by the quest for greater capacity to produce a louder sound, particularly in the field of string instruments, as builders have sought greater projection of more brilliance of sound. The same may be observed in regard to the development of the piano, which at the turn of the nineteenth century was aimed at larger sound production. Also, in regard to rhythm, the musical language of the twentieth century especially distinguished itself by the high complexity of the rhythmic component, which could be rivaled only by the rhythmic and metric intricacies of the fourteenth century.

It is important, then, to understand that the stimulating effects of music are not the result of an isolated rhythmic pattern (such as syncopation, for example), a distinctive turn of melody, or a particular instrumental sound (such as the saxophone, for example). The stimulating effect of music is the result of the combination of a number of different factors. When, in addition, certain extramusical elements are added to the musical elements—performance setting, deportment of the musicians, electronically enhanced sound (especially of the deep basses, etc.)—the factor of stimulation can be exponentially increased. One needs to keep in mind this complexity of the musical experience and to be aware of how the various factors that make up a musical style can impact an individual. This certainly is a greater concern today—because of how music is approached in terms of balance between tension and relaxation—than it was during earlier centuries. Care should also be taken that the degree of stimulation sought is appropriate to the occasion, such as worship, healthy and re-creative entertainment, etc.

Associations

The diverse effects of music (intensification, beautification, stimulation) combine to create what we call *associations*. Musical experiences always happen in a context, and we naturally establish a connection—an association—between the musical event and the environment in which it takes place. Our brains function according to the multiple trace memory model, which causes the brain to cross code the music we are listening to with the events that accompany the listening experience.[66] These events may involve places, people, thoughts, actions, or any other simultaneous happening. The emotional impact of music is magnified by this process of association with an event. We all have experienced the powerful impact of memories coming back at the taste of a familiar flavor, such as a cake our mother used to bake when we were children, or at the scent of a familiar smell, such as candles at Christmas, etc. The same happens with music: as we hear the strains of familiar pieces, they transport us back to the event that was marked by this music.

The forming of associations is a highly subjective process and must be carefully understood and evaluated before it is used to draw universal conclusions. Let me illustrate this point with the following examples.

For most people who love classical music, Mendelssohn's Violin Concerto in E minor is one of the finest of its kind. For years my daughter was unable to listen to this concerto without feeling very nauseated and sick. We used to play this selection when she was very young while we drove to the beach on a very bumpy, winding road that made her feel carsick every time we traveled it. For her, this Mendelssohn concerto was associated with car sickness and had lost all of its beauty. Even though this was wonderful music, to her it was associated with a disagreeable experience. Similarly, while I may find profound meaning in a particular hymn because it is associated with a specific spiritual moment in my life, the same hymn might be completely insignificant—even meaningless or unpleasant—for someone else.

These examples demonstrate that the meaning one individual attaches to a musical selection, by means of his or her own personal associations, can be entirely different, even completely opposite, from the meaning given by another individual to the same music. These differences stem from the fact that the musical experiences are tied to entirely different types of events. What can be a negative musical experience for one may very well be a positive experience for another. What may distract one person from a relationship with Christ may be the very reason another person is drawn to Him. It is very dangerous to use such personal experiences to set up universal principles for a whole group.

Associations, however, are not limited to individuals. Groups and communities often have a consensus on certain associations that are formed through communal experiences. These must be taken into serious consideration when making decisions for a group about appropriate or inappropriate use of music. For instance, a hymn played on steel drums would be a thrilling experience for anyone living outside of the Caribbean. For most of the churches in the West Indies, however, such a performance presents a problem because of the association of these instruments with the carnival and other immoral situations.[67]

As we deal with congregational worship music, the issue of associations becomes even more complex since every single individual who is part of the community comes from a different background or way of life, and each person will have different associations connected with this or that style of music.[68] Encountering musical cultures different from our own should stimulate our search for an understanding of how these musical cultures are an expression of a spirituality similar to our own, though the message is expressed in a different language. Our interest should be awakened as to how these other musical cultures could enrich our own musical language and experience.

Since associations form such an essential part of our musical experience, it is important to understand how the association mechanism functions. When isolated musical components that are neutral in themselves (such as a rhythmic pattern, a melody, a chord, or an instrumental sound) combine to form a musical discourse, this discourse is interpreted in a given cultural context. Thus it is given a particular meaning. Music does not exist in a vacuum. It is a cultural phenomenon that happens within a specific cultural setting and is given meaning in situ. In other words, as music is created and played, the society or cultural group within which this takes place impresses meaning upon it. This happens as the music is associated with the time, place, and situation in which it is played, or with the people who perform it and, through association again, their lifestyles. "The more a piece of music is repeated in the same context, the more it will begin to 'mean' that context," writes Harold Best.[69]

This may, but does not necessarily, signify that the meaning given to the music corresponds to the original intent of the composer. Those two "truths" may even be contradictory. Remember the saraband, which is today a stately piece often played for church services. Originally it was a sensual dance imported from South America. If we want to ensure that a style of music is appropriate for a particular circumstance, it is important to consider which meaning is connected to that style in a given cultural setting and at a given time. In the same way that a society has its common understanding of how to express rejoicing, mourning, respect, or worship, there is generally also a common understanding with regard to the interpretation and use of a particular type of music. This common understanding needs to be taken into consideration.

The meaning of music shifts according to time. Music has no "interior beacon"[70] that guarantees a permanent meaning. Therefore, associations change over the course of time because the musical event becomes associated with new circumstances. This reality also needs to be taken into consideration. What one generation has interpreted as unfit for worship (for instance, the use of electric organs in the nineteenth century and electric guitars in the twentieth century) is not necessarily an obstacle to another generation. New ways of playing these instruments, in venues and on occasions different from previous ones, have created new associations.

It is still important that this new interpretation can be subscribed to by a large segment of a cultural group. It may happen that one individual, because of his/her particular experience in the past, will forever be uneasy with a given style practiced in church. This is true for any style of music in church. It can be the case with a former Catholic believer who gets uneasy at hearing a performance of Schubert's "Ave Maria" or chantlike singing. I have often encountered in my classes students who relate how they had been actively involved in earlier times of their lives as musicians in pop/rock bands. They still find it very difficult, if not impossible, to worship in the contemporary style or to accept any music in church that reminds them remotely of rock, whether it be through the use of certain instruments (electric guitar, saxophone, etc.), lively rhythms, or other characteristics. It brings back strong memories of lifestyle and other practices associated with that music. We need to respect this reaction since, for those individuals, this type of music is intimately linked to and associated with the cultural package they experienced while being part of a band (lifestyle, performance style, etc.).

On the other hand, these individuals should also respect the musical choices of those who do not have the same history of association. Most of the young people who listen to "Christian rock" and who play and sing in church in contemporary style were never exposed to the cultural package of secular rock music. Therefore, they do not live the experience with the same associations and the same effect. To them, it is an energizing and lively experience. This example is another illustration of the principle of the acquired character of the musical experience. We need to accept the reality that we all react in different ways to similar types of musical experiences.

Again, it is important to consider the issue with balance and common sense and to make sure that the interpretation and understanding of a style within a social or cultural group as a whole are considered before making a decision. The church, in the way she expresses and lives the truth, is not a static entity but a living body of people who grow together and toward one another through time, all along their journey.

The impact of associations on how we understand and interpret music is of great importance. As the music is associated in our minds and hearts with a specific situation, it is only a small step from there to associating an event's music with the qualities of the event. The context plays a great role in the meaning given to music.

Associations can, and do, change over time. Through careful and appropriate use of a practice, new and wholesome associations can be created. Though this process of transformation takes time, the past has shown that it is, in fact, a very basic principle. I still remember that when I was a child in Europe, radio and television were criticized as tools of the devil that would lead people to perdition. The association of these channels of communication were so intimately associated with entertainment and frivolity that nobody would ever have thought of using them one day as a primary means of worship or evangelism. History has written the rest of the story!

The Social Factor of Music

So far we have looked into the effects of music on the individual. But music is also a great facilitator of human interaction. It has a community building effect for the same reasons discussed above: it intensifies and embellishes the community event and has an empowering impact on the gathered group or crowd. Mass demonstrations, whether political or artistic, predominantly take place with some singing or chanting of slogans. This is how mass hysteria is achieved, creating a feeling of empowerment, as can be observed easily in political or artistic rallies, as well as in the physical outcome of most of these. Very seldom do such rallies happen in silence, although this would be more typical of peaceful demonstrations, which seem to purposely avoid intensification and excitement.

Beyond its bonding role in human interaction, music is a powerful tool of communication. From social interaction and observation one can, indeed, learn to understand the meaning given to music within a social group and, at the same time, learn a proper response to that music. In this way the musical experience creates social understanding and, ultimately, meaning. Association, of course, plays an important role in this. We all learn, from our personal experiences of watching movies, how "happy" or "scary" music evokes meaning and helps in the understanding of a particular situation.[71]

But there is more to the role of music as communicator. Music can also contribute to the formation of habits and identities. Music that corresponds to the memory paths established in our brains, through our cultural or educational exposure to certain styles, will be perceived as pleasurable based on feelings of expectation and anticipation. We are, therefore, motivated to seek more of it in order to satisfy these senses of anticipation and expectation.[72] Such motivation has the potential to result in a real addiction to music. As early as 1987 American philosopher Allan Bloom commented: "Though students do not love books, they most emphatically love music. Nothing is more singular about this generation than its addiction to music.

This is the age of music and the states of soul that accompany it. . . . Today, a very large portion of young people between the ages of 10 and 20 live for music. It is their passion; nothing else excites them as it does; they cannot take seriously anything alien to music."[73]

The listening experience can thus become habit-forming, especially if it is geared predominantly toward a single style. In that sense, our musical choices can be revealing about who we are as individuals. Mary Devereaux justly comments that "if virtue consists (in part) in taking pleasure in the right things and not in the wrong things, then what is my character now such that I can take pleasure in these things?"[74]

While most often our musical choices are dictated by our personalities or the social context in which we grew up, there are also times when individuals make deliberate choices in matters of music preferences, especially at an age or period in their lives when forming identities. An young person in search of identity will readily associate with other individuals or groups of people he/she wants to be like (role models) or with whom he/she has something in common (ethnic background, for example). There is a strong desire to create a bond and to embrace common values, which can be externalized through common dress or hairstyle, shared activities, or listening to the same style of music. In this case, musical preferences become a mark of personal or group identity.[75]

It is important to remember at this point that, as is true for any habits, the habits we form in matters of musical experiences contribute to shaping our character. In *Messages to Young People*, Ellen G. White made this connection very clear: "Actions, often repeated, form habits, habits form character."[76]

Music is indeed a powerful agent in human activities, daily or sacred, individual or communal. The above explanations have revealed the increasingly complex ramifications of the musical experience, on both the individual and social levels. The question of the meaning of music by means of its associations, and its social role, must therefore always remain at the forefront of our minds. Are the values of the music—as I learned to understand them or as they are understood by the social group I am part of—compatible with Christian values and a Christian lifestyle? Are they fostering Christlike attitudes or, on the contrary, eliciting from me inappropriate thoughts and behavior?

Such questions certainly point to the importance of our personal responsibility in matters of musical choices.

A Responsible Use of Music

There are a number of ways in which we can create a responsible musical experience:

1. Our musical choices help us *understand who we are*. Because music intensifies our natural tendencies, we will "naturally" be drawn to types of musical experiences that respond and cater to our desires and inclinations. Paying attention to these "natural" choices will help us to discover our preferences and penchants. This can become an avenue of self-discovery and a beginning for change.

2. We need to remember that musical styles come with a *cultural package*. They are often associated with places, people, and actions. If my musical choices lead me into situations or relationships that are not in harmony with my values and beliefs, I need to make changes.

3. We need to be aware that music may affect the *emotional and physical well-being* of an individual. It is important to observe to what degree an individual is stimulated, energized, or, on the contrary, depressed by the music he or she is listening to. These effects vary from one individual to another, and one's personal reaction to a certain type of music cannot necessarily be applied to someone else's experience.

4. We need to relearn how to *listen actively* and to *create a "musical conscience."* Too often, our musical experiences are passive. That is, we let music wash over us without even paying attention to it. We need to relearn how to listen to music in a conscious and active way. To do so will help us in pursuing musical experiences that affirm the values that define our lives: the values of respect and care, life and health, moral, mental, and spiritual well-being—all of these applied to ourselves as well as to people with whom we interact.

5. It is also important to find out honestly about our *expectations* when we indulge ourselves in a musical experience. What attracts me in this music? What does it bring me that makes me feel good about it? What kind of experience do I seek? What is the nature and degree of the excitement I pursue? What are my motivations in pursuing it? When I listen to this music, what does it make me want to do? To what extent is this music conducive

to indulge in and maintain undesirable thoughts or actions? Does this music bring me closer to God, or does it draw me away from Him? Am I primarily interested in losing myself in the experience, or do I look, instead, for re-creation in this experience? Our investment in a musical experience should be the result of a conscious, selective, and intentional choice that affirms our value system and our cultural and social setting.

6. Finally, we want to *create musical experiences that intensify, embellish, and re-inforce high moral standards.* In going to a concert or a musical event, I might believe that I am choosing a musical experience, when in reality I am choos-ing to enter into particular activities or to associate with certain individuals whose values might be far removed from mine. These *moral* decisions precede the musical choices. Where we go, with whom we associate, and what we do, do not belong to the realm of musical choices but rather to that of lifestyle decisions. As it accompanies and emotionally heightens an event we choose to attend, the music participates in the elaboration of our value sys-tem. This takes place independently of the style presented, popular or clas-sical. When used on inappropriate occasions, music can become a coagent in detracting from the high principles we are called to. When used in appro-priate venues, music becomes positive affirmation of life and creation, not only on the individual level but also on a communal level.

CONCLUDING REMARKS

Music experiences certainly do affect, inflect, and stimulate our senses, thoughts, and behavior. We all have our own idiosyncrasies and weaknesses; we all are tempted by different things in our lives. Temptation can come in the form of food, books, music, movies, sex, sports, work, etc. Some of these were God's gifts to man and woman, originally meant for their benefit, health, and enjoyment. As these gifts are misused and abused by individuals, they may take on negative connotations. But what becomes a temptation for me is not necessarily a temptation for another. Temptation is not associ-ated only with pop or rock music. Some fall under temptation while listening to classical music, folk music, or even religious music. Satan uses every pos-sible venue to tempt us. Rather than being perceived as the evil itself, music should be understood as a *vehicle*, an *avenue*, for Satan to tempt us to evil. Thus Ellen G. White comments on how Satan makes music a "channel through which to gain access to the minds of the youth."[77] She does not refer there to any specific kind of music. Even classical music or sacred music could be used to manipulate thoughts and feelings—and this, even in church.

Temptation has to do with a personal decision about indulging oneself in thoughts, attitudes, or behaviors that are not in harmony with biblical principles and Christian values. It is each individual's responsibility to make choices in his or her musical preferences and practices in a way that he or she can control desires, tendencies, and temptations. In much the same way, another individual might have to control his or her eating, sex, or work behavior.

Our answer to the question "Is music neutral?" must be articulated very carefully. There are two predominant views on the matter. One view approaches it from a quasi mystical, almost superstitious perspective, lending music a magical power. The other takes a materialistic stance: music has no moral effect whatsoever on the human being.

I do not subscribe to either view, but take into account the dynamic character of the musical experience. Musical meaning cannot be attached to isolated elements of the musical language, such as an instrument, a chord, a melody, a rhythmic pattern, or a style. Those elements are neutral in themselves. However, music does affect us strongly when it acquires meaning within an event, an experience. As such, music cannot be said to be neutral. One should not, though, forget that music affects various individuals in different ways. But it always does so within a given context that determines the understanding of the meaning of a certain type or style of music.

This teaches us, then, a twofold lesson of responsibility and tolerance. We have a responsibility toward ourselves concerning the nature of our musical choices, and a responsibility toward others regarding the musical choices we present or grant to our youth groups and the congregation at large. We learn a lesson of tolerance, in that we do not necessarily understand the full meaning of a style of music if we have not learned, through experience, how to interpret it. Music is a very complex phenomenon, both in itself and as it happens in the reality of an actual experience, whether individual or collective.

We will always celebrate life in its manifold aspects. We will always worship a holy and divine God. And we will always be doing so with our limited and inadequate musical language. In the presence of our human limitation and the great diversity observed in sacred and secular music styles, there is a need to raise our reflection, discussion, and practice of music above and beyond the limits of the personal, the relative, or the simply cultural. In order to find the right and adequate musical language, we need to turn to criteria outside of the subjective and human realm, to criteria that transcend both and go beyond culture or education. We need to find an external and universal source to help us determine how to make music for God. We will find those criteria in the Word of God and in the counsels of Ellen G. White.

---

[1] For more details, see Harold Best, *Music Through the Eyes of Faith* (San Francisco: Harper, 1993), p. 92.

[2] See Anthony Hicks, "Handel, George Frideric, sec. 10: Oratorios and musical dramas," *Grove Music Online*, http://www.grovemusic.com.

[3] For a more in-depth discussion of this concept, see Harold Best, p. 92.

[4] The expression is by Karen Hanson, "How bad can good art be?" *Aesthetics and Ethics: Essays at the Intersection,* Jerrold Levinson, ed. (Cambridge, U.K.: Cambridge University Press, 1998), p. 214.

[5] Paul Edwards, ed., *Encyclopedia of Philosophy,* (New York: The Macmillan Co. and The Free Press, 1967), s.v. "Aesthetics, Problems of," by John Hospers.

[6] Best, pp. 43, 44, 151.

[7] John Calvin, "Epistle to the Reader," *Cinquante Psaumes en français par Clém. Marot (1543),* in *Corpus Reformatorum,* Wilhelm Barum, ed. (Brunschwig, Germany: C. A. Schwetschke and Sons, 1867), vol. 34, chap. 6, pp. 165-172.

[8] Justin Martyr, *The Dialogue With Trypho,* transl. A. Lukyn Williams, D. D. (New York: The Macmillan Co., 1930), chap. 2:4, p. 5.

[9] Clement of Alexandria, *Paedagogus,* J. C. M. Van Winden, ed. (Boston: Brill, 2002), book 2, chap. 4, par. 41; idem, "The New Song," in *Protreptikos,* transl. Thomas Merton (Norfolk, Conn.: New Directions, 1962), par. 9, pp. 15-18.

[10] Basil the Great, "Homily on Psalm 1:1-2," in J.-P. Migne, ed., *Patrologia Cursus Completus, Series Graeca* (Paris: Excecudebatur et venit apud, 1857-1866), vol. 29, col. 209, quoted in James McKinnon, ed., *The Early Christian Period and the Latin Middle Ages,* vol. 2, *Strunk's Source Readings in Music History,* rev. ed., Leo Treitler, general ed. (New York: W. W. Norton and Co., 1998), p. 11; Basil the Great, *Exhortation to Youth as to How They Shall Best Profit by the Writings of Pagan Authors,* vii, in J.-P. Migne, ed., *Patrologia Cursus Completus, Series Graeca,* vol. 31, cols. 581-584, quoted in James McKinnon, *The Early Christian Period and the Latin Middle Ages,* p. 69.

[11] John Chrysostom, "*Exposition of Psalm 41,*" in J.-P. Migne, ed., *Patrologia Cursus Completus, Series Graeca,* vol. 55, cols. 156-159, quoted in James McKinnon, *The Early Christian Period and the Latin Middle Ages,* p. 13.

[12] Saint Augustine, *De Musica,* transl. Frank Hentschel, Philosophische Bibliothek, 539 (Hamburg: Felix Reiner, 2002), book 6, chap. 17, par. 56.

[13] Boethius, *Fundamentals of Music,* transl. Calvin M. Bower, ed., Claude V. Palisca (New Haven, Conn.: Yale University Press, 1989), pp. 2, 3.

[14] Cassiodorus, *An Introduction to Divine and Human Readings,* transl. Leslie Webber Jones (New York: Columbia University Press, 1946), book 2: *Secular Letters,* part 5: "On Music," p. 190.

[15] Isidore of Seville, *Etymologies,* book 3, chap. 17, transl. Helen Dill Goode and Gertrude C. Drake, Colorado College Music Press Translations, 12 (Colorado Springs: Colorado College Music Press, 1980), p. 14.

[16] For more detailed information on this topic, see James McKinnon, ed., *Music in Early Christian Literature* (Cambridge, Mass.: Cambridge University Press, 1987); idem, "The Church Fathers and Musical Instruments" (Ph.D. dissertation, Columbia University, 1965); idem, *The Early Christian Period and the Latin Middle Ages*; David W. Music, *Hymnology: A Collection of Source Readings,* Studies in Liturgical Musicology, No. 4 (Lanham, Md.: The Scarecrow Press, 1996); and Johannes Quasten, *Music and Worship in Pagan and Christian Antiquity,* transl. Boniface Ramsey, O. P. (Washington, D.C.: National Association of Pastoral Musicians, 1973).

[17] Any survey of such a broad topic must, by necessity, remain schematic. The reader will understand that the following explanations are conducted in such a way as to focus narrowly on the topic under discussion and make complex concepts available to a broad public.

[18] The term *harmonia* is often wrongly translated as "harmony." In Greek antiquity it was used to indicate the various musical modes (Dorian, Phrygian, Lydian, etc., later called *tonoi*), referring more precisely to melody as a complex of relationships among the pitches that constituted a given mode. E.g., the Dorian mode consisted of the relationships of tone-semitone-tone-tone-tone-semitone-tone (the equivalent of the white keys on the piano, from D to the next highest D), which additionally could be arranged into patterns of smaller (microtones) or larger (minor third) intervals. It was these rational orderings of pitches that were understood to have an influence on the soul. Beyond this use, the term *harmonia* was also applied to concepts outside of the musical realm, such as the harmony of the universe, the harmony of the soul, the harmony of the city, etc. Similarly, the term *musical* was used by the Greeks to refer to the harmonious state of the soul, the city, etc. (Plato, *The Republic,* transl. by G. M. A. Grube [Indianapolis: Hackett Publishing Co., 1974], book 3, par. 403a, p. 72).

[19] Plato, book 3, par. 401d, p. 71. It is noteworthy to observe that in this passage Plato does not refer exclusively to music but to the rhythms and *harmoniai* that define the arts in general. The two concepts, rhythm and harmony, must then be understood in a broader sense. Rhythm can be found in the temporal divisions of architecture (e.g., the principle of repetition) or sculpture, or poetry (poetic feet as subdivisions of verses), etc. *Harmonia* refers to harmonious relationships (harmony) on a broader level, such as orderings according to the fundamental ratio 1:2, which in music yields the octave that contains all the other numerical relationships of pitches. The same ratio 1:2 can be verified in temple architecture (such as the temple to Zeus in Agrigentum, Sicily) or the human body (cf. Polyclitus' theory of the proportions of the human body, as illustrated by Leonardo da Vinci's famous drawing "Study of the Human Proportions according to Vitruvius"). The principles of proportion and unity were, then, placed within the larger context of their respective interrelationships and their relationships to the universe as a cosmic dimension.

Both criteria (rhythm and harmony) give importance to the principle of unity, in which all parts are seen as fractions or multiples of a basic common measure. Herein lies the fundamental criterion for the classification of rhythms into virtuous or vulgar. Since the good is also the indivisible, the one, and since the highest pursuit of humankind is the soul's fusion with the one, the ideas of unity, indivisibility, and simplicity were fundamental qualities to be emulated in the pursuit of all human endeavor.Variety, divisibility, and excess were considered as contrary to the acquisition of virtue.

Only simple divisions were acceptable as good in the various pursuits of the human city. E.g., one should fulfill only one function in the city (see Plato, book 2, par. 370b, p. 40).As applied to rhythm, both Plato and Aristotle pointed to the intimate connection between poetic meters and musical rhythm and advised that one "must not pursue complexity nor great variety in the basic movements" (Plato, book 3, par. 399e, p. 70).The same reason of unity and simplicity also lies at the basis of the acceptance or rejection of some instruments: the use of those that are capable of producing multiple sounds, such as the aulos (double reed instrument) or the kithara (harp) was discouraged (see Aristotle, *Politics,* book 8, par. 6, in Thomas J. Mathiesen, ed., *Greek Views of Music,* vol. 1 of *Strunk's Source Readings in Music History,* rev. ed., Leo Treitler, ed. [New York: W.W. Norton, 1998], p. 31).

[20] Not all Greek philosophers shared this belief.The Greco-Roman philosopher Sextus Empiricus (second century A.D.) refuted the theory: "It is not conceded offhand that by nature some of the *mele* [songs] are exciting to the soul and others are restraining." He also stated this: "That the cosmos is ordered in accord with harmonia is shown to be false in various ways; even if it is true such a thing has no power in reference to happiness—just as neither does the *harmonia* in the instruments" (from "Against the Musicians," par. 27, in Mathiesen, ed., *Greek Views of Music,* pp. 99, 103).As examples to the contrary, he mentioned the failure of music to prevent Clytemnestra, in a fit of excessiveness, from slaying her husband,Agamemnon, who had especially appointed a bard to endow her with discretion. He attributed the effect of music not to its power of imparting manly courage or discretion, but rather to its power to *distract,* either from the painfulness of work or the agony of warfare (*ibid.,* p. 100): "It is not because it [music] has the power of discretion that it restrains the heart, but rather because it has the power of distraction" (idem). Similar views were shared by the Epicurians (*ibid.,* p. 101).

[21] "The form of the Good is the greatest object of study, and it is by their relation to it that just actions and the other things become useful and beneficial" (Plato, book 6, par. 505a, p. 159; cf. book 7, par. 517c, p. 170).

[22] See Plato, book 7, pp.168-191.

[23] For a more detailed account, cf. Nicomachus, *Enchiridion harmonices,* transl.Thomas Stanley (1701), in John Hawkins, *A General History of the Science and Practice of Music* (London, 1776; reprint of 2nd ed., New York: Dover Publishing, 1963), vol. 1, pp. 9, 10; partially reproduced in Piero Weiss and Richard Taruskin, eds., *Music in the Western World: A History in Documents* (New York: Schirmer Books, 1984), pp. 3-6.This principle of a rational and mathematical ordering of the universe was applied to all the arts: architecture, sculpture, drama, poetry, the human body, and music.

[24] See Aristotle: "*Mele* [melodies] do actually contain in themselves imitations of *ethoses* [character]," and "we seem to have a certain affinity with the *harmoniai* and rhythms" (*Politics,* book 8:5:1340, in Mathiesen, ed., *Greek Views of Music,* p. 29).

[25] Cf. Plato, book 3, pars. 400d, 401d, pp. 70, 71, in which the author makes a connection between beauty and order in music and the notion of order and harmony in the soul. (For excerpts from the *The Republic,* see Mathiesen, ed., *Greek Views of Music,* pp. 9-19). See also Aristotle, *Politics,* book 8.5-7, in Mathiesen, pp. 24-34.

[26] Related by Sextus Empiricus, "Against the Musicians," in Mathiesen, p. 98. Harmonia, in regard to the soul, refers to the harmonious relationship between the different parts of the soul

(rational, emotional, and appetitive). Similarly, harmonia, applied to music, refers to the harmonious relationship among the various pitches that form a mode. Moreover, another parallel relationship between the virtues and the harmoniai can be seen in the fact that both deal with affections or character traits. The harmoniai were attributed characteristics that corresponded to the various virtues (represented by balance), or the lack thereof, as expressed in a number of excessive attitudes. Thus the Dorian mode, considered as of a sedate and manly ethos, represented the virtue of bravery. The Mixolydian was a mournful, restrained mode, used for lamentation, i.e., a lack of discretion or temperance. The Lydian mode was understood as decorous and educative, therefore suited to the age of boyhood. It was, however, rejected for mature men because of its lack in imparting power to the warrior, etc. (See Aristotle, *Politics*, book 8:7, in Mathiesen, ed., *Greek Views of Music*, pp. 33, 34).

[27] As explained by Pythagoras and related by Gaudentius' *Harmonic Introduction* (see Mathiesen, pp. 66-85).

[28] Philo of Byzantium, *Mechanicus*, 49.20, in "From the Fourth Book of Philon's *On the Making of Artillery*," par. 2, in Philon and Heron, *Artillery and Siegecraft in Antiquity*, transl. James G. DeVoto (Chicago: Ares Publishers, 1996), p. 7.

[29] Plato, book 7, pars. 529a-531c, pp. 180-182.

[30] "Is not the right love a sober and musical love of the orderly and the beautiful?" (Plato, book 3, par. 402d, p. 72). For this reason, poetic inspiration in the sense of imitative poetry (best represented by tragic poetry, with its emphasis on the excessive affections, cf. Plato, book 10, par. 595a-c, p. 240) was considered as something undesirable and dangerous for the ideal city (*polis*) precisely because this type of poetry was about individuals who let their passions, rather than reason, govern their behavior (cf. Plato, book 10, pars. 602c-605c, pp. 246-249). Excessive emotional reactions (such as joy, fear, mourning) were perceived as corruption because they prevented individuals from being led by reason (Plato, book 10, pars. 603b-608b, pp. 247-252). Incidentally, Plato's derogative view of rhythm must be understood in this context: rhythm was a poetic ornamentation that heightened the intensity of the emotion (Plato, book 10, par. 601b, p. 245).

[31] The four virtues were wisdom, bravery, temperance, and justice (Plato, book 4, par. 427e, p. 93).

[32] See Aristotle: "All agree that the Dorian harmonia is more sedate and of a specially manly ethos. Moreover since we praise and say that we ought to pursue the mean between extremes, and the Dorian harmonia has this nature in relation to the other harmoniai, it is clear that it suits the younger pupils to be educated rather in the Dorian mele" (Aristotle, *Politics*, book 8, par. 7, in Mathiesen, ed., *Greek Views of Music*, p. 34). Aristotle had a more nuanced view of the use of the different harmoniai (modes) than his predecessors. In his view there were two objectives in choosing a particular mode: the possible and the suitable. For the pleasure of older people he recommended the more "relaxed harmoniai" (relaxed Lydian), which were likened by Socrates to "intoxication" because they failed to produce power; for children he favored the Lydian mode, "capable of being at once decorous and educative" (Aristotle, *Politics*, book 7, in Mathiesen, ed., *Greek Views of Music*, p. 34). The Greeks did not reject, however, the use of excited modes, such as the Phrygian. On the contrary, they recommended their use for the purpose of purification (*katharsis*: "a pleasant feeling of relief") rather than for the education of the young (Aristotle, *Politics*, book 7, in Mathiesen, ed., *Greek Views of Music*, p. 33).

[33] Plato, book 4, par. 430b, p. 95.

[34] Joy represented another extreme state of the soul; therefore, excessive laughter was also dis-

couraged (see Plato, book 3, par. 389a, p. 59). Similarly, grieving was not seen as a desirable emotion because it prevented one from thinking and acting with efficiency (see Plato, book 10, par. 604d, p. 249).

[35] Aristides Quintilianus, *On Music: In Three Books*, transl. Thomas J. Mathiesen (New Haven, Conn.: Yale University Press, 1983), book 1, par. 1, p. 72.

[36] Plato, book 3, par. 401e, p. 71.

[37] Plato, book 3, par. 401c, p. 71.

[38] The Greek term *mele* must be understood as the functional complex of text, rhythm, and pitches, all three of which make up a melody (cf. note by the editor, "Plato, From the *Republic*," in Mathiesen, ed., *Greek Views of Music*, p. 10, note 2).

[39] Aristotle, *Politics*, book 8, par. 5, in Mathiesen, ed., *Greek Views of Music*, p. 29.

[40] The soul "is a *harmonia*" or "has a *harmonia*" (Aristotle, *Politics*, book 5, in Mathiesen, ed., *Greek Views of Music*, pp. 29, 30).

[41] Aristotle, *Politics*, book 8, par. 5, in Mathiesen, ed., *Greek Views of Music*, p. 29.

[42] Ellen G. White, *Christ's Object Lessons*, p. 355.

[43] Cf. E. G. White: "We are to contemplate Christ, and through Him . . . the willing and obedient will gain victory after victory [transformation]" (*ibid.*, p. 404).

[44] Samson Raphael Hirsch, *Der Pentateuch*, vol. 2: *Exodus* (Frankfurt am Main, Germany: Verlag der Kauffmann'schen Buchhandlung, 1869), pp. 555, 556.

[45] On this common confusion of terminology, see Karen Hanson, "How bad can good art be?" in *Aesthetics and ethics: Essays at the intersection*, Jerrold Levinson, ed. (Cambridge, U.K.: Cambridge University Press, 1998), pp. 214, 215.

[46] Characterizations about music such as these can, of course, be seen as very personal. While it is true that there is an element of subjectivity in such statements, there is a general consensus in a given society or culture of what is good quality versus cheap quality, even in music. As we discussed earlier, the level of exposure to, and the education an individual received in, a certain type of music will greatly influence such judgments. We are not advocating here that there is no place for anything other than classical music. On the contrary, there is a whole body of good quality folk, popular, and world music with all the crossover forms available today—music of the people—which in its simplicity can equally feature depth, craftsmanship, and art.

[47] For more insight into this phenomenon, cf. Alessandro Baricco, *L'âme de Hegel et les vaches du Wisconsin* [*The Concept of Soul in Hegel and the Cows of Wisconsin*] (Paris: Albin Michel, 1998).

[48] Donald P. Hustad, *Jubilate! Church Music in the Evangelical Tradition* (Carol Stream, Ill.: Hope Publishing Co., 1981), p. 11.

[49] This topic will be dealt with in detail in Part Two.

[50] Iris Yob, "The Arts as Ways of Understanding," p. 14.

[51] Jacques Barzun, *Music Into Words*, a lecture delivered in the Whittall Pavilion of the Library of Congress, October 23, 1951. The Louis Charles Elson Memorial Fund (Washington, D.C.: The Library of Congress, 1953), pp. 18, 19.

[52] Jules Combarieu, *La musique et la magie: Étude sur les origines populaires de l'art musical, son influence et sa fonction dans les sociétés* (Paris: Alphonse Picard and Sons, 1909; reprint Geneva, Switzerland: Minkoff, 1978), p. 86.

[53] *BBC Music Magazine*, June 2002, p. 61.

[54] Best, p. 54.

[55] Daniel Levitin, *This Is Your Brain on Music: The Science of a Human Obsession* (New York: Dutton, 2006), pp. 110, 168.

[56] "Listening to the Silence: African Cross-rhythms," video recording (Princeton, N.J.: Films for the Humanities and Sciences, 1996).

[57] Baruch Spinoza, *Ethics*, transl. Samuel Shirley, ed. Seymour Feldman (Indianapolis: Hackett Publishing Co., 1992), pp. 153, 154: "As for the terms 'good' and 'bad,' they likewise indicate nothing positive in *things* considered in themselves, and are nothing but modes of thinking, or notions which we form from comparing things with one another. For one and the same thing can at the same time be good and bad, and also indifferent. For example, music is good for one who is melancholy, bad for one in mourning, and neither good nor bad for the deaf" (italics mine).

[58] Best, pp. 57, 151.

[59] "Today, when the altar is cracked and tumbling, today, when pulpit and ceremonies have become objects of doubt and derision, art must emerge from the temple, must spread out and accomplish its far-reaching evolution outside. . . . The creation of a *new music* is imminent; essentially religious, strong, and effective, this music, which for want of a better name we will call *humanitarian*, will embrace within its colossal dimensions both the Theater and the Church. . . . All classes of society, finally, will merge in a common religious sentiment, grand and sublime. And art shall say: 'Let there be light'" (Franz Liszt, "Concerning the Situation of Artists and Their Condition in Society," *Gazette musicale de Paris*, August 30, 1835; in Jean Chantavoine, ed., *Fr. Liszt: Pages romantiques* [Paris: F. Alcan, 1912], pp. 65–67, quoted in Piero Weiss and Richard Taruskin, eds., *Music in the Western World: A History in Documents* [New York: Schirmer Books, 1984], pp. 366, 367).

[60] For a life reaction to this incongruent situation, see the testimony of a former member of the orchestra at the concentration camp of Birkenau, in *Bach in Auschwitz*, videorecording (New York: WinStar TV and Video, 2000).

[61] This was already observed by John Calvin: "Now in treating music I recognize two parts, to wit, the word, that is the subject and text, and the song, or melody. It is true, as St. Paul says, that all evil words will pervert good morals. But when melody goes with them, they will pierce the heart much more strongly and enter within. Just as wine is funneled into a barrel, so are venom and corruption distilled to the very depths of the heart by melody" (John Calvin, *Oeuvres choisies* [Geneva, Switzerland: Chouet and Cie., 1909], pp. 173–176; translation by Richard Taruskin; quoted in Piero Weiss and Richard Taruskin, *Music in the Western World: A History in Documents*, p. 108).

[62] Willem Van de Wall, *Music in Hospitals* (New York: Russell Sage Foundation, 1946), p. 11.

[63] The nature of the musical experience is much too complicated to be pinned down in a categoric and schematic way. There are too many factors involved in the listening experience, such as general health, mood, physical condition, preoccupations, education, etc., of the individual. Research about the effects of rock music has indeed brought about contradictory results. More recent research, about the effects of music in general on the brain, has again underlined the complexity of the phenomenon and revealed how little is known about how the brain processes music and affects our thoughts, feelings, desires, and behavior. See, for instance, Levitin, pp. 4, 8, 9, 107, 140.

[64] See Joseph Lanza, *Elevator Music: A Surreal History of Muzak, Easy-Listening, and Other Moodsong*, rev. ed. (Ann Arbor, Mich.: University of Michigan Press, 2004), p. 4.

[65] Mary Devereaux comments on this concern by way of the movie "Triumph of the Will," which presents Nazism as attractive and therefore good ("Beauty and Evil," in *Aesthetics and Ethics*, p. 241).

[66] Cf. Daniel Levitin: "A song playing comprises a very specific and vivid set of memory cues. . . . The music is linked to events of the time, and those events are linked to the music" (p. 162).

[67] The fact that drums are associated with such events does not make them ipso facto evil in themselves. Contrary to general belief, drums are not used only in animistic or orgiastic ceremonies involving sorcery. They are also used in everyday communication and general music making, accompanying work or play (in Africa) or serving as the expression of a very complex and sophisticated type of "classical" music (in India). The question comes to mind, then, "Why not rather linger on *those* associations?"

[68] A more in-depth look at this issue will be provided in Part Two.

[69] Best, p. 54.

[70] *Ibid.*

[71] The contrary is, interestingly, equally true. Some movies feature silent moments in which the absence of music purposefully evokes a dramatic or eerie atmosphere.

[72] Cf. Levitin, pp. 107-110.

[73] Allan D. Bloom, *The Closing of the American Mind* (New York: Simon and Schuster, 1987), p. 68.

[74] Mary Devereaux, "Beauty and Evil," in *Aesthetics and Ethics*, p. 242.

[75] Cf. Levitin, *This Is Your Brain on Music*, p. 226.

[76] E. G. White, *Messages to Young People* (Nashville: Southern Publishing Assn., 1930), p. 148.

[77] E. G. White, *Testimonies for the Church* (Mountain View, Calif.: Pacific Press Publishing Assn., 1948) vol. 1, p. 506.

PART TWO

*Music In the Bible and the
Writings of Ellen G. White:
Principles and Lessons*

CHAPTER 4

{ *A PHILOSOPHY OF MUSIC* }

The Bible does not give us direct instructions as to the use of music. Unlike the handling of the themes of love and faith, there is no specific chapter that provides a definition of sacred music or clear instructions about styles of music to be used or not. In the Bible, we encounter events that deal, to a variety of degrees, with music making, or we find instructions given about lifestyle values. It is from these events and recommendations that we can draw principles and guidelines to help us use music in such a way that it truly reflects the character of God and becomes an avenue for worship to the glory of God. In studying these passages, we first encounter a philosophy of music. Then the texts that deal with music address the subject from a twofold perspective: music for God and music among the people.

Early in the history of the people of Israel, God presented a project to His people that strikes us in its modernity and scope. In Deuteronomy 31:19-22 He addressed Moses shortly before his death and gave him a specific command: "Now write down for yourselves this song and teach it to the Israelites and have them sing it, so that it may be a witness for me against them. . . . And when many disasters and difficulties come upon them, this song will testify against them, because it will not be forgotten by their descendants. . . . So Moses wrote down this song that day and taught it to the Israelites."

Beauty

From the very outset music is here presented as a gift from God. It is remarkable that someone would have the idea to associate a practical document that comes with overtones of difficulty and effort, a text labeled by Moses himself as "law,"[1] with music. Nobody today would think of teaching or learning law through singing or to the accompaniment of musical instruments. Song and instrumental music are generally associated with leisure, enjoyment, or entertainment. When God puts these two apparently unrelated, even opposed, activities together (duty and enjoyment), it indicates how important it was for Him that the "good" goes hand in hand with the "beautiful."[2] From the very beginning, then, God makes it clear that beauty is not only a gift from Him but also an important and indispensable ingredient of life. He gave us the first demonstration of this principle at Creation as He stepped back periodically to assess His work, saying that it was "good" (Genesis 1:3, 9, 12, 18, 21, 25) and even "very good" (1:31).

The same principle of beauty is conveyed in the example of the schools of the prophets. Here again, we learn the lesson of music as an art, as beauty and aesthetic expression.

The schools of the prophets were launched by the prophet Samuel. He "gathered companies of young men who were pious, intelligent, and studious" in order to create a "barrier against the wide-spreading corruption, to provide for the mental and spiritual welfare of the youth, and to promote the prosperity of the nation by furnishing it with men qualified to act in the fear of God as leaders and counselors."[3]

The curriculum in these schools went beyond the study of the Law and the history of Israel. For practical reasons students were also required to study sacred music and poetry.[4] This was the time of young David, who later was to be associated with the planning of the Temple service. There was, then, a need to set up and structure a body of liturgical literature, both texts and melodies. The creation of this literature became one of the responsibilities of the students at the schools of the prophets. The task was later carried over into the Temple service, as several of these former prophet students took on positions as music leaders (1 Chronicles 16:37, 42; 25:1).[5]

What we encounter here is a desire to beautify the service of God. The Old Testament gives us a wealth of examples in which this aim is realized, first in the building of the tabernacle, then in the preparation of the Temple. There is an aesthetic preoccupation: render something beautiful and introduce art, beauty, and wonder. This principle was already present in the wilderness command to "sing" the law of God. We find it expressed again in the words of the psalmist when he describes the attributes of the Lord's ordinances in terms of beauty, comparing them to light, gold, and honey (Psalm 19:7-11). To sing the law meant to beautify it, to render it wonderful and admirable from an aesthetic point of view, in addition to its already existing moral beauty. Later, in the Temple service, the same concern was applied to the ordinances of sacrifice and found an expression in the permanent presence of music accompanying the sacrifices night and day.[6] This only echoes the theme of the beauty of God Himself, so often encountered in the Psalms: "One thing I ask of the Lord, this is what I seek: that I may dwell in the house of the Lord all the days of my life, to gaze upon the beauty of the Lord and to seek him in his temple" (Psalm 27:4). "Ascribe to the Lord the glory due his name; worship the Lord in the splendor of his holiness" (Psalm 29:2; see also Psalm 96:9).

Mental, Spiritual, and Social Growth

Beyond the aesthetic dimension, the text in Deuteronomy 31:19-21 also tells us that the music was meant to be an avenue for relationship and communication between God and the people of Israel. God used the song to remind Israel of His love and care, and through this song, Israel would be given a chance to enter again into relationship with their God. Ellen G. White pushes the implications of the text even deeper. In the books *Education* (Ed)[7] and *Patriarchs and Prophets* (PP),[8] she comments extensively on this passage and sees in this divine command a comprehensive program for a harmonious development of the entire individual.

1. *Music making affects the mental development of the individual by intensifying the memory process:*

"The more deeply to impress these truths upon all minds, the great leader [Moses] embodied them in sacred verse. . . . The people were directed to commit to memory this poetic history, and to teach it to their children and children's children" (PP, 467, 468).

"In later years they retained in their minds the words of the law which they learned during childhood."[9]

"Many precious lessons were fixed in their minds by means of song. . . . The principles of truth were implanted in the memory" (Ed, 39).

"God's commandments . . . were forever fixed in the memory of many a child and youth" (Ed, 42).

"There are few means more effective for fixing His words in the memory than repeating them in song" (Ed, 167).

We all can verify this principle in our own experience: when we start remembering a song, the tune comes back first, and only then, little by little, will the words follow. The memory of the music helps to bring back the memory of the words.

2. *Music making affects the spiritual well-being of the individual:*

Music "is a precious gift of God, designed to uplift the thoughts to high and noble themes, to inspire and elevate the soul. . . . It is one of the most effective means of impressing the heart with spiritual truth" (Ed, 167, 168).

"With a song, Jesus in His earthly life met temptation" (Ed, 166).

"Temptations lose their power, life takes on new meaning and new purpose, and courage and gladness are imparted to other souls" (Ed, 168).

"As He grew older He was tempted, but the songs His mother had taught Him to sing came into His mind, and He would lift His voice in praise."[10]

3. *Music is a valuable tool in character building:*

"Their thoughts were uplifted from the trials and difficulties of the way, the restless, turbulent spirit was soothed and calmed" (Ed, 39).

Song "has power to subdue rude and uncultivated natures; power to quicken thought and to awaken sympathy . . . and to banish the gloom and foreboding that destroy courage and weaken effort" (Ed, 168).

4. *Music promotes social skills:*

Song "promote[s] harmony of action" (Ed, 168).

"Concert of action taught order and unity, and the people were brought into closer touch with God and with one another" (Ed, 39).

The various effects and benefits of music have been the subject of recent research in education,[11] health,[12] religion,[13] etc., that demonstrates that these age-old purposes of music are universal and still valid for today. This should encourage us to increase our own musical practice at home, at school, etc., and indicates the importance of musical education as part of school curricula at all levels.

To the biblical writer music was a gift from God, a gift of beauty that brings us to wonder, to stand in amazement. Through music we are able to catch a glimpse of the beauty of the Lord. He also saw music as a means for communication, education, and spiritual growth, and as a way to build a well-rounded human being. For the biblical writer, then, the natural response was to return this gift to God.

---

[1] "Take to heart all the words I have solemnly declared to you this day, so that you may command your children to obey carefully all the words of this law" (Deuteronomy 32:46).

[2] A number of early church fathers commented on this association of duty and beauty: "The Holy Spirit sees how much difficulty mankind has in loving virtue, and how we prefer the lure of pleasure to the straight and narrow path. What does he do? He adds the grace of music to the truth of doctrine. Charmed by what we hear, we pluck the fruit of the words without realizing it" (Basil the Great, "Homily on Psalm 1," in J.-P. Migne, ed. *Patrologia Cursus Completus, Series Graeca*, vol. 29, col. 211).

[3] Ellen G. White, *Education* (Mountain View, Calif.: Pacific Press Publishing Assn., 1952), p. 46.

[4] "The chief subjects of study in these schools were the law of God, with the instructions given to Moses, sacred history, sacred music, and poetry" (E. G. White, *Patriarchs and Prophets*, Mountain View, Calif.: Pacific Press Publishing Assn., 1958, p. 593).

[5] For the connection between the schools of the prophets and the music leaders appointed by David for the Temple service, see 1 Samuel 10:5 and 1 Chronicles 25:1. Indeed, both texts refer to prophesying while being accompanied by harps and lyres. On the connection between the tenth-century prophets and the Levite Temple service, see A. Neher, *Histoire biblique du people d'Israël* (Paris: Adrien Maisonneuve, 1962), pp. 186-189.

[6] See Psalm 27:6; 1 Chronicles 23:30, 31; 25:6-8.

[7] E. G. White, *Education*, (Mountain View, Calif.: Pacific Press Publishing Assn., 1952).

[8] E. G. White, *Patriarchs and Prophets* (Mountain View, Calif.: Pacific Press Publishing Assn., 1958).

[9] E. G. White, "Training Children for God—No. 1," *The Advent Review and Sabbath Herald*, Sept. 8, 1904, p. 7.

[10] E. G. White, *The Voice in Speech and Song* (Boise, Idaho: Pacific Press Publishing Assn., 1988), p. 412.

[11] See the numerous articles on the effects of music on school performance, social skills, and the psychological development of the individual in general. For research publications on these topics, consult the electronic databases ERIC (Educational Resource Information Center), PsycINFO, etc. As for the "Mozart effect" (which, by the way, can also be observed by playing music written by other composers of the classical period, such as Schubert, for example)—the improvement of spatial-reasoning tasks immediately after listening to the music—recent research has shown that this theory is not scientifically defendable. The effect lasts, on average, not longer than 10 minutes, and similar results can be obtained with different inputs. There are, though, benefits to be reaped from the musical experience, especially through the actual practice of music. Those are, among others, more highly developed motor skills and coordination, a significantly larger number of neural connections between the two hemispheres of the brain, and increased concentration of gray matter that accounts for information processing (see Daniel Levitin, *This Is Your Brain on Music*, pp. 219-221).

[12] Music therapy as a discipline, a relatively recent development, is now taught in many colleges and universities.

[13] An increasing number of publications on music and its role in the church have appeared on the market in recent years.

CHAPTER 5

Music for God

To be a musician in a church setting means more than just to play an instrument or to sing. To be a church musician means to participate in something special, in something that is set apart and goes beyond the human realm. It means to participate in the divine. As we look at the biblical account of the Temple musicians, we notice that this was the way music making was understood in those times.

Music as a Ministry

A careful reading of the account of music organization in the Temple (1 Chronicles 23) reveals that only the tribe of Levi was chosen to be part of it. To understand the reasons behind this choice, one must go back to the episode of the golden calf at the foot of Mount Sinai. Chapter 32 of the book of Exodus relates how Moses and Joshua came down from Mount Sinai, Moses holding the tables of the law in his hands. As Moses and Joshua approached the camp, still unable to see the scene below them, they heard unusual activity in the camp. To Joshua it sounded like war: "When Joshua heard the noise of the people shouting, he said to Moses, 'There is the sound of war in the camp'" (verse 17). But Moses knew better. God had already told him about the incident (verses 7, 8). He was also familiar with the religious practices of Egypt, because he had been educated at the Egyptian court for the role of a pharaoh, which included training as an Egyptian priest. Moses knew how to interpret the sounds coming from the camp: "It is not the sound of victory, it is not the sound of defeat; it is the sound of [antiphonal] singing[1] that I hear" (verse 18). In relating this story, we are not so much interested in the type of music produced around the calf as in the outcome of the event, which teaches us a profound lesson in regard to the responsibilities of a musician making music to the Lord. Exodus 32:25, 26 relates the end of the episode of the golden calf: "Moses saw that the people were running wild and that Aaron had let them get out of control and so become a laughingstock to their enemies. So he stood at the entrance to the camp and said, 'Whoever is for the Lord, come to me.' And all the Levites rallied to him."

The Levites had been chosen to serve in the Temple because of their faithfulness to the Lord while all the rest of the people had fallen into idolatry: "It was found that the tribe of Levi had taken no part in the idolatrous worship. . . . The Lord honored their faithfulness by bestowing special distinction upon the tribe of Levi" (PP, 324). The special distinction consisted of being set apart[2] by God for service in His Temple, including the position of Temple musicians.

The situation has not changed for today's church musician. Serving the Lord in church is still a special distinction, a holy office. It still has the same presupposition as for the Levites of biblical times, namely, faithfulness. Seen in this light, the function of the church musician becomes a ministry, a position in which he/she is set apart to serve the Lord in a special way.

The Seventh-day Adventist Church at large has not yet considered the function of church musician as an essential one. With a few exceptions for larger churches, musicians typically are not part of the pastoral staff and render their services on a voluntary basis. With the increasing need for music leadership in our church today, hiring trained musicians as music ministers would provide leadership and the possibility to mentor other musicians, thus helping to alleviate the problems so many churches encounter.

The criteria for qualifying to play or sing for the service are generally limited to being able to play or sing more or less decently. In most cases the concern with faithfulness does not seem to be a priority. What does the word "faithfulness" really imply? Does it refer to someone who attends church regularly? Someone who is a "good" member of the church or a baptized member of the church? Someone who expressed his/her desire to participate in the worship service, using his/her talent?

The concept of faithfulness, as applied to the church musician, goes beyond these simple technicalities. To be a faithful musician means that one's everyday lifestyle is in harmony with the biblical values and principles, that there is a willingness for growth and maturation in bringing the musical talent more and more into harmony with the proposed ideals. It implies that this person has experienced what it means to walk with God every day, to communicate with God: "Music is acceptable to God only when the heart is sanctified."[3] It also means that the musician has an interest in, and an understanding of, the role of the church and of worship, as well as a burden to serve the congregation, to minister to the congregation through musical talent. Being a church musician goes beyond talent and skill; it brings in a spiritual dimension and a willingness for service. To lead out in a musical moment means to draw the congregation together into a spiritual journey. This can happen only if the musician has already experienced such a relationship in his or her own personal life with God. In order to lead someone, you must already be familiar with the place where you are going.

Music, a God-centered Activity

The concept of music as a ministry, of music for the Lord, something set apart, is paramount in the biblical texts that deal with music. We find this theme to be particularly prominent in the Psalms. The psalmist sings and plays *to the Lord*: "I will praise *you*, O Lord, with all my heart; I will tell of all *your wonders*. I will be glad and rejoice *in you;* I will sing praise *to your name*, O Most High" (Psalm 9:1, 2). "At his tabernacle will I sacrifice with shouts of joy; I will sing and make music *to the Lord*" (Psalm 27:6). "Sing for joy *to God* our strength; shout aloud *to the God* of Jacob" (Psalm 81:1). "Come, let us sing for joy *to the Lord;* let us shout aloud *to the Rock* of our salvation" (Psalm 95:1). "Give thanks *to the Lord*, call on his name. . . . Sing *to him*, sing praise *to him*" (Psalm 105:1, 2). Music done for the Lord is God-centered music. Its only focus is God, not the self or the congregation.

The physical arrangement of the musicians during the Temple service confirms that this principle, repeatedly expressed by the psalmists, was not just a poetic image. It was indeed put into practice in the very way the musicians were placed for singing and playing.

The Temple compound was made up of three courts (see Diagram A, p. 93): (1) the outer court of the Heathen, (2) the inner court of the women, and (3) the court of the Israelites, where the sacrifices were actually performed. Only male Israelites were allowed to pass through the Nicanor Gate and access the court of the Israelites, up in a reserved area, to watch the sacrifices being performed. The Mishnah,[4] which covers the time of the Second Temple Period (536 B.C.-70 A.D.), gives us an insightful description of the way the sacrifices were done and the role the musicians played during these ceremonies. The trumpet players were placed west of the altar, whereas the singers/instrumentalists were placed east of the altar (cf. 2 Chronicles 5:12; see Diagram B, p. 94). Thus the musicians, as they performed their music, were physically oriented toward the sacrifice, indeed playing and singing *to the Lord*. Even in the detail of the placement of the musicians, the very gesture of music making, the biblical principle of singing to the Lord was faithfully observed.

The purposeful placement of the musicians contains a number of lessons for today's worship. Music in churches is typically performed from the front, thus prominently displaying the musicians themselves, whether a choir, a soloist, an organist/pianist, or a praise team. It would be very impractical to suggest, nowadays, that the musicians should be placed out of sight of the congregation. Musicians typically lead out in congregational singing and should be able to make eye contact and communicate. Because of their particular location in church, however, their position and function may come through in an ambiguous, misleading manner, both for the congregation and the musician himself/herself. Could the music be perceived as a performance (same setting as in a concert), as a show or display? Could the position of the musician—up front, often elevated—instill in him/her an inappropriate attitude of self-centeredness and display? Many of us have been exposed to such ambiguous "performances" in church. I believe the lesson to learn from the biblical model of music making is that we need to be aware that the focus in worship music should happen on a totally different level, namely, on the level of the divine. Musicians are, then, encouraged to honestly check their motivations, to reconsider the function of music in worship, and to explore new ways in which their very placement can contribute to conveying the meaning of music in worship. Our creativity should be challenged even in such simple matters of organization.[5]

Music Pleasing to God

The Scriptures go a step further in the way the focus of the musical ex-

DIAGRAM A : TEMPLE MOUNT

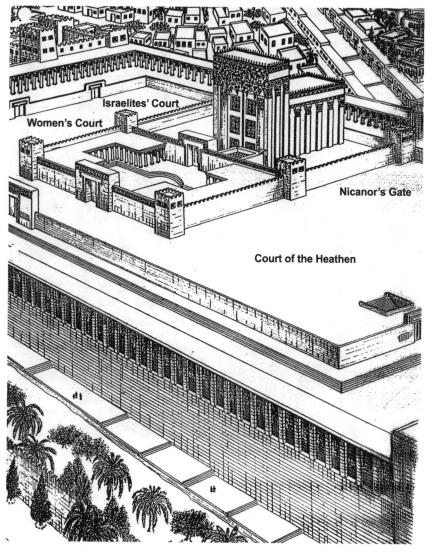

DIAGRAM B:
BLUE PRINT OF THE TEMPLE

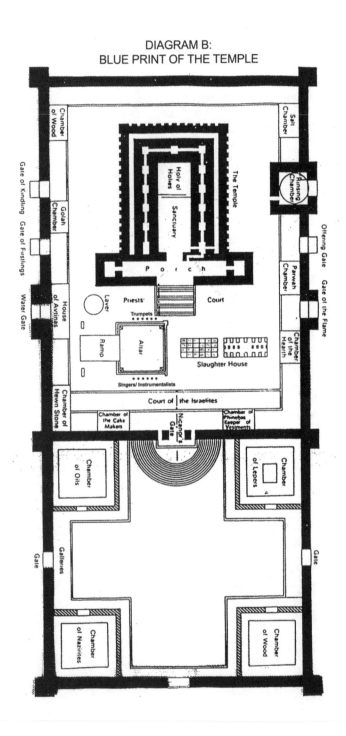

perience is related: music should be done in such a way that it *pleases* God. "May the words of my mouth and the meditation of my heart *be pleasing* in your sight, O Lord, my Rock and my Redeemer" (Psalm 19:14). "Therefore, I urge you, brothers, in view of God's mercy, to offer your bodies as living sacrifices, holy and *pleasing* to God—this is your spiritual act of worship. . . . Then you will be able to test and approve what God's will is—his good, *pleasing* and perfect will" (Romans 12:1, 2)[6]. "I will sing to the Lord all my life; I will sing praise to my God as long as I live. May my meditation *be pleasing* to him, as I rejoice in the Lord" (Psalm 104:33, 34).

The way music is performed in churches today often does not indicate a primary focus on pleasing God. The main concern seems, on the contrary, to lie with the congregation. Pastoral staff discussions about musical styles often revolve around the aim to plan and deliver something that pleases the congregation, that can attract a certain kind of *audience*. We already mentioned how placing the instrumentalists, choir, or praise team up front—in full view of the congregation—sends the message, voluntary or involuntary, that the playing and singing is done for the enjoyment of the congregation. Similarly, anybody who has been involved with singing/playing in church remembers the embarrassment of being in front of everybody, the fear of not *performing* well, and the self-conscious concern with one's dress or hairstyle.

Indeed, the physical arrangement of the congregation, facing the platform, naturally creates a spectator setting—watching something that happens up front. Specific attitudes, such as expressing criticism about the quality of the performance, or hand clapping as an expression of approbation or appreciation, can also be seen as indicators of spectator attitudes, drawing the worshipper away from the focus on pleasing God.

Clapping can, indeed, be a very ambiguous expression in worship. Congregations clap after baptisms, testimonies, sermons, and, of course, music. In Western cultures clapping is traditionally understood as applause, that is, a mark of appreciation of a performance. When asked, though, why they clap during worship and what this gesture represents to them, people generally indicate that their clapping is meant as a physical expression of affirmation, a way to enter into and participate in the experience of what was said or sung. Clapping, then, is an example of how associations can be of a different nature and even change according to time or place, as discussed in Part One, pages 60-64.

Still, it is interesting to analyze in what musical circumstances clapping generally happens in church. Typically, people give applause after rousing or spectacular performances or after a presentation by a children's choir or instrumental ensemble. One would be hard-pressed to remember clapping after a meditative song or a quiet instrumental piece. But isn't there also reason to be affirmative for quiet moments in worship? Similarly, it is telling that people never would think to clap after a prayer, even though there are beautiful prayers offered in churches. Ellen G. White sees singing "as a part of religious service . . . as much an act of worship as is prayer" (Ed, 168). The *selective* character of clapping after music should, then, make us wary about the true motivation of clapping after music.

Many music directors feel uncomfortable with the clapping after a "performance." One among them found a solution that will make us smile at its simplicity and creativity and, at the same time, bring us to wonder about the real meaning behind clapping after music in worship. In order to send the message to the congregation that their singing was not a performance but an offering to the Lord, this director of a children's choir had a child come up to the pulpit before the singing started and invite the congregation to pray with the choir through the song. Then the child would quietly resume his or her place in the choir, and they would start singing. Not once was their singing mistaken for a performance: people never even thought about clapping, having been invited to join in a prayer!

Clapping after music is still too closely associated with the acknowledgment of an artistic performance in order not to be mistaken as applause. It is true that clapping takes on different meanings in different cultural settings, and these differences must be respected. It is, therefore, up to every church to look at this issue with their musicians and members and evaluate which direction—and how far—they want to go with this "expression of affirmation." The concern for a God-pleasing rather than a congregation-pleasing musical experience during worship will be of great help when making such decisions.

There are two fundamental truths that should be communicated to and impressed upon church musicians, namely, (1) that they are indeed playing for God and (2) that as they do so, their primary concern should be to please God, not to please the worshippers or themselves.

How do we please God? How do we know what He likes us to do for Him in terms of music? As human beings, we will, of course, never be able to live up to God's expectations. In searching for an answer to this question, I like to use an image from our everyday life. Whenever we are about to offer a gift to someone we know and love, our first thought is about who the person is and what he or she likes—what would he/she find pleasing? Then we try to find a gift to fit the personality.

It should happen the same way with our musical gifts to God. We first need to find out who God is—His character, His attributes—so that we can match our gift as nearly as possible to His personality. Our music should express all the facets of the character of God: His holiness, His creatorship, His majesty and grandeur, His love, mercy, and faithfulness. Our music should also be an expression of our gratitude for these aspects of His character. This is what we find in the Word of God when it deals with music or with praising God. The two faces of God are consistently presented side by side. One reveals God as the Creator and Master of the universe—the great, distant God. The other reveals God as the Redeemer—the loving, sustaining, close God.[7] This twofold message is given in the very first words of the Lord's Prayer: "Our *Father* who art *in heaven*" (Matthew 6:9, RSV). The music we present in worship should evoke and emulate the full spectrum of God's character: the holiness, beauty, and perfection of His heavenly side, as well as the goodness, mercy, and loving-kindness of His fatherly side.

The task of the musician is to evoke these characteristics from any given musical style used in worship, whether it be classical, folk, popular, or ethnic. In all these styles, the musician must search to come as closely as possible to an authentic reflection of the attributes of God's character. It is only under this condition that a given type of music can qualify for the high calling of giving glory to God. In their unique ways styles carry the possibility to live up to such a high goal. However, on the part of the composer or performer, it takes a keen understanding of how each style functions and enough experience in the art of music to *transform* a style, making it useful for sacred purposes. At the outset all music is secular music because all music uses the same basic vocabulary and grammar. We have previously established that there is no such thing as sacred chords or chord progressions, sacred rhythms or melodies, or even sacred instruments. All music must undergo a transformation in the hands of the musician, based upon the musician's understanding of the sacred character of God and the event.

We can look at the great Renaissance and baroque sacred masterpieces by Josquin des Prez, Palestrina, Vivaldi, Handel, or Bach, or we can look at the nineteenth-century folklike camp meeting or gospel songs. All use the same musical language in their contemporary, secular counterparts. The key to their appropriateness lies (1) in the understanding those composers had of the holy and merciful character of God and the sacredness of the moment of adoration and (2) in their knowledge of how to use and manipulate the musical language of their time. The great classical works of the sixteenth, seventeenth, and eighteenth centuries predominantly celebrate and give glory to the great Creator of the universe. On the other hand, situated at the very opposite spectrum in terms of an aesthetic perspective, and closer to today's praise songs, the nineteenth-century gospel or camp meeting hymn speaks about the close, personal God within reach of the most humble person seeking Him. The earlier works found their musical origin in the great courtly or operatic secular repertoire, the latter in the secular folk or popular style of their time. For the earlier works, it was the understanding of the character of God or the event as a sacred moment that reshaped them into sacred music. With the folk songs, it was the personal experience of deep and transforming repentance and surrender that shaped them into sacred songs. Both types of music are needed to provide true worship.

Joy and Reverence

The whole Bible, from the Creation story to the book of Revelation, is pervaded by this twofold presentation of God's character.[8] It is, therefore, natural to find the same theme in the texts that were specifically written for a worship setting, namely, the Psalms. The Psalms present God, on one hand, as the close, loving God Redeemer and, on the other hand, as the distant, powerful God Creator, who rules and judges the earth (consider these pairs of psalms: 19 and 20, 23 and 24). Psalm 95 expresses this theme in a very explicit way and reveals, at the same time, one of the secrets to an authentic way of worshipping God.

In liturgical circles Psalm 95 is known as the venite psalm. *Venite* is the Latin word for "come" and represents the first word of this psalm in the Latin translation of the Bible, the Vulgate. Time and again, a great number of composers have chosen this psalm and set it to music. The word "come" indeed articulates the structure of this poem and functions as a keyword. The worshipper is twice invited to "come" for a specific act of adoration. The first time (verse 1), he/she is summoned to sing, shout aloud, and make music to celebrate God the Redeemer. The second time (verse 6), he/she is summoned to bow down and kneel as he/she acknowledges God, the Creator of the universe. These two sections are then followed by an invitation to "hear his voice" and to respond with obedient hearts. This is in exact parallel with the structure of themes in the biblical key text on worship, Isaiah 6, verse 1-8, in which the worshipper first encounters the high and exalted Holy God (verse 1), then comes into the presence of the healing, forgiving God (verse 7), and finally offers himself/herself in a spirit of obedience (verse 8).

Psalm 95 and Isaiah 6 present a biblical model of the worship experience that should characterize our earthly worship.[9] Too often, our worship services are defined by either reverence or joy. When reverence is favored to the exclusion of joy, we end up with a dry and stiff worship experience in which the emotions are banned and "truth" reigns supreme. When there is too much joy to the exclusion of reverence, the worship service can get out of hand and has more to do with emotionalism than truth. It seems very difficult to find a way to combine both attitudes. All through the history of the church this very issue has torn churches and theologians apart. The secret to an acceptable worship lies right here, in the achievement of this balance. The vertical and the horizontal must intersect in order to create an authentic partnership between God and people. We are invited by the biblical text to achieve both together, so that in our adoration the whole nature of God is addressed, expressed, and pleased. This is the greatest challenge we encounter in the realization of our worship. True worship cannot be achieved by looking for external or mechanistic means, such as music, for example, in shaping our services. It can happen only as the result of an inner attitude that has grown as our personal relationship with Christ deepens through our daily walk with Him. When the hearts of the musicians and worship leaders are transformed, their music will also be transformed as the result of their inner attitude. This will be visible in the musical choices made, the performance manner, and the spirit that governs the musical experience and spreads into the congregation. The musicians' minds will be taken off self-conscious pre-occupations to focus on the essential, namely, God Himself.

Skillfulness and Excellence

This spirit, however, does not exempt the musician from cultivating qual-ities that will enable him or her to offer an acceptable gift of music. We men-tioned earlier how goodness and beauty go hand in hand in God's work and character. Beauty as an aesthetic quality responds to certain standards of form and structure and is generally associated with craftsmanship[10] and excellence. The concern for excellence has been a traditional preoccupation in the Scriptures when dealing with matters pertaining to the sanctuary or the Temple. The various craftsmen working on the realization of the sanctuary were endowed with specific qualities. Exodus 35 introduces Bezalel, the goldsmith, as being filled "with the Spirit of God, with skill, ability and knowledge in all kinds of crafts" (verse 31). The words "skill" and "skillful" are mentioned repeatedly in the following verses (Exodus 35:35; 36:1, 2) with reference to other artisans and craftsmen, so as to underline the impor-tance of skill and ability in addition to being filled with the Holy Spirit.

The same concern can be found in the texts that speak, a few centuries later, of the musicians involved with Temple music and, just before that, with those who brought the ark to Jerusalem: "Kenaniah the head Levite was in charge of the singing; that was his responsibility *because he was skillful* at it" (1 Chronicles 15:22). "Asaph, Jeduthun and Heman were under the su-pervision of the king. Along with their relatives—all of them *trained and skilled* in music for the Lord—they numbered 288. Young and old alike, teacher as well as student, cast lots for their duties" (1 Chronicles 25:6-8). "Sing to him a new song; play *skillfully*, and shout for joy" (Psalm 33:3).

It is often assumed that being filled with the Spirit is the essential precon-dition, or even sole condition, for making music for the Lord. While it cer-tainly is an essential quality, it is not the only one. As the biblical texts demonstrate, the Spirit of God is the starting point that sets the scene and assures the faithfulness of the musician, which sets him/her apart for the task. This is, however, only the beginning. The next step is to develop the God-given talent into skill, ability, and knowledge of one's trade.[11] This means, then, that to play or sing to the Lord presupposes the Spirit *and* talent, training, preparation, as well as organization. In commenting on our responsibility with regard to the talents God entrusts to us, Ellen G. White says: " The development of all our powers is the first duty we owe to God and to our fellow man. . . . We should cultivate every faculty to the highest degree of perfection, that we may do the greatest amount of good of which we are capable. . . . God will accept only those who are determined to aim high. He places every human agent under obligation to do his best."[12]

To reach this point means hours of disciplined and often frustrating practice and rehearsals as one strives to become better prepared, more proficient, and more creative in praising God through music. (Temple musicians had to go through five years of thorough training before being admitted to serve at the sacrifices.[13]) This is particularly true for public worship, in which the musician actually "speaks" to God on behalf of the whole congregation or to the congregation on behalf of God. The musical language and skill of the church musician must be able to convey the word of God with clarity and without any distraction caused by poor preparation or lack of skill or talent, so as not to interrupt, or even prevent, the worshipper in his journey into the presence of God.

The Psalms as a Model for Worship Music

The psalms offer an excellent example of the principles discovered in our study so far, principles of focus, motivation, and excellence. But even beyond these principles, the psalms also become a model for worship and worship music because of their harmonious blending of the subjective and objective elements in worship.

The subjective component is found in the literary genre used in the psalms: they are written as poetry, using the free imagination and creativity of the poet. Their tone is predominantly personal, and they are filled with an outpouring of every imaginable human emotion and feeling. In fact, most of the psalms are emotional outcries that come from deep within the heart of the psalmist.[14] Those psalms can be seen as early praise songs.

The objective component in the psalms is found in the subject matter, the topics that are dealt with, namely, objective truth. The psalms speak to us of the history[15] and Messianic hope[16] of Israel, of the law of God[17] and His grace through salvation,[18] of creation[19] and judgment,[20] of prophetic exhortation,[21] the kingdom of God,[22] and worship and adoration,[23] including a number of specifically liturgical psalms that situate the believer at the gates of the sanctuary.[24]

In this superimposition of the subjective and the objective, of the heart and the mind, the psalms offer a way to address the tension that comes with every act of adoration, namely, the tension between the horizontal and the vertical, between joy and reverence. Objective truth is carried through subjective emotions into our innermost beings.

Addressing both mind and heart is still essential for today's worship. Expressing our heart's desires and needs should always be accompanied by the learning and remembering of the biblical truths and vice versa. Worship leaders should take great care to provide avenues for both subjective and objective expressions of faith. Hymns have traditionally fulfilled the role of teaching congregations and believers about truth and doctrine. For today's generation the expression of the heart passes through praise songs whose primary aim is not so much teaching, but rather focusing on the personal aspect of the worship experience. Some churches have well understood the benefits of using both repertoires during worship and, combining the two genres, are able to provide a more wholistic worship experience for their congregations.

Diversity

Another biblical model for music in worship comes to us in the book of Revelation. Musical events in John's letter are distinguished by their focus on the character and acts of God—they have a doxological character. The songs in chapters 4 and 5 revolve around the holiness of the everlasting God and His worthiness because of His deeds (Creation and salvation).

What mostly characterizes the singing and sounds of music is diversity. Revelation 7:9 presents a "great multitude . . . from every nation, tribe, people and language," addressing their acclamations to God. Music in the book of Revelation is predominantly a corporate undertaking. Hosts of angels sing and play instruments, and groups of people shout acclamations and proclamations (Revelation 4:10, 11; 5:8-14; 7:9-12). The way the music is organized appears as a combination of symmetry and spontaneity. The singers and musicians are gathered around a throne in concentric circles (4:4; 5:6, 11; 7:11, etc.) and sing, shout, or cry in the manner of spontaneous acclamations

(4:11; 19:1, etc.). There is a great array of sounds—we hear singing (4:11; 5:9, 12; 15:3, etc.), shouting of acclamations (19:1, 6), sounds that remind of roars of rushing water or peals of thunder (14:2; 19:6), harps playing (5:8; 15:2), trumpets sounding (8:6ff.), and the sounds of powerful natural happenings, such as earthquakes and hailstorms (11:19). In spite of this variety, however, there remains a strong sense of unity. The singing and sound making are generally done by a group that is united by a common cause or fate.

Our churches would do well to take inspiration from these examples. Often, the very qualities of worship music that are presented in the book of Revelation are lacking in our services and, for that matter, in our dealings with music. These characteristics are of utmost importance: an exclusive focus on God, the organized and simultaneously spontaneous character of the music making, the sense of unity and belonging among the people that anchors the diversity of their styles and expressions, and, above all, the corporate character of the musical experience.

In contrast, a good deal of music in churches today is done by individuals or selected groups through special musics, choir numbers, and organ introits, preludes, and postludes. Though the congregation participates in a few songs or hymns (generally too few), the worshippers spend most of their time listening and enjoying the performances. The participatory experience has been replaced by a spectator experience. While listening is not negative, the whole Bible, as well as the writings of Ellen G. White, teaches us that our music in church should be done primarily through corporate singing. Ellen G. White writes, "The singing is not always to be done by a few. As often as possible, let the entire congregation join."[25]

If there were more corporate participation, many problems encountered with music could be avoided before they even start.

The Old and the New

In commenting about the schools of the prophets and their interest in sacred song and poetry, Ellen G. White observes that "sanctified intellects brought forth from the treasure house of God things new and old."[26] The New Testament demonstrates the same interest in both the old and the new, as it encourages the singing of psalms, hymns, and spiritual songs (Ephesians 5:19; Colossians 3:16).

The psalms themselves were written over several centuries, and new ones were continually added to the old ones. They were, then, taken over by the New Testament church, and new types of song were added, i.e., the hymns.[27] The addition of hymns in the New Testament demonstrates a principle that will repeat itself again and again throughout the history of the church: every time a renewal of the religious experience takes place, it will bring about a new repertoire of music.

Change and renewal in music are part of a lively religious journey. They witness to the dynamic character of a church in that they express a forward movement, an experience in progress. It is, though, essential to also hold on to the old, as the biblical record teaches us—the former hymns, the way music was done in church in the past, and the experiences of those who came before us. The songs of the past speak about former struggles, hardships, and experiences of the church. They teach about the great truths of Scripture as they were cherished and understood in earlier times. They connect us to our roots, to the church at large from its very beginnings. For this reason the old songs are a rich heritage for today's church and should be treasured and kept alive. As in the time of Samuel, the Temple, and the early church, we also should value the "things new and old" "brought forth from the treasure house of God."[28]

---

[1] The original term anah is a technical expression for singing in a cultural context (G. Johannes Botterweck, Helmer Ringgren, and Heinz-Joseph Fabry, eds., *Theological Dictionary of the Old Testament,* transl. David E. Green [Grand Rapids: William B. Eerdmans, 2001], vol. 11, p. 221) and refers probably to the practice of responsorial, or antiphonal, singing, i.e., a group responding to a foresinger, or two groups answering back and forth in singing (see R. Alan Cole, *Exodus: An Introduction and Commentary,* Tyndale Old Testament Commentaries, D. J. Wiseman, ed. [Downers Grove, Ill.: Inter-Varsity Press, 1973], p. 226; cf. John I. Durham, *Word Biblical Commentary,* vol. 3: *Exodus,* [Waco, Tex.: Word Books, 1987], p. 430). This practice of singing was associated with the cult of Apis, the god represented by the golden calf. The level of noise associated with this celebration (reminding Joshua of a war scene) indeed corresponded to the orgiastic practices that generally accompanied the cult of the golden calf (cf. R. Alan Cole, *Exodus,* p. 218; cf. Francis D. Nichol, ed., *The Seventh-day Adventist Bible Commentary* [Washington, D.C.: Review and Herald Publishing Assn., 1976], vol. 1, p. 667).

[2] See *Seventh-day Adventist Bible Dictionary,* rev. ed. (Washington, D.C.: Review and Herald Publishing Assn., 1979), p. 235, s.v. "Consecration."

[3] E. G. White, *Evangelism* (Washington, D.C.: Review and Herald Publishing Assn., 1946), p. 512.

[4]I. Epstein, ed. *The Babylonian Talmud* (London:The Soncino Press, 1938), vol. 12: *Sukkah* 51a, pp. 238-242. See also 2 Chronicles 29:27.

[5]There are many different ways in which musical contributions can renew and refresh the service, such as processions, placement of the musicians in the middle of the congregation, singing or playing from a place where the musicians cannot necessarily be seen (from the back, for example), etc. In withdrawing the visible element of the musical performance, it is possible to create a greatly intensified listening experience. For some of the newest trends on this matter, see Dan Kimball, *Emerging Worship: Creating New Worship Gathering for Emerging Generations*, David Sanford, ed. (Grand Rapids: Zondervan, 2004).

[6]See also Philippians 4:18 for the same association of an "acceptable" and "pleasing" sacrifice to God.

[7]See, for example, Isaiah 6:1-7; Revelation 4 and 5; Psalms 33, 95, 100, 145, etc.

[8]See especially Genesis 1 and 2; Revelation 4 and 5.

[9]See Ellen G.White's statement on the relationship between earthly and heavenly worship: "God is high and holy; and to the humble, believing soul, His house on earth, the place where His people meet for worship, is as the gate of heaven. The song of praise, the words spoken by Christ's ministers, are God's appointed agencies to prepare a people for the church above, for that loftier worship" (*My Life Today* [Washington, D.C.: Review and Herald Publishing Assn., 1952], p. 286).

[10]Craftsmanship is understood as the artistic elaboration of the different parts of a creative work, in terms of unity and variety, in more or less complex relationships of references, transformations, recalls, and allusions. This happens on the levels of both external factors (concerning the various sections of a piece) and internal factors (concerning thematic materials).

[11]Ellen G.White also underlined the importance of quality performance: "Let the singing be accompanied with musical instruments *skillfully* handled" (*Testimonies for the Church*, vol. 9, p. 144. [Italics mine.]).

[12]E. G.White, *Christ's Object Lessons*, pp. 329, 330.

[13]See *The Babylonian Talmud*, vol. 3: *Hullin I*, 24a, pp.118-120.

[14]See, for instance, Psalms 5, 7, 22, 31, 38, 62, 63, 88, 102, etc.

[15]See Psalm 114 on the Exodus; Psalms 78, 105, 106, 126, and 137 on the Exile.

[16]See Psalms 2, 22, and 110.

[17]See Psalms 1, 15, 19, 24, 119.

[18]See Psalms 18, 79, and 149.

[19]See Psalms 8, 33, and 104.

[20]See Psalms 52, 68, and 82.

[21]See Psalms 12, 14, 53, and 75.

[22]See Psalms 2 and 48.

[23]See Psalms 66, 95, and 100.

[24]See Psalms 8, 15, 42, 43, and 46.

[25]E. G.White, *Testimonies for the Church*, vol. 9, p. 144.

[26]E. G.White, *Patriarchs and Prophets*, p. 594.

[27]Spiritual songs date from the Old Testament as, for instance, the songs of Deborah, Hannah, etc. Even though scholars do not yet agree on the meaning of the expression "spiritual songs," it is generally admitted that it represents more of a spontaneously created song, akin to the Old Testament canticles. New Testament canticles include the songs of Mary, Zechariah (also Zacharias), Simeon, etc. (see Luke 1 and 2). Some scholars believe that spiritual songs refer rather to the ecstatic utterances that may have happened during speaking in tongues.

[28]E. G.White, *Patriarchs and Prophets*, p. 594.

CHAPTER 6

Music in the Temple

ORGANIZATION OF MUSIC IN THE TEMPLE

During their time of wandering, war, and conquest, Israel was predominantly occupied with survival activities. The first and second Temple periods, however, brought times of peace and political stability favorable to the development and flourishing of the arts. Sacred music was provided by a guild of professional musicians.

The organization of music and the musicians in the Temple is a vivid illustration of the importance that was put on the development of talent. One Chronicles 25:6-8 describes a full-fledged music academy of 4,000 members,[1] consisting of teachers and students, all under the supervision of King David.[2] Young and old worked in carefully arranged shifts (verses 9-31). Not everyone was occupied as a performing musician; many Levites were taking care of manufacturing and maintaining the instruments and garments, which were kept in storage rooms in the Temple vicinity.

The highly professional organization of the music in the Temple speaks to the concern Israel's leaders had for excellence. But excellence does not necessarily have to be synonymous with professional expertise. Not every church has the human resources or the financial means to maintain a professional musician. Rather, the concept of excellence must be understood as a goal to tend toward, whatever the level of the musician. There are amateur musicians who are very professional in their own way. Excellence, in this perspective, means to constantly develop one's abilities to the highest level possible, and to strive to offer the Lord the best possible gift of music the musician can achieve in his/her musical journey at a given time. Excellence is a continuous commitment to give one's best, rather than a stage reached once and for all.

The question of talent must be considered when dealing with public worship. There will always be people who misidentify their talents so that they often overlook where their real gifts lie. God gave out talents to "each according to his ability" (Matthew 25:15) and encourages us to use them to the best of our abilities. He never asked us to use and develop a talent that He did not give us or that we do not possess. For some reason, however, musical talent seems to be a favorite, one many would like to possess. It is very difficult to dissuade people from their convictions about their musical abilities.

Our culture has created an image of music making that brings individuals to believe that all they need is a microphone, a pair of speakers, the ability to play a few chords on the piano or the guitar, good intentions, and, of course, an audience. While this is acceptable as long as we remain in a private setting looking for some personal pleasure and enjoyment, it does not correspond with God's expectations when we come to worship Him. This is made very clear as we take a look at the circumstances that surrounded the service in both the tabernacle and the Temple, and realize how carefully the musicians were chosen and prepared for the service of the Lord. Paul subscribed to the same standards in matters of public worship. As he put it very bluntly: "Since you are eager to have spiritual gifts, try to *excel* in gifts that *build up* the church" (1 Corinthians 14:12).

The point Paul wants to make here is that whatever is contributed to worship should be intelligible, edifying, and strengthening to the church. If what I believe to be my gift distracts from, rather than enhances, adoration by its poor quality of delivery, and if there is the "spirit" without the "mind," then this gift should not have a place in the church. Of course, such a position might easily be condemned as elitist and exclusive. However, it becomes meaningful from the perspective of Paul's concluding words on the matter of public worship: "Everything should be done in a fitting and orderly way" (verse 40).

Ellen G. White addressed the same issue in several of her writings: "There should be system and order in this [the matter of singing] as well as every other part of the Lord's work. Organize a company of the best singers, whose voices can lead the congregation, and then let all who will, unite with them. Those who sing should make an effort to sing in harmony; they should devote some time to practice, that they may employ this talent to the glory of God."[3] "Music forms a part of God's worship in the courts above. We should endeavor in our songs of praise to approach as nearly as possible to the harmony of the heavenly choirs. I have often been pained to hear untrained voices, pitched to the highest key, literally shrieking the sacred words of some hymn of praise. How inappropriate those sharp, rasping voices for the solemn, joyous worship of God. I long to stop my ears, or flee from the place, and I rejoice when the painful exercise is ended."[4]

This concern for quality and excellence should not absolutely exclude, however, the possibility of moments that are of a more spontaneous order. Such moments, though, are meant to be rare occasions in order to avert disorder or excess.

Functional and Participatory Music

The music performed in the Temple was not art for art's sake, art as an end in itself. The Israelites would not come to the Temple to listen to a beautiful concert. The Temple music was functional and liturgical. When used in liturgical settings, music was meant to accompany and beautify acts of adoration. In the Temple the main act of adoration took the form of sacrifices: "The duty of the Levites was to help Aaron's descendants in the service of the temple of the Lord. . . . They were also to stand every morning to thank and praise the Lord. They were to do the same in the evening and whenever burnt offerings were presented to the Lord on Sabbaths and at New Moon festivals and at appointed feasts" (1 Chronicles 23:28-31).[5]

The Mishnah relates how the priests went about their liturgical duties accompanied by the Levite musicians singing and sounding their instruments, as the worshippers, assembled in the court of the Israelites, were bowing in prayer.[6] In the same way that God had planned to embellish the difficult experience of learning the law, He had made provisions for the sacrifices—in themselves a physically repulsive act—to be embellished by musical offerings. This music was not meant to be listened to as an aesthetic experience per se. Its purpose was to lend beauty to an act of worship, to set it apart, to elevate it above the ordinary so as to mark its particular character.

The participatory character of the music attached to the Temple can be observed on occasions when all the people of Israel were involved in the celebration, such as journeys to Jerusalem in order to celebrate high feasts or the Feast of Tabernacles. Ellen G. White remarks, "The service of song was made a regular part of religious worship, and David composed psalms, not only for the use of the priests in the sanctuary service, but also to be sung by the people in their journeys to the national altar at the annual feasts."[7] On those occasions the people would join in the singing. Ellen G. White gives a lively account of one such event, namely, the Feast of Tabernacles: "The temple was the center of the universal joy.... Here, ranged on each side of the white marble steps of the sacred building, the choir of Levites led the service of song. The multitude of worshipers, waving their branches of palm and myrtle, took up the strain, and echoed the chorus; and again the melody was caught up by voices near and afar off, till the encircling hills were vocal with praise.[8]

A number of liturgical psalms were written with the explicit function of inviting entry into the house of God (e.g., Psalms 15, 24, 27, 95). These psalms present beautiful examples of participatory moments and are well suited for congregational reading at the beginning of a worship service.

Music in worship should be, foremost, music done by all the people. The greatest musical offering to God comes in the form of congregational singing, as all the voices join together in common praise.

Instruments in the Temple

The instruments used in conjunction with the Temple service,[9] as well as on the occasion of the bringing of the ark to Jerusalem, are systematically listed as harps, lyres, trumpets, and cymbals (1 Chronicles 15:16, 19-22, 28; 16:5, 6; 25:1-6; 2 Chronicles 5, 7). The instrumentation characteristic of the Temple service is often referred to in order to make a point with regard to the use of instruments in our church services. More specifically, this list of instruments is used to justify the exclusion of some instruments from today's worship. The following reflections on that matter propose to help put the situation in the right perspective and to clarify a number of confusions and misconceptions so as to enlighten discussions and decisions on this matter.[10]

The musical practices in the Israelite Temple had many parallels in surrounding cultures. In Egyptian, Assyrian, and Sumerian civilizations, for instance, harps, lyres, cymbals, and trumpets were the prominent instruments in the temple service. Percussive instruments were of minor importance.[11] The stress was on "vocal music and sweet singing," and the ceremonies "had a certain dignity and holiness, inasmuch as those instruments employed were not held conducive to arousing sensuality."[12] In contrast to these religious cultures and to the Israelite practices, Phoenician ceremonies were of a noisy, sensuous, and exciting character, with louder instruments, such as double-pipes, cymbals, and drums being "used so to stimulate the youths to a frenzied craze that they would emasculate themselves."[13] These Phoenician practices featured female musicians who functioned at the same time as sacred prostitutes.[14] The reader familiar with the story of Elijah's competition with the prophets of Baal on Mount Carmel will easily recognize the kind of celebration described here. It appears, then, from these examples, that the use of instruments was partly determined by the particular character of the worship sought after.

Harps and Lyres

Both the harp and the lyre were plucked string instruments that produced a soft tone. The lyre, held in front of the musician's chest, featured from three to eight asymmetrical strings plucked with the fingers or a plectrum. The harp had a resonant body and was placed on the ground; according to Josephus,[15] it had 12 strings that were plucked with the fingers. It could be compared in size to the Celtic harp of today that is used in folk singing. Both the harp and the lyre were used to accompany singing—they were not meant for solo performance.

Every single mention of music making related to the Temple service lists those two instruments. They were foundational to the music that was part of liturgical or extraliturgical celebrations. There is, however, no reason to conclude that they were "sacred" instruments, set apart for this particular purpose. On the contrary, both the harp and the lyre are presented many times by the prophets in association with prostitutes, drinking, and reveling (e.g., Isaiah 5:12; 23:16; 24:8, 9; Amos 6:5, etc.). The use of the same instrument in situations both of adoration and immorality indicates that the Bible does not attribute particular virtues to instruments and does not label a particular instrument as good or bad.

Cymbals

The ancient Near Eastern cymbals were small idiophones,[16] pairs of bell-shaped bronze disks approximately 2.5 to 4.5 inches in diameter. In the Temple they were used to signal events in the process of a musical or liturgical action,[17] such as the beginning of a song or stanza, a stop in the performance to allow for a particular liturgical happening (acceptance of sacrifice, prayer, etc.), or a signal for the priests officiating at the altar. Cymbals are generally associated with the word "selah,"[18] which marks off sections in the psalms. They were not intended to be sounded like a modern, large, orchestral cymbal that adds resonance to climactic moments in a musical performance. Their size was much too small for them to function as resonating instruments. Cymbals were worn on the tips of two fingers of one hand, in the manner of castanets, and were clashed together by finger action. The Bible indicates that only the chief music leaders were to sound the cymbals,[19] another hint at the signaling function of this instrument. Cymbals were not sounded during the singing and were not used to produce noise, as was the case in pagan ceremonies (Phoenician).[20]

It is noticeable that the Hebrew word "*tseltselim*," used to designate the cymbals in earlier texts (2 Samuel 6:5), was traditionally associated with the pagan Canaanite cult. In later texts, especially those referring to Israelite religious events or ceremonies (1 Chronicles 13:8; Ezra 3:10), these cymbals came to be designated by a different word, "*metsiltayim*," probably to avoid any connotation with pagan practices.[21] The biblical writers obviously wanted to keep the liturgical situation clear of any ambiguities.

Trumpets

The word "trumpets," as used in modern translations of the Bible, refers to several types of wind instruments: the short and widemouthed military trumpet, the long silver trumpets, and the ram's horn (shofar). Often the various translations of the Bible do not differentiate among them, and call them, indiscriminately, trumpets. They were all used for the same purpose though—to signal events. None of them was used for melodic playing, since they could produce only the natural harmonics of the fundamental tone (approximately three to five sounds). The silver trumpets were mainly associated with the wilderness era—when various signals were used to communicate within the camp (Numbers 10:1-10)—or with the Temple service.

There is, however, a significant difference in use and symbolism among these instruments, especially between the long silver trumpets and the shofar. The shofar's symbolic meaning was for the rabbis associated with the event of the sacrifice of Isaac, when a ram was caught by its horns in a thicket, becoming the substitute sacrifice for Isaac. (See *Talmud Babli, Rosh* Hashanah 16a.) From this time on, the ram's horn was linked with sacrificial and liturgical events. Even today the shofar is sounded to herald in the Jewish New Year and to end the Day of Atonement. In ancient Israel it was also sounded for specific feasts and to welcome the Sabbath on Friday evening. Its symbolic use in the Bible is attested to by many important events, such as the circling of the wall of Jericho, the battle of Gideon, etc.

Flutes and Drums

The biblical texts do not mention either flutes or drums as part of the Temple instruments. With regard to the flutes, the biblical records distinguish between the *ugav*, a small pipe made of reed that produced a sweet tone, and the *halil*, a big pipe with a mouthpiece that produced a sharp and penetrating tone similar to that of the oboe (cf. the Greek *mono-aulos*). According to the traditional texts, these instruments seem not to have been part, as a general rule, of liturgical events in the Temple. Some texts, though, mention the ugav as "retained from the first temple;"[22] it appears, however, that it was never used on Sabbaths.[23] Also, the list of instruments given in the Mishnah[24] mentions the "sweet-sounding" flutes as being used in the Second Temple, but only on 12 days during the year around the altar—during the Passover and Pentecost ceremonies and at the Feast of Tabernacles. The flute was, then, considered by the Israelites as an extraliturgical instrument.

The flute known as halil (big pipe), which featured a sharp and penetrating tone and was considered to be an exciting instrument, was allowed during the Second Temple period for processions and weddings and during joyous festivities around the Temple area. According to these descriptions, the ancient Israelites made a distinction, with regard to instrument use, between extraliturgical celebrations (festivals and other religious popular events or gatherings) and the liturgical moments set apart for Sabbath services at the Temple.

The same situation applied to the drums. The *tof*, in ancient Israel, was a small handheld frame drum similar to today's tambourine (without the bells). The tambourine is mentioned several times in the Bible as being part of extraliturgical events, generally out of doors, such as the song after the crossing of the Red Sea (Exodus 15:20), the reception of David after the slaying of

Goliath (1 Samuel 18:6), the victorious return of Jephthah the warrior (Judges 11:34), and the journey of the ark to Jerusalem (2 Samuel 6:5; 1 Chronicles 15:28, 29).[25] The tambourine was also part of certain celebrations (e.g., the water libations) during the Feast of Tabernacles, when great festivities were organized within the area of the court of the women in the Temple, and men would dance[26] and throw burning torches.[27] Given the rhythmic character of the tambourine, its playing was typically associated with dancing. Even though the tambourine did not have a place in liturgical settings, its presence was, then, still very strong in extraliturgical religious contexts.[28]

With few exceptions, the playing of the tambourine was generally associated with women who used the instrument to accompany singing and dancing.[29] The cultural practice of the ancient Near East to associate drums with women may provide one answer to the absence of drums in the Temple service. Indeed, only men were allowed to serve in the Temple, and the music was exclusively provided by male Levites. Even though women certainly played an important role in extraliturgical events, they were not allowed to go beyond the court of the women and enter into the court of the Israelites, even less to officiate for the sacrifices in the priestly court.[30] It is, then, quite possible that the gender specific character of the tambourine led to its exclusion from the Temple service.

The use of the tambourine on the Temple premises on the occasion of different religious events (such as the Feast of Tabernacles in the court of the women) indicates that the problem does not lie with the instrument itself in the sense that it is not appropriate for adoration. In that case the tambourine would also have been inappropriate and banished from the extraliturgical celebrations (such as the bringing of the ark to Jerusalem). The problem seems to be more of a cultural nature, namely, particular conventions practiced in a given time and space.

If today one would argue that the drums had to be excluded from church on the basis of the biblical practices in the Temple, one also would have to exclude women from our church services! Along the same lines, one could advance the reasoning that, since flutes were not accepted in liturgical settings at the time of the Temple, there should be no place for the organ in our churches today since organs are but a series of "flutes" (incidentally, the modern Hebrew word for organ is the same as the one used for the sweet sounding flute, "ugav"). And in order to stay consistent and in keeping with the same rationale, one also would have to accept only harps and lyres for use in church. This would be problematic since harps are too expensive to afford and lyres no longer exist today.

Concluding Remarks

As we look at the use of instruments in the Temple service, it becomes clear that there were many parallels between Israelite practices and those of surrounding Near Eastern cultures. These parallels point to generally accepted standards for liturgical instrumentation for a given geographic area and/or time period. While we do notice the use of some similar instruments and musical practices in pagan and Israelite worship, some instruments/practices were conspicuously absent from Temple worship, probably in order to prevent association with, or forms of, pagan worship.[31] Yet the opposite process may also be observed: instruments that at one time were not accepted found their way into the Temple at a later time (though in slightly different circumstances), such as was the case with the flutes.

Out of a similar concern, care was taken to change the meaning or symbolism of a given instrument or musical practice in case of a danger of misunderstanding or ambiguity, such as happened with the cymbals. Though they were part of the unacceptable Phoenician worship, the cymbals found an essential place in Israelite Temple worship by being given a new name and meaning. Instead of being used as noise makers, they fulfilled, under their new name, the function of signaling moments in the musical performance. This reinterpretation of the meaning of certain elements surrounding cultural practices is steeped in the concern for appropriate worship and music making devoid of any ambiguity.

These observations underline the importance of an objective and balanced approach to the appropriateness or inappropriateness of certain instruments for worship. Rather than condemning the use of an instrument because of its association with pagan rites, etc., the Scriptures indicate that such instruments can, on the contrary, be given an important place in God's worship. Their meaning and associations can be changed and transformed. Such a procedure is, in fact, a basic principle throughout the Bible.[32]

In regard to instruments in worship, the decisions must be made within the context of performance. We have seen how the flute, though it was holding the reputation of a sensuous instrument and was associated with unacceptable worship practices, found its way into extraliturgical Israelite celebrations and festivities because it was capable of creating a joyful and festive atmosphere.

The same was true for the drum. It was perfectly fitted for various extraliturgical religious ceremonies, but it did not find a place in Temple worship probably because women were not part of the liturgical setting in Temple ceremonies, and because it was an instrument closely associated with dancing, which was not part of Temple worship practices.

It finally all comes down to the context in which an instrument is played and the way in which it is played. The Bible shows clearly that instruments in themselves do not carry *evil* or *sacred* values. The cultural understanding of an instrument (associations), the manner of performance, and the spiritual disposition of the musician are the criteria that determine the appropriateness of an instrument for worship. Associations can be changed, and thus a new meaning can be given to an instrument. In keeping with this principle, ethnomusicologists who were wrestling with the issue of indigenous music in a non-Western Christian worship setting raised the question, "If a culture understands a certain instrument's association with evil spirits, can't the instrument be redeemed with the understanding that it can now be associated with the Spirit of God?"[33]

The observation of Temple practices in terms of instrumentation indicates that there was a real concern to parallel, in the music, the worship values expressed by the other liturgical actions. Temple worship, primarily focused on sacrifices, was not of an excited character, but favored dignity and reverence. It therefore avoided anything that would foster sensuous or exciting reactions. But joy and animated celebration were not shunned from biblical religion. The numerous religious festivals, spread over the whole year, provided many opportunities for joyful, loud, and exuberant expression, in which instruments otherwise absent from the Temple found a place. Appropriate use of music occurs when the music holds true to the values of the occasion and to an authentic worship of God while, at the same time, maintaining a spirit of joy and reverence.

Music for God is music that is done at its best according to the abilities of the musician. It is music that strives to reflect the perfect character of God—music worthy to be offered to our Lord and Maker. In the presence of the sublime, of the holy, there is no place for mediocrity or for the quickly thrown together. Only the best is acceptable.

While music is our offering to God and we strive to make it as worthy as possible, we must not forget that our music happens in a setting that includes a whole congregation. Besides being music for the Lord, it then also becomes music among the people.

---

[1] Two hundred eighty-eight among them were the professional singers (cf. 1 Chronicles 23:5) who officiated for the sacrifices in 24 groups of 12. The minimum age for a singer to be able to assist at the sacrifices was 30 years; the maximum age was set at 50 years (cf. *The Babylonian Talmud, ibid.*).

[2] The expression "under the supervision of the king" uses the Hebrew phrase *'al yad David* (literally, "on the hand of David"), which points to the practice of chironomy. In this practice the leader's hand movements would indicate the shape of the melody (ascending, descending, etc.). This was a common practice in the ancient Near East that served as a mnemonic device for the singers and instrumentalists in an exclusively oral tradition. This practice was then carried over into plainchant and was in use until the advent of Western notation, around the eleventh century A.D.). See Eric Werner, *The Sacred Bridge: Liturgical Parallels in Synagogue and Early Church* (New York: Schocken Books, 1970), pp. 107, 108.

[3] E. G. White, "Cooperation With Ministers," *The Advent Review and Sabbath Herald,* July 24, 1883, p. 2.

[4] E. G. White, *Evangelism*, pp. 507, 508.

[5] See also Psalm 27:6: "At his tabernacle will I sacrifice with shouts of joy; I will sing and make music to the Lord." Cf. *Babylonian Talmud, vol. 12: Sukkah* 51a, p. 236.

[6] Jacob Neusner, ed., *Mishna* (New Haven, Conn.: Yale University Press, 1988), *Tamid* 7:3, pp. 872, 873. Cf. Diagram B, p. 81.

[7] E. G. White, *Patriarchs and Prophets*, p. 711.

[8] E. G. White, *The Desire of Ages* (Mountain View, Calif.: Pacific Press Publishing Assn., 1940), p. 448.

[9] In this section we will consider only the instruments used during the liturgical Temple service. For a more comprehensive study of the general use of instruments in the Old Testament and the Bible overall, see Joachim Braun, *Music in Ancient Israel/Palestine: Archaeological, Written, and Comparative Sources*, transl. Douglas W. Stott (Grand Rapids: William B. Eerdmans, 2002); Jeremy Montagu, *Musical Instruments of the Bible* (Lanham, Md.: Scarecrow Press, 2002); *Encyclopaedia Judaica,* s.v. "Music;" and the article "Musical Instruments of the Ancient Hebrews," *The Seventh-day Adventist Bible Commentary,* vol. 3, pp. 29-42.

[10] For an overview of the use of instruments in the Bible and the musical system featured in the ancient Near East, see L. Doukhan, "Music in the Bible," *Shabbat Shalom,* Autumn 2002/5763, pp. 18-25.

[11] Only one or two small drums (tambourines) and one or two cymbals ("modest noise-

makers") were part of those sacred orchestras (cf. A. Z. Idelsohn, *Jewish Music in Its Historical Development* [New York: Schocken Books, 1975], p. 7).

[12] *Ibid.*, pp. 4, 5.

[13] As commented on by the second-century A.D. thinker Lucian, quoted in Idelsohn, *Jewish Music*, p. 6. The exciting character of the shrill sound of the double pipes was still acknowledged as such during ancient Greek civilization.

[14] Cf. Horace, quoted in Idelsohn, p. 6.

[15] Josephus, *Antiquities of the Jews*, 7:12.3, in Josephus, *Complete Works*, transl. William Whiston (Grand Rapids: Kregel Publications, 1960), p. 165.

[16] An idiophone is an instrument made of resonant material; it is made to resonate by hitting, shaking, or scraping (cf. bells, woodblocks, maracas, etc.).

[17] The use of cymbals for signaling pauses and interruptions is attested to in all of the ancient Near East, cf. Joachim Braun, p. 20.

[18] John Arthur Smith understands this term to be a "rubric indicating a break in the singing for the worshipers to prostrate themselves" ("Musical Aspects of Old Testament Canticles in Their Biblical Setting," *Early Music History* 17 [1998]: 255).

[19] Such as Asaph, Heman, and Jeduthun (in 1 Chronicles 6:44 Jeduthun is called Ethan; they are the same person (cf. *The Interpreter's Dictionary of the Bible*, s.v. "Jeduthun"), see 1 Chronicles 15:19; 16:5; 25:6; 2 Chronicles 5:12; Ezra 3:10). In later times it was their descendants who were to continue this task (see, for example, 1 Chronicles 25:3).

[20] Cymbals typically were used as signaling instruments throughout the whole ancient Near East. In pagan cults (Phoenician) they were also used to create noise. They were made of very costly material and according to a complicated production process that excludes their use as mass instruments by common people (see Braun, p. 109).

[21] See Braun, p. 107.

[22] *The Babylonian Talmud*, vol. 5: *Arakhin* 10b, pp. 56, 58; *The Talmud of the Land of Israel*, transl. Jacob Neusner (Chicago: University of Chicago Press, 1988), vol. 17: *Sukkah*, 5:6, p. 130. Cf. Idelsohn, *Jewish Music*, pp. 11-15.

[23] *The Mishnah, Sukkah* 5:1, p. 288; *The Babylonian Talmud*, vol. 22: *Sukkah* 50b, p. 236.

[24] Jacob Neusner, *The Mishna: A New Translation*, Arakhin 2:3, 4, pp. 811, 812.

[25] The text in 2 Samuel explicitly mentions the tambourine. 1 Chronicles 15 acknowledges only David's dancing; the tambourine is not listed specifically with the other instruments. This should not lead us to think, however, that the tambourine was absent from the procession accompanying the final journey of the ark to Jerusalem, since dancing, in ancient cultures, was inevitably connected to the playing of drums.

[26] Cf. *The Talmud of the Land of Israel*, vol. 17: *Sukkah* 5:4, pp. 123, 124; cf. also *The Mishna, Sukkah* 5:4, p. 289. In ancient Israel, dance seems to have been part of certain religious ceremonies (see David dancing before the ark; cf. also Psalm 149:3 and 150:4). Though it was used during the second Temple period for certain nondevotional celebrations (as at the Feast of Tabernacles), dancing never was part of the Temple service per se. The only form of dance present in the Temple was the processions around the altar, accompanied by the singing of the Levites (cf. Idelsohn, *Jewish Music*, pp. 15, 16).

[27] *The Mishna*, vol. 17: *Sukkah* 5:4, pp. 123, 124. Cf. E. G. White, *The Desire of Ages*, p. 448.

[28] The mention of the drums in Psalms 149 and 150 may appear to place their use in a liturgical context. Mention is made here of praising God "in the assembly of the saints" (149:1) or "in his sanctuary" (150:1). These passages are often used to justify the playing of drums in our worship services. It is, however, important to remember that Psalms 148-150 are so-called eschatological psalms, i.e., they point to a situation at the end of times. Psalm

148, in fact, reveals the direction in which these psalms must be understood: as a totality of praise. Psalm 148 makes the eschatological intention clear in its reference to the universal dimension of the praise giving. All the elements indebted to God join in universal praise: the heavenly bodies, human creatures, and anything in, on, and under the earth. In Psalm 149 the emphasis is on the totality of praise and the ultimate salvation (see the reference to Isaiah 42:10 with the words "Sing to the Lord a new song"). Psalm 150 presents a culmination of praise (in heaven and on earth) through a participation of all the instruments available, including the flute and the drums.

[29] The playing of tambourines by male musicians appears, indeed, to have been exceptional. The text in 1 Samuel 10:5 relates how Saul encountered a band of prophets "coming down from the high place with lyres, tambourines, flutes and harps." These prophets were part of a movement known today as *ecstatic prophecy*, a unique and relatively short-lived phenomenon in Israel that flourished at the time of Samuel, then disappeared temporarily during the times of David and Solomon (the Great Temple era). It came to a definite end during the ninth century, when it took on characteristics of the Baal cult (cf. André Neher, *L'essence du prophétisme* [Paris: Calmann-Lévy, 1972], pp. 188-190). A gender specific association of a particular instrument can also be observed in regard to the cymbals, exclusively used by male musicians.

[30] The female singers mentioned in Ezra 2:65 apparently belonged to the court musicians rather than to the Levite Temple singers (cf. Idelsohn, *Jewish Music*, p. 16).

[31] E.g., the use of "percussive, stirring and signal instruments, as well as dances and participation of women" as was customary in Phoenician cult (see Idelsohn, *Jewish Music*, p. 18).

[32] See, for instance, the pagan practice of circumcision, which was reappropriated by God as the sign par excellence for His covenant with Israel (cf. Gordon J. Wenham, *Genesis 16–50*, Word Biblical Commentary, vol. 2, pp. 23, 24 [Dallas, Tex.: Word Books, 1994). By receiving a new meaning, an old pagan symbol was to become one of the most fundamental biblical symbols.

[33] Roberta King, quoted in "Musicianaries," *Christianity Today,* October 7, 1996, p. 52.

CHAPTER 7

Music by the People and Among the People: A Collective Experience

The professional environment that characterized music in the Temple was to undergo dramatic changes during the Exile. As the Israelites were deported to Babylonia, instrumental music was suspended from the services as a sign of mourning for the loss of the Temple.[1] Psalm 137:1-4 stands as a witness to this resolution: "By the rivers of Babylon we sat and wept when we remembered Zion. There on the poplars we hung our harps. . . . How can we sing the songs of the Lord while in a foreign land?"[2] At this time the responsibility of worship and music started to shift from the professional to the layperson.[3]

A similar situation characterized the times of the early church after the destruction of the second Temple.[4] Every believer now became a priest and was endowed with the responsibilities of a "priestly" lifestyle. The responsibility for worship and music was now carried by laypeople. While this was already true for synagogue worship, it became particularly characteristic of the early church in places where worship was conducted in home churches that featured a more informal setting.

In spite of little mention of music in the New Testament, there was intense musical activity present in the early church.[5] The Gospel of Luke, in its first two chapters, features four canticles, three of which were composed by nonprofessionals: the *Magnificat* by Mary (Luke 1:46-55), the *Benedictus* by Zechariah (Luke 1:68-79), and the *Nunc dimittis* by Simeon (Luke 2:29-32).[6] The young Christian church also created its proper liturgy, based upon the traditional Jewish practices carried over from the synagogue and the Temple service, such as the chanting of Scripture and prayers or the singing of psalms and Old Testament canticles. It complemented this heritage by the addition of new genres, hymns, and spiritual songs inspired by a new event, namely, Christ's life and ministry on the earth.

The shift from the professional to the lay leader brought with it a need for instruction and guidance. Today's situation in churches is in many ways similar. Often, the burden of organizing and conducting worship and music lies upon the shoulders of lay members (church musicians, worship leaders, elders, etc.). It is, therefore, essential that guidance and counsel are sought in order to assure appropriate and relevant worship.

The absence of a professional framework of music that functions as an objective control element makes it necessary to look at the issue of church music from a twofold perspective: (1) music as a corporate act, an event that happens within a community, "by the people and for the people," and (2) music as a lifestyle issue—an individual's use of music in his/her personal and community life as related to attitudes, thoughts, and behavior.

Throughout his writings Paul gave advice and admonition to the young churches on how to cope with the difficulties that grew out of their new situation.[7] Many of his counsels dealt with matters of church life and Christian lifestyle, and these passages will become relevant for our purpose, considering the close relationship that exists between music and lifestyle. It would certainly be appropriate to apply the advice Paul gave to the Ephesians to issues dealing with music in the church: "Be very careful, then, how you live—not as unwise but as wise, making the most of every opportunity, because the days are evil. Therefore do not be foolish, but understand what the Lord's will is" (Ephesians 5:15-17).

Many of Paul's writings to the churches address issues and attitudes that affect community life. The same concern for the community is indeed in order when dealing with church music issues. Because church music happens as a collective experience, it is not a matter of personal preferences or taste. Church music, as well as worship in general, comes with a moral responsibility. Because music in worship is an activity that happens on the level of a community and implies human relationships and interaction, it cannot be done without ethical considerations.

Music as a Means for Edification, Encouragement, Thanksgiving, and Relationship Building

Paul, as well as some of the other New Testament writers, found in music benefits similar to the principles we discovered in our study of Deuteronomy 31.[8] In Paul's time music was still seen as a means for *learning, instruction, and edification*. Paul encouraged the church to "teach and admonish one another with all wisdom, and as you sing psalms, hymns and spiritual songs" (Colossians 3:16). Here instruction and warning take place through the singing of psalms, hymns, and spiritual songs.[9] Addressing the church of Corinth, Paul identified hymn singing as a contributor to "the strengthening of the church" (1 Corinthians 14:26).

Music was, moreover, presented as a source of spiritual well-being, an agent of *encouragement*. In order to uplift and encourage each other in prison, Paul and Silas started "praying and singing hymns" in the middle of the night (Acts 16:25).

More than once, singing was also used as an avenue to express *thanksgiving* and gratitude to God: "Sing and make music in your heart to the Lord, always giving thanks to God the Father" (Ephesians 5:19, 20). The apostle James also encouraged the expression of joyfulness through song: "Is anyone happy? Let him sing songs of praise" (James 5:13).

Finally, Paul saw in music an agent for social development. He admonished the Ephesians to create *relationships* by speaking "to one another with psalms, hymns and spiritual songs" (Ephesians 5:19).

Music making in the church is, then, according to the biblical model, meant to be achieved by a group of people who are supposed to interact and whose goal is to approach God as a unified body in order to offer Him a common response. Whenever several individuals are involved in a common action, ethics come into play. This is even more important when dealing with music, because people tend to have very strong personal opinions about music. These opinions were acquired and strengthened over the years through their cultural environment, their education, and their personal taste and preferences. When people come together to worship, these differences in taste clash and prevent the congregation from worshipping together in a spirit of unity. It is at this point that Paul's advice becomes vital.

Music as an Agent for Tolerance and Respect

In the context of Romans 14 and 15 and 1 Corinthians 8 and 10, Paul addresses the issue of the weak and the strong in relation to the observance of certain practices, and the passing of judgment on those who are weak. He warns us to "stop passing judgment on one another" (Romans 14:13), to not "destroy [our] brother" (14:15), to "bear with the failings of the weak" (15:1), and to "please [our] neighbor for his good, [and] build him up" (15:2). Even though Romans 14 does not speak directly about music, we find in the context of this passage a situation similar to our present concern. Paul is not dealing here with matters of law or doctrine, but rather with divergences in spiritual discernment, conviction, and practices that were the result of differences in background, education, former beliefs or experiences, or human conventions. Those different practices would in no way lessen or destroy the truth of the law or the gospel,[10] but they had the potential to bring about intolerance, a judgmental attitude, and self-righteousness.

Issues about music today are embedded in a very similar context—one of divergent convictions and practices—and create the same type of reactions. Paul's rationale may be directly applied to musical matters in the church. His advice in the following passages is striking in its wisdom and balanced approach. Although at first glance Paul's approach seems contradictory, his overall approach to this situation is far from simplistic, but rather, full of nuances.

I invite you, in reading the following passages taken from the epistles to the Romans and Corinthians, to substitute a music-related term for some of Paul's expressions, as suggested: "One man's faith allows him to [listen to] everything, but another man, whose faith is weak, listens only to a particular style [eats only vegetables]. The man who listens to [eats] everything must not look down on him who does not, and the man who does not listen to [eat] everything must not condemn the man who does, for God has accepted him. Who are you to judge someone else's servant?" (Romans 14:2-4). "One man considers one [musical style] more sacred than another; another man considers every [musical style] alike. Each one should be fully convinced in his own mind. He who regards one [style] as special, does so to the Lord" (verses 5, 6). "Therefore let us stop passing judgment on one another. Instead, make up your mind not to put any stumbling block or obstacle in your brother's way" (verse 13). "If your brother is distressed because of what you [sing or play], you are no longer acting in love. Do not by your [singing or playing] destroy your brother for whom Christ died" (verse 15). "For the kingdom of God is not a matter of [music making], but of righteousness, peace and joy in the Holy Spirit" (verse 17). "We who are strong ought to bear with the failings of the weak and not to please ourselves. Each of us should please his neighbor for his good, to build him up" (15:1, 2). "Be careful, however, that the exercise of your freedom does not become a stumbling block to the weak" (1 Corinthians 8:9). "So whether you [sing or play] or whatever you do, do it all for the glory of God. Do not cause anyone to stumble, . . . even as I try to please everybody in every way. For I am not seeking my own good but the good of many, so that they may be saved" (10:31-33). However, it is equally important, in this context, to also remember these words of Paul: "Do not allow what you consider good to be spoken of as evil" (Romans 14:16).

This series of texts teaches us that in matters of music in the church, personal taste must give way to considerations of common good. Whenever I make decisions in regard to music, I will have to consider the needs of the whole congregation and might have to step back from my own preferences, whichever those are—popular, contemporary, or classical. Whenever I consider music making in the church, I will have to ask myself whether this particular style of music will lead the congregation into a worshipful experience or whether the music will distract the congregation from worship. If my music making will prevent part of the congregation from entering into the presence of the Lord, then I become a stumbling block for my brother or sister.

The text 1 Corinthians 10:31 provides the real answer to our issue: "Whether you [sing or play] or *whatever* you do, do it all for the glory of God." Discussions about musical styles arise primarily out of strong personal opinions in matters of music, because some believe that *their* taste and preferences are to be used as standards against which all the others must be measured. Thus, the debate generally happens on a horizontal level: my opinion and my preferences versus your opinion and your preferences. When we place the discussion on a vertical level, asking ourselves "How will this contribute to the glory of God?" we deal with criteria that are outside our personal realm and that touch upon the essential in music making. Music that contributes to the glory of God is music that reflects God's character, directing our thoughts and feelings upward toward eternal things and beyond our petty discussions of one style against another. Just as there is more than one way in which a person can speak about God's character, there *should* also be more than one musical language and style by which one can speak about God's character. Today, most of our churches are composed of a multiplicity of individuals coming from different places around the world and from various cultural backgrounds. Each one of these people groups has its own way to speak about God. They should, then, also be given a chance to express their faith in their own characteristic musical language.

On the next level, the question must be asked, "How far can one go in the consideration of the weaker brother?" Who is our weak brother or sister? Is he/she the one who holds on to a particular style of music just because this is the way it has always been done in this church and because tradition is often mistaken for authority? Or is he/she one who is used to speaking with authority in the church and who has a "mission" to safeguard what he/she considers to be the only acceptable style? In other words, we need to probe the issue to determine whether it is indeed one of inappropriateness or, rather, a matter of reluctance to accept any change—for the sake of control, authority, comfort, or tradition.

Augustine, the great church father of the fourth and fifth centuries, had to deal with a similar problem in his time. As he was confronted with the issue of varying musical practices in churches, his answer was as follows: "About practices which vary from place to place, there is a single helpful rule to keep in mind, that when they are not contrary to faith nor to good morals, but help exhort us to a better life, that wherever we see them or know of their existence, we do not criticize them, but praise and imitate them, unless this will be a hindrance to those whose faith is weak. But even on that account, if there is greater hope of gain than fear of loss, they should be performed without question, especially when they can be strongly defended from the Scriptures."[11]

Our weaker brother may also be that particular group of people, often in the minority, who come to church and find that the musical language does not speak to them, that they do not understand it, or that it is not relevant for them in expressing their adoration. These individuals will certainly go through the motions of worshipping, but their hearts will not be able to join profoundly in the act of adoration. Brian Schrag, a missionary in Zaire (now the Democratic Republic of the Congo) in central Africa, relates an experiment he tried in one of the local churches when he had a choir of *kundi* (an indigenous instrument similar to a five-string wooden lyre) players perform a song on Creation. At the end of the song the congregation remained silent for a long time, overwhelmed by the effect of the music. Then they exclaimed, "We have been worshiping all this time, but today for the first time, we have been worshiping with our hearts. The music cut right to our hearts. We couldn't do anything but sit." Schrag remarks that "for the first time they had heard the gospel with the music of their souls."[12] In the words of Roberta King, ethnomusicologist at Fuller Theological Seminary, there is a need to "reconnect people's 'heart music' with their Christian faith."[13] The same principle, of course, holds for the music in any church with multicultural and multigenerational congregations.

The rule of the weaker brother is a two-way rule. Whatever prevents people from worshipping completely with their hearts, minds, and souls becomes a stumbling block. It is, therefore, our duty to open our eyes and seek to find the extent to which our music making in the church is either offensive or irrelevant to our congregation. In order to do so, we might have to forego someone's complaint—if it is not founded on the right premises—and continue ahead with a different practice of music "if there is greater hope of gain than fear of loss." The new element, of course, must be able to "be strongly defended from the Scriptures." The Word of God is the only yardstick against which any musical practice should be measured and evaluated. As we so probe our music making, if it is found to be good, then, in Paul's own words, we should not allow it to "be spoken of as evil" (Romans 14:16).

Music as a Factor of Spirit and Truth:
Balance Between Ecstasy and Discipline

In the context of 1 Corinthians 14, Paul relates a number of actions pertaining to worship, such as speaking in tongues, praying, and singing (verses 13-15). He discusses these three acts of worship within the context of worshipping "with the spirit" versus worshipping "with the mind," and of prophesying versus speaking in tongues (verse 4). In our modern day language we would translate this in terms of truth versus emotionalism, or formal worship versus emotional worship.

Formal Worship

Many of our churches today suffer from a one-sided approach to worship. Some focus primarily on a formal style centered around the Word (Scripture reading, responsive readings, sermon) and allow only a small place, within a well-determined framework, for emotional involvement and community interaction.

The danger of putting emphasis on the cognitive side of worship to the exclusion of emotions, is that worship can easily degenerate into a dry and formal exercise. It seems that Isaiah had fallen victim to this attitude without even knowing it, as Ellen G. White comments: "Isaiah had denounced the sin of others; but now he sees himself exposed to the same condemnation he had pronounced upon them. He had been satisfied with a cold, lifeless ceremony in his worship of God. He had not known this until the vision was given him of the Lord."[14]

She denounced such worship repeatedly: "Churches have had the labors of unconverted, inefficient men, who have lulled the members to sleep, instead of awakening them to greater zeal and earnestness in the cause of God. There are ministers who come to the prayer meeting, and pray the same old, lifeless prayers over and over; they preach the same dry discourses from week to week and from month to month. They have nothing new and inspiring to present to their congregations, and this is evidence that they are not partakers of the divine nature. Christ is not abiding in the heart by faith."[15] "Our meetings should be made intensely interesting. They should be pervaded with the very atmosphere of heaven. Let there be no long, dry speeches and formal prayers merely for the sake of occupying the time. . . . His service should be made interesting and attractive and not be allowed to degenerate into a dry form."[16] "That which is done for the glory of God should be done with cheerfulness, with songs of praise and thanksgiving, not with sadness and gloom."[17] "Our God should be regarded as a tender, merciful father. The service of God should not be looked upon as a heart-saddening, distressing exercise. It should be a pleasure to worship the Lord and to take part in His work."[18]

Jesus, as quoted in John 4:23, was very clear about how we should worship: "The true worshipers will worship the Father in spirit and truth, for they are the kind of worshipers the Father seeks." True worship must be done with both heart and mind. Worship done in a predominantly cognitive style needs to be enlivened by the emotions. Otherwise, it will remain false worship.

Emotional Worship

Other churches favor predominantly emotional worship, strongly emphasizing extensive musical expression and community interaction, leaving only a small part to the presentation of the Word. Ellen G. White emphasizes how emotional worship needs to be checked by reference to the Word of God and serious heart searching. She makes the following recommendations: "If we work to create an excitement of feeling, we shall have all we want, and more than we can possibly know how to manage. . . . The Holy Spirit of God alone can create a healthy enthusiasm. . . . In our speaking, our singing, and in all our spiritual exercises, we are to reveal that calmness and dignity and godly fear that actuates every true child of God. It is through the *Word*—not feeling, not excitement—that we want to influence the people to obey the truth."[19] "We have no time now to spend in seeking those things that only please the senses. Close heart searching is needed. With tears and heartbroken confession we need to draw nigh to God that He may draw nigh to us. The hearts of God's professed people are so thoroughly selfish and depraved, so passionate and self-indulgent, that He cannot work through them."[20]

Whenever we encourage emotional worship, we should be aware of its ultimate implications and the potential to draw away from true worship by neglecting the rational aspect. True worship always addresses the whole person: heart, mind, and spirit. Our purpose is neither to lead the church on a temporary emotional trip—this would be synonymous with manipulation—nor on a rational exploration, but rather into a deeper and lasting experience of the presence of God. This happens only if we involve both the mind and the heart.

The balance between the emotional and the rational aspects of worship, between the horizontal and the vertical, stands at the core of our reflection on music and worship. Two examples—one taken from early Advent history, the other from the church of Corinth—will illustrate this point. Both deal with a strongly developed emotional emphasis in worship.

Up to the 1870s the early Adventist Church practiced a style of worship that was quite exuberant.[21] By the 1850s Ellen G. White had already voiced her warnings against abusing spiritual exercises and practicing religion based on experience without the control of the Word of God. She was mostly concerned with the results of uncontrolled emotionalism: "I saw that there was great danger of leaving the Word of God and resting down and trusting in exercises. I saw that God had moved by His Spirit upon your company in some of their exercises and their promptings; but I saw danger ahead."[22]

The danger she sensed was the ever-increasing need for emotional expression and emphasis that come with highly emotional activities. She rightly understood the stimulating character of such activities, which are in contradiction with a true and lasting worship experience: "Still others . . . [make] religious emotions prominent. . . . Their religion seems to be more of the nature of a stimulus rather than an abiding faith in Christ.[23]

Because emotional events are stimulating experiences, they will result in ever-increasing levels of need for emotional content in order to provide satisfaction. Emotions are a powerful and necessary force in the worship experience, but when driven to excess, this otherwise beneficial aspect of the experience can become a factor that drives one away from the truth.[24]

Paul confronted a similar situation in the church of Corinth, which struggled with the gift of speaking in tongues. Chapter 14 of his letter to the Corinthians shows how he tried to restore the balance between ecstasy and discipline, between the emotional and rational elements, in worship. It is not so much the actual practice of spiritual exercises that Paul condemns, but its use in public worship: "He who speaks in a tongue edifies himself, but he who prophesies edifies the church. . . . He who prophesies is greater than one who speaks in tongues, unless he interprets, so that the church may be edified" (1 Corinthians 14:4, 5). "Since you are eager to have spiritual gifts, try to excel in gifts that build up the church" (verse 12).

Going beyond the issue of emotionalism, Paul hit the core of the purpose of any worship action performed during public services. He makes the point that speaking in tongues is a self-edifying exercise, while prophesying is an activity that edifies everyone present. Public worship is a communal act, meant to strengthen and edify the congregation, not primarily to allow for indulgence in emotional self-gratification. Emotional self-gratification, according to Paul, is a private matter meant to edify oneself rather than the whole church. He says, "I will sing with my spirit, but I will also sing with my mind" (verse 15), implying that both the heart and the mind must participate in our music making. While the heart is needed to inspire the mind, the mind (truth) is needed to control the heart. Both are necessary to achieve true worship, not only for the edification of the members but also to convince the unbeliever of true worship. When these two characteristics are present, worship will be done "in a fitting and orderly way" (verse 40).

Successful, balanced worship is that to which an entire congregation can respond with an amen—whether that response is verbal or otherwise. If what we are doing during worship cannot be understood by the whole church, we should instead keep quiet and speak privately to ourselves and God (verse 28). As we apply this principle to music, this means that when we present music in the church, the congregation at large should be able to respond to it truly with "Amen, so be it."

If a large part of the congregation cannot join in doing so, then we do not facilitate worship, but distract from it and create dissent and criticism. This does not mean, though, that we should expect everybody to be happy with the music. That day will come only when we worship in heaven! But it reminds us as musicians of our responsibility to be open to our congregations, to find out about their needs and different cultural and generational backgrounds. The next step is to learn how to speak their musical language and to enjoy doing so.

In 1 Corinthians 14 Paul wants to drive home two points. 1. Worship actions should be done with the purpose to edify, to build up, and to strengthen the church: "Try to excel in gifts that build up the church" (verse 12). When we come together, whatever is done should be done "for the strengthening of the church" (verse 26) and not for our own self-gratification. 2. Worship should be done in a "fitting and orderly way" (verse 40) because "God is not a God of disorder but of peace" (verse 33). Too often the things of worship are left up to chance and last-minute arrangement, hiding negligence and carelessness under the cover of "being open to the Spirit." Such attitudes result only in lack of order and purpose, and open the door to uncontrolled outcomes and mediocrity. This is true especially if too much is left up to the inspiration of the moment, which in fact is nothing but the result of last-minute whims and imagination or personal preferences. Such an inconsiderate attitude prevents the submission of plans and ideas to scriptural scrutiny: "The Lord desires to have in His service order and discipline, not excitement and confusion. . . . This is a time when we must watch unto prayer. . . . We need to be thoughtful and still, and to contemplate the truths of revelation. Excitement is not favorable to growth in grace."[25]

In order to "sing with our minds," every musical aspect of the worship service—the music, musicians, and performance mode—must be true to the spirit of biblical worship. Only when we have "truth in music" will the "singing with our spirits" be worthy of presentation to God in worship. But how is it possible to speak of truth in music? How can the concept of truth be applied to a form of art?

Truth and Music

It is, indeed, quite challenging to establish a relationship between the two concepts of truth and music. Music is generally considered a subjective reality, occurring in a personal or social setting associated with enjoyment. Music may also merely provide an almost neutral background against which other things are taking place. Truth, on the other hand, is associated with objective realities, with Scripture and with teachings and doctrine.

Ezra Pound, an American poet of the early twentieth century, wrote about the issue of truth in art and left us the following statement: "Bad art is inaccurate art. It is art that makes false reports. . . . If an artist falsifies his report as to the nature of . . . god, . . . of good and evil, . . . the force with which he believes or disbelieves this, that or the other . . . if the artist falsifies his reports on these matters . . . then that artist lies. By good art I mean art that bears true witness, I mean art that is most precise."[26]

Pound refers in this statement to two levels of truth: truth as opposed to deceit or falsehood and truth in the sense of loyalty or faithfulness to a given set of values. He makes a clear point that there exists a necessary relationship between what the artist believes—the *content* and message of his work—and the way he expresses it—the *form* of his artwork. Art that bears true witness is art in which both form and content convey the same message: "A work's aesthetic achievement consists in the skill with which it expresses its content."[27]

Applied to music, this means that the *style* of the music must convey the same message as the *lyrics,* in the case of vocal music, or the main theme or thought, in the case of an instrumental composition. With purely instrumental music, only the composer will know to what extent the true relationship between form and content has been achieved. When music has words, however, the degree of correspondence will become apparent to any attentive or concerned listener.

The process in which truth is conveyed to the worshipper through music can be compared to the way water is conveyed to the thirsty individual. The truth can be communicated by diverse cultural expressions, just as water can be channeled by all sorts of materials—metal, plastic, cement, wood, a dirt ditch, etc. These carriers depend upon time in history, geographical location, cultural practices, etc. What is essential, however, is that when the water reaches its destination, it is still the same as it was at the source, pure and unaltered. If the water comes down to us changed by the chemical constitution of the channeling factor, it can become poisonous and life-threatening. If I use a lead pipe to transport water to the faucet, it will ultimately pick up enough lead to make me sick. The source of life has, then, become the cause of sickness and death.

This illustration teaches the importance of *form* in conveying the content. When the message transmitted in worship through a particular form of music is not the same as the one transmitted by the lyrics, we have false worship. A number of factors contribute to the form of music: the musician's disposition of his/her heart, a particular song style, the manner of performance, dress and deportment, etc.

I will always remember a Sabbath morning when the pastor of my church was about to start a very difficult series of sermons on the "unpopular" topic of the sanctuary and judgment. The special music on that day was meant to set the tone for—and serve as an introduction to—the sermon. Even though the lyrics ("Holy, holy, holy") were appropriate for the solemn and serious character of the occasion, the style of performance was easygoing, almost trivial and carefree, creating an atmosphere of letting go and feeling good rather than one of reflection and inner searching. In the debriefing sessions shortly after that service, the pastor related the sheer physical difficulty he had experienced in getting up, moving to the pulpit, and starting his sermon.

The musical style had created an atmosphere completely opposite to the theme and spirit of the sermon. In this case content and form did not agree and resulted in bad art, inaccurate art—art that did not bear true witness.

In dealing with worship music, the primary truth to consider is the concept of God. Everything in worship centers around God and is focused on God. That is the essence of worship. As we look at the biblical texts describing heavenly scenes of worship (e.g., Isaiah 6; Revelation 4, 5), we find that they start out with the vision of God seated high on His throne, acclaimed as the Holy God. The *vision* of God is the crucible for worship and worship style. The Scriptures are very clear about the nature of God, as we can see in the words of God Himself as He spoke through His prophets: " 'For my thoughts are not your thoughts, neither are your ways my ways,' " declares the Lord. 'As the heavens are higher than the earth, so are my ways higher than your ways and my thoughts than your thoughts' " (Isaiah 55:8, 9). "For I am God, and not man—the Holy One among you" (Hosea 11:9).

This radical difference in character between God and human beings is often overlooked. In evangelical circles especially, the numinous—the sense of the unfathomable God who can be met only with humility—has been replaced by a "domesticated" God, a God in our image, in whose presence we feel very comfortable. The vision of the loving, saving, and merciful God has come to overshadow and almost eliminate the vision of God's essentially different character, that which sets us apart from Him as creatures in the presence of their Creator. Even though God incarnated Himself and came down to us, enabling us to speak to Him, He still remains the One different from us. I do personally believe that if, as musicians, we can recapture this numinous aspect of God and keep our sensitivities open to the transcendent, it will enable us to place our music making on a higher plane and will help us in rendering our music different, setting it apart from the common and everyday. Being aware simultaneously of the transcendent character of God and His immanence will ensure a balanced biblical approach in our worship services and will lend *truth* to our music making.

Remembering that worship music, by its very essence, is meant to be a collective experience provides a perspective that assists us in keeping our priorities straight. It reminds us of the primary focus of this experience, the raison d'être for our music making in the first place. It helps us to accept that it is not personal opinion, but *the good of many*, that is paramount to this experience. And it guides us in making choices in our personal musical experiences that prepare our hearts day by day for the ultimate encounter with God during worship.

---

[1] See Idelsohn, *Jewish Music,* pp. 96, 97.

[2] The custom of singing without instrumental accompaniment was observed in synagogues at large until 1810, when, for the first time, an organ was introduced in a reformed temple in Germany. Still today, one will not find instrumental or choir music in Orthodox synagogues; only the chanting of Scripture is part of the religious services (Idelsohn, *Jewish Music*, p. 96).

[3] A. Z. Idelsohn, *Jewish Liturgy and Its Development,* (New York: Schocken Books, 1967), pp. 16, 17.

[4] See Idelsohn, *Jewish Liturgy*, p. 24. Religious services were then held in synagogues, and probably some of the Levite musicians helped out with the chanting of Scripture.

[5] See the letters of Pliny the Younger (c. A.D. 62-113) to emperor Trajan in which he gives a description of the practice of singing in the early church (*Letters,* book 10, No. 96, quoted in David W. Music, *Hymnology: A Collection of Source Readings,* Studies in Liturgical Musicology, No. 4 [Lanham, Md.: The Scarecrow Press, 1996], pp. 3-5).

[6] The titles of these songs were taken from the first word of the song as it appears in the Latin version of the Bible, the Vulgate. In liturgical terms these songs are called the "New Testament canticles." A fourth canticle, also found in Luke (2:14), is the *Gloria* sung by the angels at Christ's birth.

[7] This adviser role was, all through the history of the church, carried on by statements made by church fathers, reformers, and theologians who felt the need to remind their churches of the importance of a healthy and appropriate use of music. Their writings reveal an ongoing concern and struggle with the concept of what is appropriate or inappropriate for the church. See Theodore Gérold, *Les Pères de église et la musique* [*The Church Fathers and Music*] (Paris: F. Alkan, 1931; reprint Geneva, Switzerland: Minkoff, 1973). See also James William McKinnon, "The Church Fathers and Musical Instruments" (Ph.D. dissertation, Columbia University, 1965 [Ann Arbor, Mich.: University Microfilms]); St. Augustine of Hippo, *De Musica* [*On Music*], in *Writings of St. Augustine* (New York: Fathers of the Church, 1948).

[8] See "A Philosophy of Music," pp. 83-87 of this book.

[9] See *World Biblical Commentary,* vol. 44: *Colossians, Philemon,* ed. by Peter T. O'Brien (Waco, Tex.: Word Books Publishers, 1982), pp. 208, 209.

[10] See *The Seventh-day Adventist Bible Commentary,* vol. 6, pp. 634-636, "Romans 14:1, 2"; cf. also Samuele Bacchiocchi, *The Sabbath Under Crossfire: A Biblical Analysis of Recent Sabbath/Sunday Developments* (Berrien Springs, Mich.: Biblical Perspectives, 1998), pp. 250-252.

[11] Saint Augustine, from "Letter No. 55, chapter 18," in *Patrologie Cursus Completus, Series Latina* (Paris: Garnier Frères, 1878-1889), vol. 33, pp. 219, 220; quoted in David W.

Music, *Hymnology: A Collection of Source Readings*, Studies in Liturgical Musicology, No. 4 (Lanham, Md.: The Scarecrow Press, 1996), p. 11.

[12] This story was related by Andrés T. Tapia, "Musicianaries," *Christianity Today*, October 7, 1996, p. 53.

[13] *Ibid.*, p. 52.

[14] *The Seventh-day Adventist Bible Commentary*, Ellen G. White Comments, vol. 4, p. 1139.

[15] E. G. White, *Gospel Workers* (Washington, D.C.: Review and Herald Publishing Assn., 1948), p. 437.

[16] E. G. White, *Testimonies for the Church*, vol. 5, p. 609.

[17] E. G. White, *Steps to Christ* (Mountain View, Calif.: Pacific Press Publishing Assn.: 1956), p. 103.

[18] E. G. White, *That I May Know Him* (Washington, D.C.: Review and Herald Publishing Assn., 1964), p. 263.

[19] E. G. White, *Last Day Events* (Boise, Idaho: Pacific Press Publishing Assn., 1992), p. 93.

[20] E. G. White, "A Call for Help," *The Advent Review and Sabbath Herald*, November 14, 1899, p. 1.

[21] See Ronald D. Graybill, "Enthusiasm in Early Adventist Worship," *Ministry Magazine*, October 1991, pp. 10-12.

[22] E. G. White, "Vision at Paris, Maine," Manuscript 11, 1850.

[23] White, *Evangelism*, p. 502.

[24] See the incident at the Muncie, Indiana, camp meeting in 1900. It was criticized by Ellen G. White because it demonstrated that highly emotional worship, when not governed by reason, can result in chaotic and irrational behavior, thus shedding a wrong light on the church. She writes, "The senses of rational beings will become so confused that they cannot be trusted to make right decisions" (*Selected Messages* [Washington, D.C.: Review and Herald Publishing Assn., 1958], vol. 2, p. 36).

[25] E. G. White, *Selected Messages*, vol. 2, p. 35.

[26] T. S. Eliot, ed., *The Literary Essays of Ezra Pound* (New York: New Directions, 1968), pp. 43, 44.

[27] Mary Devereaux, in "Beauty and Evil: The Case of Leni Riefenstahl's *Triumph of the Will*," in *Aesthetics and Ethics: Essays at the Intersection*, Jerrold Levinson, ed. (Cambridge, U.K.: Cambridge University Press, 1998). p. 244

CHAPTER 8

{ *Music as a Personal Experience* }

Paul's advice also deals with Christian lifestyle on the personal level. We are able to draw inferences from his writings in regard to not only the practice of music in church but also the practice of music in relationship to our personal development. This journey will be a two-way road: while our musical experiences may and should contribute to our growth as Christian individuals, our spiritual transformation, on the other hand, will exert an influence on our musical experiences.

Music as a Factor of Growth and Transformation

Ellen G. White, in her book *Evangelism*, indicates the important relationship between music making and our sanctification: "Music is acceptable to God only when the heart is sanctified and made soft and holy by its facilities."[1]

In the same spirit, Paul urges us in Romans 12:2 to submit ourselves to a process of transformation in order to find out what God's will is: "*Do not conform any longer to the pattern of this world*, but be transformed by the renewing of your mind. Then you will be able to test and approve what God's will is—his good, pleasing and perfect will."

The only way for us to be able to understand God's will for us in our music making is to make ourselves available to this transformation process. In his epistles to the churches of Colossae and Ephesus, Paul indicates how we can achieve this goal: "*Set your hearts on things above. . . . Set your minds on things above*, not on earthly things. . . . Put to death, therefore, whatever belongs to your earthly nature: sexual immorality, impurity, lust, evil desires and greed, which is idolatry. . . . You must rid yourselves of all such things as these: anger, rage, malice, slander, and filthy language from your lips. Do not lie to each other, since you have taken off your old self with its practices and have put on the new self, which is being renewed in knowledge *in the image of its Creator*" (Colossians 3:1-10). "*Be imitators of God . . .* and live a life of love. . . . Nor should there be obscenity, foolish talk or coarse joking. . . . Let no one deceive you with empty words. . . . Live as children of light (for the fruit of the light consists in all goodness, righteousness and truth) and *find out what pleases the Lord*" (Ephesians 5:1-10).

As musicians, once we set our hearts and minds on things above and try to emulate the character of our Creator rather than follow the standards of this world, our music will reflect this transformation. In our choices of music and words, in our attitudes, in the way we perform or sing, and in the way we relate to the congregation, we will convey the image of our Creator. We will not be occupied with satisfying our selfishness by gathering around those who play and sing music that our "itching ears want to hear" (2 Timothy 4:3). We will not be preoccupied with success and popularity or with pleasing ourselves or a particular group of people. The focus will shift from self and be directed toward God. This is the meaning of the concept of music as *ministry*. When that point is reached, the personal faith of the musician that informs his/her music making spills over into the collective realm of music making. Music becomes a powerful tool for transformation within the members of the congregation, not only to lift them up but also to convey to them values and truths that will be planted in their hearts in a very deep way.

The importance of maintaining truth at a high level and setting high expectations for our youth in this regard was underlined by Ellen G. White: "Never bring the truth down to a low level in order to obtain converts, but seek to bring the sinful and corrupted up to the high standard of the law of God."[2] "I was shown that the youth must take a higher stand and make the word of God the man of their counsel and their guide."[3]

Contrary to what many believe, today's youth are not looking for an easy or cheap message. In confrontations about the issue of church music, I often have heard the adults accuse the youth of lack of spirituality, immaturity in spiritual matters, and shallowness. The fact that some pastors or leaders deliver a cheap message to youth does not mean that this is what the youth want and are looking for. After all, the depth of our youth's spirituality rests upon the modeling and teaching *we* have provided in matters of worship.

Today's youth are, on the contrary, expecting a real and lasting message, even if it is a difficult one. Robert Webber, in an article published in the *Worship Leader* magazine,[4] underlines some factors that are important to youth today. He mentions a revival of interest in spirituality, the search for faith, commitment to a cause they can believe in, and commitment to service, asking "What can I do for others?" Adjectives that characterize this generation in regard to religion are real, genuine, relational, and honest. Today's youth are tired of entertainment worship and are looking for a genuine encounter with God and more depth in their spiritual journey.[5] This is where the task lies for today's youth leaders and mentors.

In the context of a recent evaluation of our collegiate worship service at the Andrews University church, we gathered a group of university students to give us some feedback. At the end of the session the senior pastor asked the students what topics they would like to hear addressed from the pulpit. Their answers came as quite a surprise to us: "We want you to address some of the essential issues that come up in our lives and on the campus, such as premarital sex, drug use, theft, etc. And we want you to give us straight talk about it, without beating around the bush."[6] The message could not have been clearer: the young people want to hear a strong, direct message that will help them to clearly discern what direction to undertake in regard to these issues, even if it is difficult.

This is exactly what Ellen G. White meant when she spoke about taking a higher stand. Even if the message is difficult, this is what the youth want to hear. The same principles should also apply to their musical practice and experiences. Considering the important part music plays in their lives, it is essential that this tool be used to reinforce high values and send strong, clear messages. Making our young people responsible for their musical choices, both in their private lives and in church, will help them reach maturity in their personal lives and within their communities.

What does it mean, then, to *reflect the image of the Creator* in music, and how can we achieve this goal?

In several instances[7] Paul paints a picture of what makes for a true Christian life, showing us attitudes that will best reflect the image of the Creator. He enjoins us as believers to be careful how we live, to use wisdom and discernment, and to seek to understand what God's will is. This subject resounds like a leitmotif throughout his epistles. As we start applying these principles to music in general, or to church music in particular, the first thing that strikes us is the objective and deliberate character of such an undertaking. To reflect the image of the Creator means to make choices for our music making, objective and well-considered decisions, based on a true understanding of the character of God and His will for us. These choices are not founded on feelings, personal taste or preferences, the latest fashion, etc. They are the result of a genuine searching by the human mind and heart for discernment, knowledge, understanding, and wisdom in our musical practice, in the perspective of the ultimate goal of the whole undertaking—to find out and embrace what God's will is, what pleases Him. They have to do with transformation.

The decisions we make concerning our lifestyle in the light of our relationship with God should inform the decisions we make as to the choice of our musical experiences. These experiences can be a particular event or context, or the lyrics of a song. Indeed, a specific piece of music may accompany morally positive events or lyrics, or morally negative situations or lyrics. A specific piece of music can accompany circumstances marked by violence, indecent behavior, the consumption of drugs and alcohol, or non-Christian values; it may also be used in another context, with different lyrics or in different company, or in connection to a spiritual experience promoting ethical and religious values.[8] For instance, it may be appropriate to listen to and enjoy Jacques Offenbach's *Gaîté Parisienne* in the setting of a concert hall or at home, but it would be improper to attend a performance of the same music at the Moulin Rouge in Paris or at a Las Vegas revue.

We should constantly make sure that any kind of experience we choose to participate in, whether associated with classical, popular, or even religious music, will affirm and deepen our relationship with God instead of distracting us from it and leading us further away from our Creator. Because of our love for a certain music, it may happen that we expose ourselves to places, the company of people, and activities that are not in harmony with the biblical principles of lifestyle. The guidelines for our orientation of life are clearly outlined in the book of Galatians, and the choice of our musical experiences should likewise be guided by these principles: "The fruit of the Spirit is love, joy, peace, patience, kindness, goodness, faithfulness, gentleness and self-control" (Galatians 5:22, 23).

Music does not happen in a vacuum, but always in context and with an established meaning attributed by society within a given cultural setting. The understanding of that meaning and the degree of deliberate engagement in the musical experience—or refusal thereof—will determine the effect of the music. We would be hard-pressed to prove that music has power to influence us without our personal consent and submission to its effect. The primary concern in the debate on music should be to build individuals with strong principles and well-founded convictions who develop a close relationship with God and learn to listen to and follow the guidance of the Spirit. If, in addition, they are well aware of how music works and are equipped with a broad education in matters of music, they will be able to make informed and responsible musical choices in terms of good taste and strong ethical values. Their convictions and understanding will determine their decisions and the extent to which they will allow themselves to submit to or refrain from a given experience. Putting all the blame on music is too easy an escape for one's personal failure to grow into a strong Christian individual.

---

1 E. G. White, *Evangelism,* p. 512.

2 *Ibid.,* p. 137.

3 E. G. White, *Testimonies for the Church,* vol. 1, p. 497.

4 Robert Webber, "Finding Hope in the Coming Generation," *Worship Leader,* September/October 2000, p. 12.

5 According to a survey related by Robert Webber, 90 percent of the people interviewed (23-year-olds from 23 countries and more than 40 denominations) responded in this sense ("Beyond Contemporary Worship," *Worship Leader,* March/April 2000, p. 12).

6 Meeting held at Pioneer Memorial Church, Andrews University, Berrien Springs, Michigan, on April 25, 2006. As a result, these topics were addressed in a series of sermons on the theme "The Chosen" during fall 2007 (available online at www.pmchurch.org).

7 See his letters addressed to the various churches of the Christian world in his time.

8 E.g., the use of J. S. Bach's music for both Christian and satanic worship.

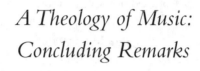

CHAPTER 9

A Theology of Music: Concluding Remarks

The picture that emerges from our study of the principles found in the Bible and the Spirit of Prophecy is rich in lessons. We have received manifold answers to our question "What was music for the biblical writers?"

Music was first understood as a gift from God—a gift received and cultivated with awe. In response it was returned to God as an offering that focused entirely on God Himself, reflecting His attributes, His character, and the biblical worship values. Music in the Bible was doxological, meaning that it was sounded for the Lord rather than for the congregation.

For these reasons worship music was understood to be a ministry that must be carried out with faithfulness. Ministry implies a spirit of service: service to God and service to the community. Talent and skill are necessary but not sufficient. Only the disposition of the heart and the nature of the personal relationship with God will make the music worthy of worship. The musician's attitude and concerns must reflect this understanding of his or her task, and he or she should serve both God and the congregation with a spirit of humility.

Music was also used in the Bible as a tool for teaching the truth and remembering it, a powerful means to enshrine the truth in the human heart through beauty and emotional impact. Beyond the aesthetic beauty it conveyed, music became, then, an avenue to convey moral and spiritual beauties, theology, and eternal values. It also functioned as a channel for the expression of personal experiences on a wholistic level.

To our question "How was music used in biblical times?" we receive a threefold answer: with skill, with discernment, and with dedication. With *skill* was the only acceptable way to play or sing to the Lord, because of the excellent and perfect character of the Lord Himself. *Discernment* can be observed in the balance achieved between the emotions and the mind (spirit and truth) and in the ethical concern that was expressed in matters of music making within a community of believers. Finally, *dedication* can be found in the concern for transformation, in the understanding of the special set-apart character of the music making for God, and in the endeavor to be pleasing to God.

Beyond these principles drawn from the Bible and the Spirit of Prophecy, we needed, however, to move one step further and ask "How will this new understanding affect my music making?"

One idea grew conspicuously out of our study: the issue of musical style for church is not primarily a musical matter, but first of all, a spiritual matter. In other words, the *individual* must be looked at before the musician and the music making. The first stage to be considered and developed is the musician's maturity in spiritual understanding as a result of the transforming power of the Spirit, the truth about the nature of God, and, consequently, the truth about ourselves and the world we live in. Only then should we consider the person's maturity as an artist, performer, composer, or singer.

At my church we make it a habit, before we choose a music or worship leader, to interview a candidate. The interview always starts with the same questions. We ask "What is your understanding of worship? How do you see the role of music in worship? How do you see your role as worship/music leader in this twofold dynamic?" Answers to these questions form the starting point of a true worship- or music-leading experience. They will provide the necessary discernment between what is appropriate or inappropriate, and will guide and influence the choices made by the musician, bringing him or her to understand their role to be that of a servant of God and of the congregation. As Paul puts it in his letter to the Philippians: "This is my prayer: that your love may abound more and more in knowledge and depth of insight, so that you may be able to discern what is best and may be pure and blameless until the day of Christ" (1:9, 10).

Only when this level of understanding and experience has been reached on the part of the musician, should we finally start considering the matter of musical style. The choice of style will be the result of a transformed individual who has a full understanding of the special character and meaning of the moment and of the responsibilities he or she is accepting as an artist in providing an avenue for the dramatic event that is going to take place between God and the worshippers.

Two concepts have established themselves in the course of these considerations: appropriateness and relevance. *Appropriateness* in the context of worship means that in my music making, in the choice of music and in the playing or singing, I will endeavor to come as close as possible to an expression of who God is in order to bring an offering that is pleasing to Him. *Relevance* in the context of worship means that in my music making, I will show sensitivity toward my fellow worshippers as I consider the diversity of cultures and ethnic backgrounds that make up my congregation. This will be manifested in my choice of a plurality of styles and instruments used, shaped, or transformed in such a way that they do not become an offense to anybody. On the contrary, they will enable us to praise God as a unified body in a multifaceted way, as God Himself taught us through the gift of diversity in His Creation.

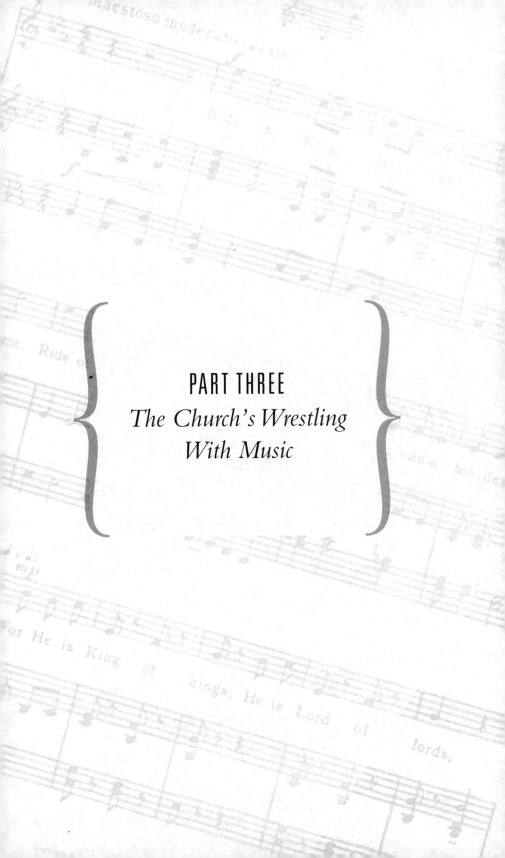

PART THREE
The Church's Wrestling With Music

INTRODUCTION

The church, by her very nature, lives in constant tension between the vertical and the horizontal. Her mission is to maintain and safeguard this tension in perfect balance in order to provide to her believers a venue that will permit an authentic relationship between God and human beings. An authentic relationship should be one in which men and women perceive and sense their Creator in the manifold aspects of His being and His doings, and may come before their Creator just as they are, communicating with Him in their very own human language. This relationship becomes particularly critical when dealing with matters of worship, a time during which the relationship is sought for in a special way and celebrated and brought to a climax in a particularly focused and heightened manner. Because worship has to do with God, there are a number of immutable principles necessary in order to have real and authentic worship, principles that have to do with the *essence* of worship. On the other hand, because worship includes the human factor, there are also changeable elements in worship, elements that have to do with the *expression* of worship. The modes of expression in worship change according to time and place and are shaped by the verbal and nonverbal languages used in various cultural groups. This tension between the divine principles and human expressions of worship is healthy and desirable because it keeps worship dynamic and alive.

When dealing with musical matters, the tension between the essence and expression of worship becomes an issue that stands at the very forefront of the debate on church music. Throughout the ages the church has wrestled with this tension and has tried to propose solutions according to various perspectives and motivations. It appears that quite often she has overlooked the reality and benefit of this tension and has opted to emphasize one side over the other, either putting the accent on the divine character of worship or, on the contrary, on the human aspect of worship.

Congregational song during worship epitomizes this tension and has repeatedly become an object of concern on the part of church leaders. Three topics in particular have retained the attention: the influence of music on the human emotions, the legitimacy of secular influences, and the use of instruments in the church. Indeed, these are the very same issues that still raise red flags in church today. Arguments have changed according to time and place. Within all this variety, though, three patterns emerge in the church's efforts to safeguard the balance between the vertical and the horizontal: the concern for truth, the concern for mission, and the concern for political status.

The purpose of studying the history of congregational song is to learn lessons from what went wrong and to take inspiration from what worked well, so as not to repeat the same errors. I propose, then, that in the following pages we undertake a short journey through the history of congregational song and find inspiration for our own practices of singing in the church.

As we study hymn singing and music making by looking at documents pertaining to the history of the Christian church, several patterns and practices emerge that will become characteristic of the development of hymnody. These patterns and practices will be like faithful companions in our overview of the singing church and will, hopefully, trigger our personal reflections on church music, encouraging us to perceive answers that fit our own times and particular situations.

This section is not meant to be a historical survey of music making in the church. Its purpose is, rather, to focus on key moments when the church wrestled with particular issues of interest to us today. Thus, we will be able to learn, from others' previous experiences, both what mistakes to avoid and what solutions to adopt.[1]

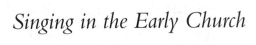

CHAPTER 10

Singing in the Early Church

The New Testament Church

New Testament congregational song had its source in the singing of psalms and canticles of the Old Testament. The psalms, primarily meant as music to accompany the sacrifices in the Temple (see 1 Chronicles 23:30, 31 and Psalm 27:6), were also a rich source of personal or congregational devotion. They contain the whole gamut of human emotions brought before the Lord in song. Israel's canticles contain songs of praise and victory (e.g., the song of Moses and Miriam, Exodus 15), of petition (e.g., Daniel's prayer, Daniel 9:4-19), of remembrance (e.g., the song of Moses, Deuteronomy 32), and of visions of the future (Daniel 8:9, 10).

The singing of psalms was practiced by the Levites in the Temple, but it was also a basic form of singing among the people apart from the Temple service. The many responsorial psalms are examples (Psalms 42, 43, 46, 57, 136, etc.), especially the psalms of ascension (Psalms 120-134), which were sung by the people of Israel during their journeys to Jerusalem in order to take part in the various religious feasts. The people would gather from all over Israel to converge on the city on the mountain. During their ascent to Jerusalem, their walk was enlivened by psalm singing.

The biblical philosophy of congregational singing, namely, participatory singing, was inscribed in the very poetic form of these oldest songs. The way a psalm was written translated this participatory principle. The typical psalm verse comes in two parallel segments, each one speaking about the same idea in different but complementary ways. The singing of psalms was done in antiphonal fashion, i.e., two groups alternating with each other, each one singing one half verse. Psalm 102:1-4 illustrates this:

Hear my prayer, O Lord;

>let my cry for help come to you.

Do not hide your face from me when I am in distress.

>Turn your ear to me; when I call, answer me quickly.

For my days vanish like smoke;

>my bones burn like glowing embers.

My heart is blighted and withered like grass;

>I forget to eat my food.

Participatory singing was to become the most characteristic and fundamental trait of congregational singing throughout history. Furthermore, the psalms were sung to melodies drawn from folk repertoire, with occasional foreign tunes added.[2]

This basic principle of singing was carried over into the New Testament church. Paul encouraged the church of Ephesus to sing psalms, hymns, and spiritual songs. In various places the New Testament refers to singing as a means to create relationships and unity (Ephesians 5:19, etc.) or as an expression of joy (James 5:13, etc.), praise (Acts 16:25; Romans 15:9, etc.), and thanksgiving (Ephesians 5:19, 20, etc.). Singing in church was also meant for the purpose of edifying and strengthening the believers (1 Corinthians 14:15, 26; Colossians 3:16, etc.). All these injunctions were addressed to groups of believers rather than individual musicians.

Early descriptions and eyewitnesses of singing during the first decade of the Common Era relate practices similar to those observed in Old Testament congregations. Philo of Alexandria, a first-century A.D. philosopher, described how the members of a Jewish or possibly early Christian sect,[3] the Therapeutae, would form into groups and sing responsively, women and men alternating:

"When, therefore, the presiding worshiper appears to have spoken at sufficient length, some one rising up sings a hymn which has been made in honor of God, either such as he has composed himself, or some ancient one of some old poet, . . . and in regular order, and in choruses, admirably measured out in various and well diversified strophes. And after him then others also arise in their ranks, in becoming order, while every one else listens in decent silence, except when it is proper for them to take up the refrain of the song, and to join in at the end; for then they all, both men and women, join in the hymn.

"And after the feast they celebrate the sacred festival during the whole night; and this nocturnal festival is celebrated in the following manner: they all stand up together, and two choruses are formed, one of men and the other of women, and for each chorus there is a leader and chief selected, who is the most honorable and most excellent of the band. Then they sing hymns which have been composed in honor of God in many meters and tunes, at one time all singing together, and at another moving their hands and dancing in alternating verses, and uttering in an inspired manner songs of thanksgiving.

"Then, when each chorus of the men and each chorus of the women has feasted by itself . . . they join together, and the two become one chorus. . . . Now the chorus of male and female worshipers . . . makes a most delightful concert, and a truly musical symphony, the shrill voices of the women mingling with the deep-toned voices of the men."[4]

The same practice of singing antiphonally and responsorially was still in use in the fourth century and throughout the Christian churches of the East, according to the writings of Saint Basil (c. A.D. 329-379): "Rising up from their prayers, they begin the chanting of psalms. And now, divided into two parts, they chant antiphonally, becoming master of the text of the Scripture passages, and at the same time directing their attention and recollectedness of their hearts. Then, again, leaving it to one to intone the melody, the rest chant in response.[5]

The biblical text, then, establishes from the very outset a tradition of singing according to the principle of participation and interaction, which would also become the primary form of singing in the early Western church. Through the efforts of Saint Ambrose (c. A.D. 339-397), bishop of Milan, this practice was imported from the Eastern church to Milan in Italy during the fourth century.[6]

It is significant that this basic principle of participation in congregational singing—and the consequences such a practice would bring about with regard to type and style of music used—would come under attack and be con-

stantly challenged throughout the history of the church. Indeed, the participatory singing lies at the heart of the tension between the vertical and the
horizontal that was discussed earlier. Congregational participation introduces
a strong human element into the dynamics of worship.

While the New Testament church took over and continued the practices
of the Old Testament church, it also brought about changes. A new religious
experience, or a renewed understanding of religious beliefs, generally results
in the creation of new forms of expression. The new experience of the early
church was the event of Christ's life and mission. These events were being
celebrated by a new type of song, called hymns. In his commentary on Psalm
73, Saint Augustine (A.D. 354-430), bishop of Hippo, defined the hymn as a
"song of praise to God."[7] More specifically, the hymn was understood as a
song "to Christ as God." Pliny the Younger, a Roman historian of the first
and second centuries, while reporting to Emperor Trajan about Christian
practices around A.D. 111, mentioned this practice of the earliest Christians
to "sing a hymn antiphonally to Christ as God."[8] Hymns were meant to
teach the new believers about Christ, His life on earth, His mission, and the
hope of His second coming. Beyond the recounting of God's wonderful
works and praise for what He is and has done, singing becomes, then, a powerful apologetic tool as well: its main purpose is to spread the truth. Throughout its use in the church, the hymn has been characterized by its emphasis
on teaching, on conveying truth and doctrine. According to Saint Jerome (c.
A.D. 347-419), Niceta of Remesiana (c. A.D. 335-414), an early missionary
to the Balkans, spread the gospel through "sweet music of the cross."[9]

The Church Fathers and Music

The role of music in teaching the gospel was recognized and encouraged
by the early church fathers.[10] Here is what Saint Basil, bishop of Caesarea,
said about the power of hymn singing: "For when the Holy Spirit saw that
mankind was ill-inclined toward virtue and that we were heedless of the
righteous life because of our inclination to pleasure, what did he do? He
blended the delight of melody with doctrine in order that through the pleasantness and softness of the sound we might unawares receive what was useful
in the words."[11]

Teaching and learning are not usually associated with pleasure and charm.

What was it, then, in these songs that *charmed* the ears of those early Christians? According to contemporary documents, it was the tunes to which these hymns were sung that had such a strong impact. They were drawn from the secular repertoire,[12] a technique used repeatedly by church reformers in the course of history when there was a desire to enable the congregation to join in the singing immediately and spontaneously without first having to learn new tunes. The teaching was focused on doctrine and truth, not on the singing. Every teacher knows that good pedagogical practice introduces only one difficulty at a time.

Instruction was an important concern for the leaders of the early church. On one hand, there was a new element in the religious understanding that needed to be taught to the traditional believer. On the other hand, there was a need to instruct the newcomers to the Judeo-Christian world. The history of congregational singing illustrates how practical and theological considerations can work hand in hand. A new need creates a new form of singing. Change in religious understanding brings about change in the practice of religion.

In pursuing the history of hymn singing during the fourth and fifth centuries, we discover still another use of the hymns, namely, as "weapons" to engage in religious warfare.

The Arian heretics, led by Bardasanes and his son Harmonius, were quick in sensing the power of hymn singing in spreading their message. They also understood the importance of using familiar tunes to spread the songs rapidly.[13] Ephraim Syrus (c. A.D. 306-373), a fourth-century church father and defender of orthodox doctrines, did not hesitate to pick up the tunes of these heretics and put new words to them in order to combat their doctrines and spread the truth.[14]

On a different occasion, in their zeal to convert people by means of religious songs, the two factions—the Arians on one side and the faithful members of the congregation of Saint John Chrysostom (c. A.D. 347-407), bishop of Constantinople, on the other side—soon became engaged in physical conflict, trying to outdo each other during their nocturnal processions of hymn singing. As things started to get out of control, people from both sides were killed, and the Arians were forbidden to sing their hymns any longer in public.[15]

Many church fathers were especially concerned that young people make good choices in terms of musical practice.[16] Saint John Chrysostom's comment about the natural inclination of youth toward popular music sounds very familiar to modern ears: "Today, your children learn satanic songs and dances in fashion . . . but no one knows a Psalm. It is as if they are ashamed (to know a Psalm), they laugh at it and ridicule it.[17]

To counteract the impact of popular songs, the church fathers wrote hymns that would provide an alternative musical repertoire for the young people. Saint Chrysostom mentions how music "arouses the soul, gives it wing, sets it free from the earth, releases it from the prison of the body," and how "in order to prevent that the demons introduce their licentious songs and spoil the whole thing, God has given the Psalms so that their effect be at the same time agreeable and useful."[18] It is interesting to notice that these songs were meant not only to be useful, to guide the youth, but also to be agreeable and attractive to them. Around A.D. 200 Clement of Alexandria (c. A.D. 150-between 211 and 215) had already shown a similar preoccupation. One of his hymns written for young people, "Shepherd of Tender Youth," can still be found in Seventh-day Adventist hymnals.[19]

Still another concern was on the minds of the church leaders, namely, music as a purely aesthetic experience during worship. Saint Augustine addressed the issue of singing or music as it pertains to distracting from the Word of God and making the worshipper forget the primary purpose of his or her coming to worship. Saint Augustine writes in his *Confessions*: "When I find the singing itself more moving than the truth which it conveys, I confess that this is a grievous sin, and at those times I would prefer not to hear the singer."[20] Saint Augustine well understood that the role of music in worship is not aesthetic, but rather functional, namely, to point to the truth and enhance the Word of God.

In early Christianity music was also used as a powerful force of unification. Saint Augustine relates how Saint Ambrose fought Arianism in the city of Milan by occupying, with his faithful, the basilica besieged by soldiers. Singing hymns kept up the Christians' spirits and helped pass the time: "In those days your faithful people used to keep watch in the church, ready to die with their bishop, your servant. It was then that the practice of singing hymns and psalms was introduced, in keeping with the usage of the Eastern churches,[21] to revive the flagging spirits of the people during their long and cheerless watch."[22]

Finally, another issue encountered by most of the church fathers was the use of instruments in church. Instrumental music usually accompanied every pagan festivity: banquets; private meetings; family celebrations; the theater, with its burlesque representations; and, of course, religious ceremonies. Some of these events were still participated in by the newly converted Christians, and in the minds of the people, there were still strong associations in regard to pagan uses of instrumental music. Thus, in the majority of cases, in order to avoid ambiguous situations, the church fathers chose to play down or out-right reject the use of instruments in the church. Their argument was that God had permitted the use of instruments, and music in general, out of di-vine condescendence for the spiritual immaturity of the believers.[23] In saying so, the church fathers simply followed the model of the ancient Greek philosophers who believed that the gods, out of pity for the weak human condition, had allowed the agreeable experience of rhythm and melody in order to ease humankind's suffering and labor.[24]

Saint Basil the Great commented on the usefulness of instruments in the following terms: "Out of the arts necessary to life which furnish a concrete result there is carpentry, which produces the chair; architecture, the house; shipbuilding, the ship; tailoring, the garment; forging, the blade. Of useless arts there is harp playing, dancing, flute playing, of which, when the opera-tion ceases, the result disappears with it. And indeed, according to the word of the apostle, the result of these is destruction."[25]

Such decisions, however, were difficult to justify because they were con-trary to the biblical model, which presents a rich palette of instrumental music used in worship, especially Temple worship. The apparent contradiction with the biblical account was solved by providing allegorical interpretations based on observations of the physical properties of the instruments and the manners in which they were played. Pseudo-Origen, for instance, in referring to Psalm 92:3, compares the ten-stringed lyre to the "soul acting in a prac-tical way when it is put into motion by the precepts of God." The harp is likened to the "pure spirit animated by spiritual knowledge." He remarks, "The musical instruments of the Old Testament are not unsuitable for us if understood spiritually. . . . The harp is the active soul; the psaltery is pure mind. The ten strings can be taken as ten nerves, for a nerve is a string. There-fore, the psaltery is taken to be a body having five senses and five faculties."[26]

In similar fashion the lyre was said to refer to the human dimension and represented practical deeds because, according to Eusebius of Cesarea, as the lyre was played, it looked toward the earth. The harp, on the contrary, represented contemplation because when it was played, it was directed toward the heavens.[27]

The Council of Laodicea

Several issues regarding music were on the minds of the early church leaders: (1) the importance of singing, but also of singing the right songs (both the possible effect of the songs and the impact of secular influences were considered); (2) the uses made of music in the church, including teaching through music, rallying the church around the singing experience, and safeguarding the functional character of the music in church; (3) the use and abuse of instruments.

The church fathers did not always agree with one another on which position to take. During the first three centuries, as the church was not yet a unified entity, bishops were their own masters over an assigned territory, and their decisions became the rules. As discussions and disputes broke out over acceptable practices of music, the issues were brought before the Council of Laodicea (c. A.D. 363, 364). Though the Council of Laodicea was primarily a regional event, the issues dealt with there concerned the larger body of believers. Indeed, the decisions made at the Council of Laodicea changed the picture of congregational singing up to the time of the Reformation. The bishops of the church, grappling with such issues as the use of instruments, nonscriptural texts, and secular tunes for congregational singing, opted for a more ascetic approach to music. They decided to put an end to the discussions by prohibiting not only all of these options but also the participation of the people in singing in the church.[28]

At this point I invite you to take a moment to reflect on the ways issues about music were dealt with in the early times of the church, and the solutions that were brought forward. The radical decision of the Council of Laodicea resulted in the exclusion of the faithful from taking an active part in the worship service. The church justified her decision, citing the poor manner of singing on the part of the congregations and the resultant interference "with the decorous performance of the chant."[29] While this argument makes sense, it is suspicious, because the characteristic complaints that led up to the decision of the council, namely, the introduction of secular elements, the use of instruments, etc., are not addressed here at all. A later decision, similar to the one of the Council of Laodicea, indicates that the exclusion of the people from singing was related to the presence of secular elements. Indeed, during the sixteenth century, the Council of Trent proceeded to a similar interdiction with regard to secular elements in church music, this time directed toward the great composers of masses and motets (e.g., the great Renaissance composer Giovanni Pierluigi da Palestrina). One would be hard-pressed to invoke, here, reasons of poor performance or absence of decor.

It appears, then, that the church, ever so subtly, changed the course of her mission. From servant of God and the congregation, she evolved into an entity serving her own interests, namely, that of being represented and recognized as a rich and powerful political authority. As the pomp and formality of the official religion became very prominent, the common people were progressively excluded from participation in worship.[30] Two centuries after the Council of Laodicea, the music of the church—plainchant, intimately tied to Pope Gregory the Great (c. A.D. 540-604) in terms of its organization—reflected in its lofty, objective, and contemplative beauty, her theology and its transcendental character. During the twelfth and thirteenth centuries, however, this music evolved into a complex edifice of sumptuous and elaborate art, paralleled by the grand edifices of the cathedrals, as both were meant to display the material and spiritual splendors and riches of the church. The rise of church music throughout the Middle Ages to hitherto unknown heights of artistic achievement that were to shape Western music, both sacred and secular, for ages to come, went hand in hand with a deep spiritual decline of the church. By now the music of the church had become the domain of the professional. There was no place for the simple folk—their role in worship was relegated to singing simple responses and amens.[31]

As we look over these early experiences in Christian hymnody, several patterns emerge that kept recurring throughout the history of the church and that are still very much alive and relevant today. They represent the core issues in the church's struggle with music that could be met either with a welcoming attitude or, on the contrary, with rejection.

Pattern One. A great amount of singing among the people testified to their natural desire to express themselves in song and music. The singing was meant for the people and was done mostly in a participatory manner. This pattern grew directly out of the biblical account, and during the first four centuries the practice flourished inside and outside the church.

Pattern Two. The borrowing of secular tunes was a permanent feature of early congregational song. It was a direct outgrowth of the popularity of congregational singing and was utilized in order to achieve a strong and enthusiastic response. Musical elements familiar to the people were used to permit and encourage spontaneous singing. Seen by the church leaders as a threat to the integrity of the message because of ambiguous associations, this practice was eliminated by radical means, i.e., taking the singing away from the people.

Pattern Three. There was a direct relationship between a new religious experience and the creation of a new body of song. Singing hymns satisfied a natural need—out of the abundance of the heart—and accommodated the newly found truth with new forms of expression. It put the truth in a concrete and tangible form, into contemporary, understandable language, so that it could be appropriated by the heart and mind of the believer.

Pattern Four. Singing was a commodity, a tool intended to reach a purpose, a goal. Music was perceived as a way to touch people. It was used as an expression of praise (see, for example, the song of Hannah, 1 Samuel 2:1-10; the canticle of Mary, Luke 2:46-55; the hymn of Paul and Silas, Acts 16:25, etc.) or as a means for teaching the truth in a wholistic and effective way. But music was also used to serve political motivations; to display the power, opulence, and success of the church; to impress an adversary or rival. When music comes to be used for such purposes, it becomes a weapon to create dissension and separation. Rifts can then happen between the professionals of the church and the simple churchgoers or between different groups of people within the church at large.

Pattern Five. In observing the various types of solutions proposed by the church to solve dilemmas of church music, it appears that the leaders in charge of the early singing church favored the "safe" way of prohibition or exclusion. They opted for prescription rather than description, thus eschewing the difficult path of balance between the vertical and horizontal. This reaction can be attributed to a number of fears on the part of the church:

fear of syncretism between the secular and the sacred; fear that the spontaneity of the people would compromise the transcendent character of worship; fear of weakened ecclesiastical power as the people received a voice in matters of worship; and, finally, fear of compromising the institution represented by tradition, conservatism, and continuity.[32] Very often, when the congregation was excluded from the singing, this was done in the name of safeguarding the truth by not allowing any "foreign" element to enter the liturgy. Nobody, though, seemed to worry about the loss in terms of worship experience as the singing was taken away from the people.

In spite of all the measures taken and all the prohibitions enacted, the church did not succeed in eradicating the singing among the people. Already at the time of the Council of Laodicea, a number of churches continued to involve the congregation, especially in the Eastern church but also in the West, predominantly in places far removed from the cities.[33] The people cherished their songs, and those ancient hymns and verses were kept alive in private devotions and during out-of-doors religious processions and celebrations, as well as at other festivities such as the medieval plays. From time to time some leaders went back to the ancient methods in order to revive the singing of the congregation.

One such leader was Saint Francis of Assisi (c. A.D. 1181-1226), the founder of the Franciscan order. Reacting against the formalism of the church, he did not hesitate to reintroduce vernacular songs, *laudi spirituali*, in order to revive the singing of the congregation, at least during their popular devotions. These *laudi* were patterned, in their poetic and musical structure, after the contemporary troubadour songs and dances. This initiative brought Saint Francis of Assisi the title, given to him by his followers, of "jongleur of God."[34]

One must, however, wait for the great fifteenth- and sixteenth-century Reformers (especially Luther and Calvin) in order to see congregational singing regain its place in the church and be returned to the people.

---

[1] For a good survey of the historical development of hymn singing and church music, see Andrew Wilson-Dickson, *The Story of Christian Music: From Gregorian Chant to Black Gospel, An Authoritative Illustrated Guide to All the Major Traditions of Music for Worship* (Minneapolis: Fortress Press, 1996).

[2] See the many references to tune names in the titles of the psalms: "The Doe of the Morning" (Psalm 22), "Lilies" (Psalm 45; see also Psalms 60, 69, and 80), "A Dove of Distant Oaks" (Psalm 56), "Song of the Winepresses" (Psalms 84, according to the Septuagint; see also Psalms 8 and 81), etc. (cf. Marvin E. Tate, *Word Biblical Commentary*, vol. 19: *Psalms 1-50*, p. 196, n. 1.a.; p. 336, n. 1.a.; vol. 20: *Psalms 51-100*, p. 65, n. 1.b.; p. 351, n. 1.b. Cf. Idelsohn, *Jewish Music*, p. 20).

[3] See Piero Weiss and Richard Taruskin, eds., *Music in the Western World: A History in Documents* (New York: Schirmer Books, 1984), p. 20. The Jewish practices of singing would become the framework for the early Christian vigils.

[4] "On the Contemplative Life or Suppliants," in *The Works of Philo Judaeus*, transl. from the Greek by Charles Duke Yonge (London: H. G. Bohn, 1855), pp. 18-20.

[5] Letter 207 from Saint Basil "To the Clergy of Neocaesarea," in Saint Basil, *Letters*, transl. Agnes Clare Way, vol. 28 of *The Fathers of the Church* (New York: Fathers of the Church, 1955), 2:82-84 (quoted in David W. Music, *Hymnology: A Collection of Source Readings*, pp. 12, 13).

[6] Cf. Saint Augustine, *The Confessions*, book 9, chapter 7, transl. Edward Bouverie Pusey, in *Great Books of the Western World*, vol. 18, Robert Maynard Hutchins, ed. (Chicago: Encyclopaedia Britannica, 1952), p. 65.

[7] "Hymns are praises of God with singing: hymns are songs containing the praise of God. If there is praise, but not of God, it is not a hymn; if there is praise, and praise of God, but no singing, it is not a hymn. Therefore, if it is a hymn, it will properly have these three things: not only praise, but of God, and singing" (Saint Augustine, "Exposition of Psalm 72, in *Exposition of the Psalms, 51-72*, transl. Maria Boulding, O.S.B., ed. John E. Rotelle, O.S.A., The Works of Saint Augustine: A Translation for the 21st Century (Hyde Park, N.Y.: New City Press, 2001), part 3, vol. 17, p. 470.

[8] Pliny the Younger, "Gaius Pliny to the emperor Trajan," book 10, No. 96 of *Complete Letters*, transl. P. G. Walsh, Oxford World's Classics (Oxford, U.K.: Oxford University Press, 2006), p. 279; quoted in David W. Music, *Hymnology: A Collection of Source Readings*, p. 4.

[9] "The savage Bessians [a Thracian tribe] . . . who used to offer human sacrifice to the dead, have now dissolved their rough discord into the sweet music of the Cross" (Saint Jerome, "Letter No. 60," in *Select Letters of Saint Jerome*, T. E. Page, ed. The Loeb Classical Library (New York: G. P. Putnam's Sons, 1933), p. 273.

[10] For a comprehensive treatment of the church fathers' approaches to music, see Théodore Gérold, *Les pères de l'église et la musique* [*The Church Fathers and Music*] (Strasbourg, France: Imprimerie alsacienne, 1931; reprint Geneva, Switzerland: Minkoff, 1973).

[11] Basil the Great, "Homily on the First Psalm," in J.-P. Migne, ed., *Patrologie Cursus Completus, Series Graeca*, vol. 29, col. 212; quoted in James McKinnon, ed., *The Early Christian Period and the Latin Middle Ages*, vol. 2, *Strunk's Source Readings in Music History*, ed. Leo Treitler, rev. ed. (New York: W. W. Norton, 1998), p. 11. Ambrose (339-397), bishop of Milan, elaborated on the same idea: "Precepts inculcated with violence do not last; but what you learned in an agreeable manner, once introduced to the mind, will not disappear" (*Enarr. in 12 psa. Davidicos*, J.-P. Migne, ed., *Patrologie Cursus Completus, Series Graeca*, vol. 14, col. 905); quoted in Théodore Gérold, *Les pères de l'église et la musique*, p. 103.

[12] Cf. Gerold, pp. 46, 47 (with reference to Theodoret); cf. also Hustad, *Jubilate! Church Music in the Evangelical Tradition*, p. 123.

[13] See Gerold, pp. 46, 47.

[14] See Sozomen, *A History of the Church in Nine Books*, book 3, chapter 16 (London: Samuel Bagster and Sons, 1846), p. 133; quoted in David W. Music, *Hymnology: A Collection of Source Readings*, p. 25.

[15] Related by Socrates Scholasticus (c. A.D. 380-450), a Christian church historian from Greece, in his *Ecclesiastical History*, transl. Edward Walford (London: Henry G. Bohn, 1853), book 6, chap. 8, pp. 314, 315; quoted in David W. Music, *Hymnology: A Collection of Source Readings*, pp. 24, 25.

[16] In many of their views about music, the church fathers, emulated by numerous theologians and church leaders, including those of our own time, were very much influenced by the metaphysical and ethical concepts about music as established by the ancient Greek philosophers. They borrowed from themes such as the harmony of the universe, number symbolism, ethics as based on aesthetics, etc. On the Greek concept of ethics, see "The Greek Theory of Ethos," pp. 49-53 of this book.

[17] Saint John Chrysostom, "In Colossenses," chapter 3:16, *Homil.* 9, 2, in J.-P. Migne, ed., *Patrologie Cursus Completus, Series Graeca*, vol. 62, cols. 362, 363, quoted in James McKinnon, ed., *Music in Early Christian Literature*, p. 87.

[18] John Chrysostom, "In psalmum 134:1," in J.-P. Migne, ed., *Patrologie Cursus Completus, Series Graeca*, vol. 4, col.156; quoted in James McKinnon, *Music in Early Christian Literature*, p. 80.

[19] See Clement of Alexandria's treatise *Paedagogus* [*The Instructor*], transl. Simon P. Wood, in Clement of Alexandria, *Christ the Educator*, vol. 23 of *The Fathers of the Church* (New York: Fathers of the Church, 1954). Only the text of this hymn is by Clement of Alexandria. The original music is no longer known—the present setting dates from a much later time. See *The Seventh-day Adventist Hymnal*, No. 555 (Hagerstown, Md.: Review and Herald Publishing Assn., 1985).

[20] Saint Augustine, *The Confessions*, book 10, chapter 33, par. 50, transl. Edward Bouverie Pusey, in *Great Books of the Western World*, vol. 18, p. 84.

[21] Reference is made here to the practice of antiphonal singing.

[22] See Saint Ambrose of Milan, "Letter No. 20," in J.-P. Migne, ed., *Patrologie Cursus Completus, Series Latina*, vol. 16, col. 1001. Cf. Saint Augustine, *The Confessions*, book 9, chapter 7, in *Great Books of the World*, vol. 18, p. 65.

[23] See, for instance, John Chrysostom, "In psalmum 149:2," in J.-P. Migne, ed., *Patrologie Cursus Completus, Series Graeca*, vol. 55, col. 494, quoted in James McKinnon, *Music in Early Christian Literature*, p. 83.

[24] Cf. Plato, *The Laws*, book 2, par. 653d, transl. Thomas L. Pangle (Chicago: University of Chicago Press, 1980), p. 33.

[25] Basil the Great, "Commentary on Isaiah 5," par. 158, in J.-P. Migne, ed., *Patrologie Cursus Completus, Series Graeca*, vol. 30, col. 377, quoted in James McKinnon, "The Church Fathers and Musical Instruments" (Ph.D. dissertation, Columbia University, 1965), p. 182.

[26] Pseudo-Origen, "Selecta in Psalmos—Psalm 32:2-3," in J.-P. Migne, ed., *Patrologie Cursus Completus, Series Graeca*, vol. 12, col. 1304, quoted in James McKinnon, *Music in Early Christian Literature*, p. 38.

[27] John Chrysostom, "In psalmum 149:2," in J.-P. Migne, ed., *Patrologie Cursus Completus, Series Graeca*, vol. 55, col. 493.2, quoted in James McKinnon, *Music in Early Christian Literature*, p. 83. This reference to the harp representing the heavenly realm has traditionally been exploited by composers of classical music (see, for example, Monteverdi's opera *L'Orfeo*).

[28] Cf. *Catholic Encyclopedia*, 1913 ed., s.v. "Congregational Singing," by H. T. Henry. Canon 15 of the Council of Laodicea prohibited the participation of the congregation in singing, and Canon 59 specified that only scriptural texts were allowed for the singing in the church, as done by the clergy ("Canons of the Council of Laodicea," transl. Henry R. Percival, in *A Select Library of Nicene and Post-Nicene Fathers of the Christian Church*, Philip Schaff

and Henry Wace, eds., 2nd series, vol. 14: *The Seven Ecumenical Councils of the Undivided Church*, pp. 132, 158). There was no need for the council to write a canon on the prohibition of instruments in church, since there was quasi-consensus among the early church fathers on the issue of instruments in church (see James W. McKinnon, "The Church Fathers and Musical Instruments" [Ph.D. dissertation, Columbia University, 1965], pp. 260-264). The *New Catholic Encyclopedia* proposes a number of reasons for the exclusion of the people from singing in church, among them, the increasing complexity of the music and the "gradual separation of the people from the altar" (*New Catholic Encyclopedia* [New York: McGraw-Hill, 1967], s.v. "Congregational Singing," by F. J. Guentner and R. B. Haller, vol. 4, p. 172). This separation lasted until the twentieth-century liturgical renewal of Vatican II, 1962-1965 (*ibid.*).

[29] *Catholic Encyclopedia*, 1913 ed., vol. 4, p. 241, s.v. "Congregational Singing."

[30] See, for instance, the Eastern Church in Constantinople, where the iconostasis (a solid partition) completely separated the congregation from the place where the priests performed worship. A similar, though less radical situation, could be observed in the Roman Catholic Church with the use of cancelli—low railings to prevent the people from accessing areas reserved for the clergy (see J. G. Davies, *The Origin and Development of Early Christian Architecture* [New York: Philosophical Library, 1953], pp. 90-92). As the Roman Catholic liturgy developed, it became a domain for the specialist and excluded the participation of the common people, except during a few sections of the Mass, such as the Kyrie and Credo. Even these two songs disappeared in later centuries. During the late sixteenth century a group of citizens of Venice found a way to give a voice back to the people by organizing private meetings in the church of the Oratory, for prayer, readings, and singing of spiritual songs (*laude*) (see Donald Jay Grout and Claude V. Palisca, *A History of Western Music*, 6th ed. [New York: W. W. Norton, 2001], p. 240).

[31] As a natural reaction to this exclusion, the people developed their own repertory of religious songs and hymns to be used during extraliturgical occasions, such as processions, feasts, and private devotions. Generally, these songs grew out of their secular counterparts and were, thus, much simpler in style.

[32] *Catholic Encyclopedia*, 1913 ed., s.v. "Congregational Singing," vol. 4, p. 241. *Ibid.*, s.v. "Iconostasis."

[33] Cf. "Congregational Singing, (b)" *Catholic Encyclopedia Online*, www.catholic.org/encyclopedia, accessed June 27, 2008.

[34] See Hustad, *Jubilate! Church Music in the Evangelical Tradition*, p. 123; see also David W. Music, *Hymnology: A Collection of Source Readings*, p. 30.

$$\left\{\begin{array}{c} \textit{Singing in the Time of the Reformation:} \\ \textit{Martin Luther} \end{array}\right\}$$

I n everybody's mind Martin Luther embodies the great musician Reformer. He was the champion of reintroduction of congregational singing into the church.[1] Today, his contribution resonates in a special way beyond his historical role, as his work becomes an important model and reference, both for supporters and detractors, in regard to contemporary style of church music. It is, therefore, important to consider carefully the nature of his contribution and to find out to what extent our reference to Luther is justified. On the way, this chapter will provide a number of insights into important issues related to congregational participation in church.

Luther and Congregational Singing
Luther's Musical Background

Luther was exposed to musical practice from early childhood. In school he was a *Kurrende* singer, that is, a youth going from house to house with other poor children, singing for a piece of bread. Later in his life, as he was studying to become an Augustinian monk, Luther benefited from extensive musical training. He became an accomplished singer and lute player, and tried his hand at composing polyphonic music. So great was his admiration of the contemporary composer Josquin des Prez that after performing a piece by Josquin with some friends, Luther exclaimed in one of his table talks (1538), "Josquin is the master of the notes, which must do as he wishes, while other composers must follow what the notes dictate."[2] Josquin was, indeed, the first composer to place expression before science in matters of musical composition. Luther was also very well acquainted with the Meistersinger[3] who had their headquarters in Nuremberg, the stronghold of the newly established printing business. One of his personal friends was the great musician Hans Sachs, who later was to be immortalized in Richard Wagner's opera *Die Meistersinger*. By his exposure to these different styles, Luther became acquainted with a rich variety of repertoire in terms of church music and also secular music.

The Role of Singing in the Church

Luther continued the tradition of the church fathers with regard to the role of singing and music in everyday life, for adoration, and as an educational tool. His great contribution to church music was to bring the music back to the people. This was the result of his profound conviction that every believer should be able to fully understand the biblical message—hence his translation of the Bible into the vernacular—and, therefore, be able to participate in responding to this message through the singing of vernacular hymns. Music, indeed, became the right hand of theology, and Luther accorded it the highest place and the greatest honor:[4] "I am not ashamed to confess publicly that next to theology there is no art which is the equal of music, for she alone, after theology, can do what otherwise only theology can accomplish, namely, quiet and cheer up the soul of man."[5]

The primary purpose of music in Luther's eyes, however, was to further the gospel. He wanted to see "all the arts, especially music, used in the service of Him who gave and made them."[6] In order to accomplish this, he published and disseminated a large number of new songs, first in the format of broadsheets, soon to be followed by hymnbooks.[7] In doing so, he established the hymnal as a means to teach doctrine and build piety. However, hymnals were not exclusively meant for use in church. They played an equally important role in homes, schools, inns and taverns, or at the workplace.

The Role of Singing in Society

The important role of singing in society, particularly outside the church, is often overlooked when considering the time of the Reformation. While everyone is informed about the importance of Lutheran congregational hymns (chorales [8]), the practice of singing outside of the church helps us to better understand why and how Luther used singing the way he did. One cannot emphasize enough the role Luther's hymns played in spreading the good news during the early Reformation years. Too often, this fact is over-looked or ignored.[9]

During the Middle Ages and at the time of Luther, singing permeated all aspects of life. It was considered the universal language of the people[10] and formed an integral part of living. People expected to hear, listen, and learn in this way. Beyond its use for entertainment, play, and dancing, people sang in homes, at the workplace, in the mines and fields, and while riding across the country. In the taverns and inns of the cities and towns, singing took on the essential function of news dissemination. Indeed, in a time when the printed word was rare and most of the people were illiterate, news was spread by itinerant heralds in the form of songs performed in public places, taverns, and the town markets. The messages were delivered through popular and well-known tunes and melodic patterns or in the manner of the ballad, a genre close to speech-song. Very often, these songs began with the phrase "Come hear ye" or "Hear the good news."[11]

From there it was but one step to use songs for propaganda. At the beginning of the sixteenth century many political songs and parodies[12] circulated in the form of broadsheets and were sung in public places or taverns to stock tunes or melodic patterns. These songs were an important means of disseminating ideas and news. A favorite time to create parody songs was carnival, the few days preceding Lent, a penitential season that lasted 40 days in preparation for Easter time.[13] In the manner of play, everything was possible and permissible during carnival. The favorite genres by which to deliver the parody songs were the *Volkslied* (popular song) and the *Volksballad* (popular ballad).

Another musical genre widely used in those times, though within a different social stratum, was the *Hoflied* (courtly song) or *Gesellschaftslied* (social song) of the Meistersinger.[14] These songs featured a more sophisticated poetic and musical language and were meant to be performed as solo songs. Favorite themes in these songs were love, honor, virtue, separation, etc. They could be heard at court, at professional guild meetings, and in the homes of the bourgeoisie, where families would spend time, often after meals, singing songs together or listening to someone perform as entertainment.

Luther would draw from all of these types of songs to disseminate the gospel. Whether propaganda, parody, news dissemination, or storytelling, all songs became part of his way to spread the *good news*, either in oral form or printed form, i.e., broadsheets and hymnals.[15] The sheet format permitted quick and broad dissemination, and the early hymnals were often pirated by printers to meet the urgent demands of the people.[16] The role of the Lutheran song outside the regular worship setting, namely, for propaganda, personal edification, and spiritual growth, has not been emphasized enough. It is an essential link to a better understanding of Luther's inspiration and extensive borrowing from a large variety of repertoire and song styles.

As we consider Luther's involvement in the German chorales and songs, we need to keep in mind the important role that singing occupied among all levels of society, as well as the various genres and styles of songs in use during his time. In this regard, two principles strongly underlie Luther's work as a Reformer and take on special meaning, considering that the majority of people at the time of Luther were illiterate and uneducated. The first principle refers to the channel used to *further* the Word of God, namely, *singing and saying*. The second principle ensures the efficiency of the process, i.e., *familiarity*.

To sing and say. Luther frequently associates these two words in his writings.[17] It is generally assumed that the newly invented printed page played a primary role in the spread of the Reformation. It was, however, oral tradition that played the major role in this task. In Luther's time printed documents were still rare and expensive. A book or a pamphlet was, therefore, meant to be read aloud to people. These *hearing* sessions were often followed by discussion circles in private houses, in inns, in workshops, or in guild houses.[18] In higher levels of society, singing the Word became part of edifying leisure activities.

The singing and saying of the Word took on a similar importance to that of reading and hearing, and must be connected to the tradition of heralding. Singing and saying the Word went beyond a mere participation of the people in praise. Singing and saying were primarily to contribute to the spreading of the Word, and the church was not the only place where this could happen.[19] True to the traditional practice of singing in society, Luther's songs were part of the everyday world. They could be heard in private houses for the purpose of family devotions or for edification after the meal,[20] for the teaching of doctrine and piety in schools[21] and in the workplace, for propaganda (in its original meaning as *propagation* of faith) for the gospel, as well as for polemic purposes in public places such as inns and taverns. The latter often were carried out by students, or even beggars, who performed Luther's songs at marketplaces and offered pamphlets and broadsheets with the songs for sale. From there, the songs often were adopted by the hearers and soon found their way into the church.[22] As Luther drew from traditional popular practice, he did so because of the principle of familiarity.

Familiarity. Following the example of the professional craftsmen and guilds of his time, Luther knew that a tool, in order to be efficient, must fit the need and be practical. Transposing this rule to singing, he built on the principle of familiarity. Out of practicality he borrowed from the familiar and substituted religious or edifying texts for the trivial and indecent ones. He did so out of a pastoral concern (1) to present the newly discovered truths in such a way that they would be close to the hearts, minds, and cultures of the people and (2) to help people focus on the teaching rather than on learning a new tune. These were the main reasons that Luther reached into the rich heritage of German song, both secular and sacred, in its diverse genres and styles. He took advantage of the well-known character of texts and melodies, and of their particular musical language, to exploit their popularity for loftier purposes. He applied the same procedures to the rich musical heritage of the church from the past, thus achieving continuity between the old and the new. Indeed, Luther never meant to break with the past. On the contrary, he even took freely and liberally from the old sources of chant, renewing or Christianizing them to a Protestant perspective for the spreading of the gospel.

For purposes of evangelism Luther appropriated a common vehicle of mass communication of his time, the popular song. In doing so, he applied the same strategy we use today when we make use of audiovisual tools and avenues of mass media communication (television, radio, video, the Internet) to reach people in their familiar languages and modes of expression. Luther embraced a cultural language characteristic of his time to convey, in a practical and efficient way, the truth of the gospel.[23]

The newly adapted religious texts of Luther's chorales often retained their original vernacular melodies. Luther was, indeed, not afraid to borrow from the secular world. His approach did not go without criticism on the part of church leaders. Initially, the concern was more one of mistrust toward people singing in the vernacular, since such practices had been a hallmark of earlier "heretic" movements, e.g., the twelfth-century Waldensians, the thirteenth-century Flagellants, and the fourteenth-century Hussites,[24] and were perceived as a threat to the integrity of the church. In subsequent centuries criticism shifted more toward possible secular associations, as expressed in the appendix to the *Hildesheimer Gesangbuch* (1757) or a number of exhortations not to play love songs or street songs on the organ.[25] Nonetheless, in subsequent times, the use of secular tunes for sacred purposes, indeed, repeatedly proved to be one of the most effective tools during spiritual revivals.[26]

Borrowing was standard artistic practice in Luther's time, but it was also just another expression of his belief of the place of the church within the world. To Luther, all music was spiritual, that is, helpful for theology. If the church wanted to reach the world, it needed to be able to communicate in the world's language. So that the chorales and songs would speak directly to the hearts of the people with simplicity and directness, the people should be able to join instantaneously in the singing.[27] Thus, Luther drew from artistic models, from sacred and secular folk melodies, and from other popular tunes that were familiar to everybody. He also kept the sturdy, lively rhythms characteristic of his time in order to adequately translate into music some of his dynamic texts, such as the one on the eternal battle against the age-old foe.[28] This technique of borrowing entire songs or tunes from the secular and sacred traditions is called *contrafacta*.

The Practice of Contrafacta

Luther's use of contrafacta has been the subject of misunderstandings, misuses, or straightforward denial of the practice altogether. It has been used as an argument both in favor of today's adoption of secular styles in church and against such practices. It is important to dispel those errors, to be able to understand how it was applied by Luther, and to draw true lessons for today's situation. We will now take a look at the real practice of contrafacta and find out how it was applied to the singing in church.

Any demonstration of the practice of contrafacta must, indeed, start with the observation that it is a very old technique of artistic composition in classical and folk music. Not only throughout the Middle Ages, but already during antiquity,[29] the principle of something already in existence becoming the starting point of something new was current in the arts. The Latin word "*componere*," at the root of our modern infinitive "to compose," means, in fact, "to put together." During the Middle Ages contrafacta generally happened from the secular to the sacred, but not exclusively so. The great composers of motets and Masses often used well-known popular or artistic secular songs as the basis for their religious works.[30] A great number of religious songs in the vernacular in use before the time of the Reformation have been traced to secular models and vice versa.[31] In many instances the author or copyist of the new text indicated clearly the borrowed melody to which the text was to be sung.[32]

The Context of Contrafacta

Before we enter into a closer study of the text, music, and rhythmic features of contrafacta, it is appropriate to find out how contrafacta was understood in its own time. Several reasons were given to support this practice. Secular songs were borrowed for the sweetness of their melodies and because people were already familiar with them. Generally, they had well-characterized tunes and were favorite songs. This would, as already mentioned, be of great help in speeding up the process of fixing the words in the memories of the people. Tunes were also borrowed with the purpose of substituting good lyrics for the evil lyrics in use so that people would forget the immoral songs by singing the new ones. Moreover, songs were adopted for purposes of propaganda, to use them as tools to teach truth and principles. And finally, there was a shortage of melodies for the great number of texts that sprang up during the early Reformation.[33]

It might come as a surprise that most of the songs based on tunes borrowed from the secular repertoire were not initially intended for use in church services. They were actually destined to be sung in homes, at work, in school, or in public places (markets, inns, taverns, etc.). One must remember that in those times religion did not happen on just one day of the week. It was the Reformers' purpose to permeate and transform every aspect of life toward positive change.

However, the borrowing did not happen only from the secular body of music. Reformers also freely appropriated songs and tunes from the traditional nonliturgical heritage of the church, namely, the hymns, chants, and sequences of the Catholic Church. When writing new hymns, composers commonly borrowed melodic and rhythmic features from old religious folk songs or shaped them in the style of the current Volkslied or Hoflied.[34] Borrowing from both sources, but especially from the secular, was an essential and integral part of sixteenth-century musical practice.

A Definition of Contrafacta

Popular wisdom wants to believe that in the process of contrafacta, major alterations were made to the original musical language, especially in regard to rhythm, in order to desecularize the music. As we look at several definitions of the concept of contrafacta, though, it is striking that all of them, without exception, refer to the treatment of the text rather than the music. The standard dictionary definition reads as follows: "In vocal music, the substitution of one text for another without substantial change to the music."[35] Christoph Petzsch formulates contrafacta in terms of a "spiritual *Umdichtung* or *Umtextierung*"[36] of a secular song, meaning the poetic transposition or recomposing of a text while keeping essential elements of it. In this process the text clings, as it were, to the original melody.[37] Werner Braun gives a more detailed definition of contrafacta, namely, as the transfer of a secular text into the spiritual realm, with a takeover of the literary form, meter, and rhyme patterns of the original text, and including some characteristic words, themes, or motives of the original (such as dawn, separation, departure, love, etc.) that would be easy to reinterpret in a Christian setting.[38] As for the melody, in the majority of cases it was kept in its original form with some minor adjustments to accommodate the new text. In general, the new texts were written in such a way as to conform to the existing music in terms of form, meter, accentuation, and rhythm.[39]

It appears quite clearly from the above examples, then, that the practice of contrafacta concerned primarily the manipulation of the original text, while the musical component was, generally, taken over as it was. This applies to secular sources as well as traditional (Catholic) sources; very often, the latter had already previously been taken over from secular repertoire. In many instances the new text shows some leaning on the old one, precisely for the sake of maintaining familiarity. The following section will take a look at the different ways the original texts and music were handled.

The Texts of Luther's Contrafacta Chorales

Only three hymns, for both text and music, can be recognized as stemming from Luther's own hand.[40] For most of the hymns he included in the hymnals, he picked models, text and music, from a variety of repertoire. Luther was very adamant that the songs of the people, "both the text and music, ought to grow out of the mother tongue, otherwise it is no more than aping."[41] His aim was to strip the secular songs of their profane texts, to "take off their beautiful *musica* and put it on the living sacred Word of God as a garment, with which to sing it, to praise and to give honor."[42]

More than 170 songs from Luther's era have been identified as contrafacta.[43] His secular sources were taken from all social strata: the art song of the Meistersinger (Hoflied, *Hofweise*); popular songs (Volkslied, *Volksweise*) such as love songs, herald songs, the syllabic songs of political parody and propaganda; dance songs; and the popular ballad, a type of speech-song used to tell stories.[44] From the sacred pre-Reformation sources, he borrowed nonliturgical sacred folk songs in the vernacular language (*Leisen*) that had been authorized by the church during certain high feasts of the liturgical year, such as Christmas and Easter; Latin liturgical hymns (including some of the oldest sequences); sacred songs of the Meistersinger; songs of penitence (*Geisslerlieder*); and Crusade songs. Since Luther did not want to abolish the Mass, he also took over a number of chants from the Mass Ordinary and rewrote their texts in a *Christian manner*, i.e., according to Reformation theology.

In order to foster quick and widespread acceptance, close reference to the original text of the song was purposefully aimed at. Often, the first stanza reproduced the original text in its entirety, followed then by newly written text. Traditionally, the first stanza of a song established the setting and mood of the story to be told and could easily be taken over into a new context. A few examples from Luther's own hymns will illustrate this important literary technique.[45]

The first hymn text Luther wrote was for the chorale "Rejoice Dear Christians" ("*Nun freut Euch liebe Christen gmein*"), to the melody of a traditional and well-known Easter processional song in the style of a ballad. He picked up the beginning lines of the first stanza from the original song and invited the singer to rejoice in the assurance of God's grace as he or she joined the author in the spiritual journey related in this song.

Original Text:	Contrafacta Text:
"Rejoice now men and women	"Rejoice now dear Christians
Because Christ has risen"	And let us be happy"[46]

In discovering the *new* song, people relived, by association, the joyous and celebratory mood of the Easter processions they attended in the past, a mood musically expressed by the "skipping" melody. The familiarity of the words of the first stanza immediately evoked and set the mood. The subsequent stanzas were original additions by Luther.

Luther used the same procedure for the Christmas song "From Heaven Above" (*Lutheran Hymnal*, No. 85[47]), a contrafacta of a heralding dance song. The text to this well-known hymn, "*Vom Himmel hoch da komm ich her*," was based on an old village song, "*Ich komm aus fremden Landen her und bring Euch viel der neuen Mär*" ("I come from foreign regions and bring you many news"). The original music that came with this text was taken over from an old dance song related to a wreath ceremony, in which the first stanza was sung by the herald singer, who entered into the circle of dancers to announce the news.[48] Luther purposefully maintained the allusion to the harbinger of good news by reproducing the text of the first stanza almost literally, but he attributed the words to the angels coming from foreign regions to bring good news.

Original Text:	[49]Contrafacta Text:
I come from far away countries	I come from heaven above
To bring you many news	To bring you good news
I bring so many news	I bring so many good news
That I cannot possibly tell them all	And I will sing and say about it

By doing so, Luther created in the minds of the people the same emotional reactions of curiosity and joy that they normally experienced when they gathered to hear the news in the marketplace or at the dancing event.

Similarly, both the text and melody of the famous chorale "*O Welt ich muss dich lassen*" ("O World I Must Leave You," *Lutheran Hymnal*, No. 554) had their origins in a secular art song, "*Innsbruck, ich muss dich lassen*," ("Innsbruck, I Must Leave You"). The text of the original song referred to the pain and suffering experienced by the composer Heinrich Isaac as he had to leave a beloved place and beloved people.[50]

As a last example, we introduce one of Luther's hymns that cannot be considered as contrafacta but that was written and composed after the style of the art songs of the Meistersinger tradition. "A New Song" ("*Ein neues Lied*") emulated the style and form of the historic popular song, the *Zeitlied*, as it was used by heralds for the spreading of news. The original song related the story of two early martyrs of the Reformation who burned at the stake in Brussels in the year 1523. The opening words to "Ein neues Lied," a new song, were typical of the herald singers when announcing current news. At the hearing of those same words in a new context, the people would be ready to listen to fresh and exciting news, which here, of course, was the good news of the gospel.

The above examples clearly illustrate the importance, for Luther, of establishing a connection between the old and the new texts in order to create specific associations or establish familiarity. He achieves this goal by reinterpreting the original text and giving it a new, transformed meaning.

Another technique applied to the texts of preexisting songs, secular or sacred, consisted of improving them in a Christian manner,[51] that is, adjusting the theological content according to the principles and understandings of the Reformation.[52] Luther applied such improvements to the texts of old secular or sacred vernacular songs, among them the German Leisen, the Latin *cantio*, and some of the traditional plainchant songs of the church. The desired result was achieved through translation of the existing Latin text into German and/or improving the literary quality of the German text by putting it into a rhymed form. This was especially the case when Luther translated the traditional texts of Gregorian chant or adjusted the number of syllables of a German text to fit the melodic pattern.[53]

From the above illustrations it appears, then, that textual adjustments in contrafacta were made on the levels of theology and prosody. Adaptation consisted of Christianizing the text while sometimes retaining, purposely, characteristic phrases or themes of the original version.[54] Prosodic adjustments were aimed at improving literary quality or simply adapting rhyme patterns, syllable count, accentuation, etc., to the melody that was to carry it.

The Melodies of Luther's Contrafacta Chorales

When Luther happened to alter the musical model, he never intended to produce a more *sacred* version of the tune. His intentions in modifying a preexisting tune were always founded on a concern for a better fitting between "word and tone" or considerations of a practical order, that is, adapting his songs as much as possible to the aptitudes of the common people.[55] He used to say that "music must make the text alive,"[56] and this could be achieved only by writing or arranging the melody in such a way that it would serve the rhythm of the words and the general character of the text.[57] Melodies in those times "were not individual creations in a modern sense; they did not melt with the text to form a higher poetic unity and did not describe it; they only helped to carry the text."[58] Melodies functioned as channels to sound the word. Vernacular melodic composition was still tributary of medieval techniques, based on sets of melodic turns and formulas. Any text that would correspond to the syllabic scheme of the melody could be fitted to that music.[59]

The following section will help us to gain some insights into the nature of the changes Luther brought to preexisting melodies, and the rationale he applied in doing so. The same techniques were also applied by Luther in the writing of his three original melodies, which he modeled on the art songs and popular songs of his time. In the modifications he brought to existing melodies, one may observe the clear and uniform tendency in favor of the simple, the plain, and the ease in singing. For this reason Luther sometimes wrote a number of different versions of a melody for the same text. When unsatisfied with his first results, he tried to provide an even better vehicle to carry the word.[60] He did not seek to obtain a melding of text and melody, that is, to mold the expression of the music to the expressive content of the text. He looked, rather, for a correspondence of text and music on the level of syllabic count per line, correct accentuation or emphasis on the text, a better rhyme scheme, or a more artistic turn of the melody.[61] Sometimes Luther composed more than one version to meet the particular context of the occasion. For instance, his first version of the Christmas hymn "Vom Himmel hoch" ("From Heaven Above") was written for children in the manner of a circular dance song to entertain them during the Christmas season. The other version was meant for congregational use in church.[62] In his 1542 Preface to the *Burial Hymns*, he makes it clear that there was room for the use of a variety of tunes, from one church to another. Congregations needed to sing the tunes they were familiar with and accustomed to: "We do not hold that the notes need to be sung the same in all the churches. Let every church follow the music according to their own book and custom. For I myself do not like to hear the notes in a responsory or other song changed from what I was accustomed to in my youth. We are concerned with changing the text, not the music."[63]

Some borrowed melodies needed no change at all because the meter (syllable count) of the translated or improved text fit the number of notes of the preexisting melody. In other cases the basic melodic outline was maintained but *transposed* into another mode. The main reason for such changes seemed to lie in the fact that certain modes were more singable than others, e.g., the Dorian mode (close to the natural minor scale pattern) and the Ionian mode (similar to our modern major scale pattern).[64]

More significant melodic changes can be found in songs drawn from old Latin hymns in the genre of plainchant that used free rhythm and melismatic text settings.[65] For the ease of singing by the common folk, Luther modified these melodies, either by simplifying the tune (deleting some notes) or by arranging the text in a syllabic manner, that is, one syllable to a note. At the same time, he changed the original free rhythm to a more patterned style, customary in the traditional folk song.[66]

Other changes to melodic contour included the shifting of melodic climaxes so that the highest notes fit either important words or the climactic moment of the whole text.[67] Luther was also concerned that the natural intonation and inflection of the text be mirrored in the melodic contour of the music.[68]

The foregoing examples demonstrate, then, that the motivation for changes applied by Luther and his collaborators to preexisting melodies did not grow out of theological preoccupations, but stemmed rather from aesthetic or practical considerations.

Rhythm in Luther's Chorales

Luther favored the joyous manner in every aspect of life. It corresponded to the nature of the message to be proclaimed, namely, the "joy of the gospel" ("*frohe Botschaft*"). It was, then, only natural that music, as carrier of the Word, should feature the same joyful character as the message it conveyed. For this reason many of Luther's melodies, his original ones as well as those arranged by him, feature either lively rhythms—in the form of short upbeats to each new line of the song—or syncopation.[69] The lively rhythms were borrowed from the folk song, the syncopation from the art songs of his time. While he would sometimes simplify the rhythmic elaborateness of a song for the purpose of ease of singing in a congregational setting, he liked to maintain this short upbeat formula. Another favored technique was to lengthen the first and last notes of each line of the hymn and have the notes in between flow easily in shorter notes, thus creating interest, structure, and an impression of movement.

Syncopation was the hallmark of art song in Luther's time, as was the typical formal pattern of the bar form,[70] as featured by the Meistersingers. Syncopation also happened to be one of Luther's favorite styles of rhythmic writing. Besides the animation and liveliness created by syncopation, Luther used this rhythmic pattern to bring out important words in the text.[71] Whenever Luther shied away from using syncopation in his hymns destined for congregational singing, his motivation was not to avoid secular associations in the music, but rather to ensure the ease of singing which is somewhat more difficult to maintain when the song features more rhythmic complexity or melismatic writing. Nevertheless, it is interesting to note that in spite of this concern, approximately 25 percent of the hymns in the 1533 Wittenberg *Gemeindegesangbuch*, which was prepared under the supervision of Luther himself, contain syncopation. Most of these hymns adopt, at the same time, the typical formal pattern of the Meistersinger songs, the bar form. The original version of Luther's best known hymn, "A Mighty Fortress Is Our God," features this very style and was also included in the 1533 Wittenberg *Gemeindegesangbuch*. Other examples of rhythmically animated hymns that entered congregational hymnbooks are the baptism song "*Christ, unser Herr, zum Jordan kam*" ("Christ, Our Lord, Came to the Jordan River"), "*Christ lag in Todesbanden*" ("Christ Lay in the Bonds of Death," *Lutheran Hymnal*, No. 195), the highly melismatic Pentecost hymn "*Veni sancte spiritus*" or "*Komm heiliger Geist, Herre Gott*" ("Come, Holy Spirit," *Lutheran Hymnal*, No. 224), and Luther's very first hymn, "*Ein neues Lied wir heben an*" ("A New Song Do We Sing").[72]

There was, then, great variety and flexibility in the use of rhythm. The congregations themselves played an important role in determining what would be preserved in history and what would be lost over the years. The factor of familiarity and grassroots power were already present in Luther's time. But with time the Lutheran hymn was to lose its rhythmic strength. An isorhythmic melodic setting, in which all the notes proceed mainly in equal time values, became common instead—and this is the form in which many churches are familiar with the Lutheran chorales today.[73] How did this change happen, and what were the reasons that stood behind it? These are the questions we shall now address.

The Derhythmization of the Lutheran Chorale

During the seventeenth century the vigorous rhythms of the Lutheran hymn were exchanged for an isometric style that lost the spontaneity and vitality of the original versions. The typical upbeat, the dotted rhythms, and the syncopated patterns disappeared from the hymnals. Several arguments have been advanced over time to explain this change.

Some would like to see in this change the result of an effort on the part of the church to desecularize the hymn—an effort to eradicate secular elements from church music, especially the strong and lively rhythms of the Lutheran chorale.

An observation of the development of art music in the Lutheran church at about the same time (from the end of the sixteenth through the seventeenth and eighteenth centuries) suggests a different interpretation. Choral and instrumental music—cantatas, oratorios, passions, church sonatas, preludes, fugues, and fantasies—were built on chorale melodies and demonstrate the exact opposite pattern of development. The sacred works feature the same style characteristics as their secular counterparts, including the rhythmic element. The same compositional principles were applied to chamber (secular) and church cantatas, to the recitatives and arias of operas and oratorios, to preludes, fugues, and fantasies on secular or sacred themes. Johann Sebastian Bach was criticized in his time for using theatrical instruments in church performances.[74] The most striking example for the fusion of secular and sacred styles is found in his works, especially in the secular and sacred cantatas. Both genres were written in the same style, and for his *Christmas Oratorio*,

BWV 248, he borrowed extensive passages—both choral and solo—directly from his secular cantatas (BWV 213, 214, and 215).[75] The same is true for some of the sacred works of George F. Handel. Not only did Handel borrow profusely from his own or other composers' secular works for his oratorios,[76] but many of his oratorios were operas in all but name.[77] They used the same formal outlay, musical genres (recitatives and da capo arias), instrumentation, musical figuration and techniques, and were performed by opera singers in theaters. While his later oratorios, faithful to a long-standing English tradition, integrated more choral sections, musical virtuosity was still characteristic of both the choral and solo parts of these works.[78]

The motivation for the derhythmization of the Lutheran hymn must, then, be looked for elsewhere. There appear to be four categories of reasons that might have contributed to this change: musical, architectural, theological, and practical. They all show one common denominator—the slowing of the singing tempo. Indeed, as the pace of singing became slower and slower, it was more and more difficult to maintain distinctive rhythmic patterns because they simply disappeared in the drawing out of the original note values. This resulted in a delivery of the song in equal note values, possibly with longer values at the beginning and end of each phrase. However, this transformation took place only during performance. In print the hymns continued to feature their syncopated, lively rhythms until the seventeenth century.[79]

On the musical level, the seventeenth century was marked by a particular interest, on the part of composers, with time and meter. Renaissance music, which was mainly vocal, typically featured free and flexible rhythm (except for dance music), following the natural flow of speech, and a sense of timing based on the natural heartbeat. Theorist and composer Michael Praetorius (1571-1621) was one of the first to standardize tempo in relationship to real time.[80] These developments indicate that the concern for regulated time in musical performance had taken on importance. They also shed light on future discussions dealing with the perception and prescription of appropriate tempi for diverse moments or events in life.

Moreover, the invention of a new style of music, the *cantional* style, must also be accounted for in the slower pace of singing. This new style of music became apparent toward the end of the sixteenth century, probably inspired by the practical needs of congregational singing. Lukas Osiander, a composer who had been involved with hymn writing for the Lutheran Church in the later sixteenth century, came up with the idea to put the melody, in polyphonic settings of the chorales, in the top voice in order to make the hymn melody more perceptible to the worshipper's ear. Up to that time the traditional practice of melodic writing in a polyphonic setting—i.e., music that uses more than one voice simultaneously—was to put the melody in the tenor voice, where it was literally hidden to the unprofessional ear. Churchgoers had been exposed to such polyphonic versions of the hymn melodies by hearing the choirs sing hymn stanzas in alternation with their own unaccompanied singing and organ interludes, but it was difficult for the churchgoers to clearly distinguish the melodic part. The new cantional style featured the melody in the top voice, which was of great help in leading the congregation in their singing. Ultimately, at the turn of the seventeenth century, it became the generally accepted style of musical writing, a style still found in our hymnals today. Osiander's homophonic settings of the Lutheran hymns would not as easily accommodate rhythmic variety, since four voices were now to sing simultaneously. In such cases an even pace with all the voices together at a moderate tempo is a much more adequate style. This was also the time when organs started to accompany hymn singing. The then current style of organ playing was to embellish the melody with ornaments or, especially in the time of Johann Sebastian Bach, fit the chorale melody with rich harmonizations. Both procedures, in order to take their full effect, did not accommodate for fast playing.

On the architectural level, the high ceilings of the churches created an echo effect that made it difficult for the congregation to sing at a quick pace. The singer was actually led to listen to the sound and continued singing only when the echo vanished. This might have contributed considerably to a slackening of the tempo in congregational singing, similar to what happened earlier in plainchant performance.

Possible theological factors for the slower singing tempo may be found in a general change of attitude toward religion. Spirituality and devotions were associated more and more with the idea of formality or, as Friedrich Blume, a specialist in Protestant church music, puts it, "the dogmatization of a monotonous 'solemnity.'"[81] Early eighteenth-century prefaces to hymnbooks feature a number of remarks in this direction. The general opinion about hymns seemed to be that the slower they were sung, the more edifying and enlivening they were. More specifically, the following instructions were given: "It is advised that the preacher and singers, together with the congregation, strive earnestly to the end that the singing be orderly, slow and devotional and that each verse be held a little longer, and also that each word be allowed its time for devotion."[82] An 1847 account of the singing of Lutheran chorales in Germany confirmed that this way of singing had, indeed, been put into practice: "The hymns of Luther have had their wings clipped and have put on the straightjacket of 4/4 time. And so it came about that the more inflexible the singing of the chorale was, the more solemn it was thought to be."[83]

This attitude toward congregational singing was the exact opposite of what Luther had intended the hymns to be, namely, a *joyful* expression of the gift of salvation. It indicates how theological considerations can affect the understanding and performance of the music in church.

As for practical considerations, the manner of singing, as it was done in most churches, certainly contributed to slowing the singing pace. Since most people were not able to read and printed hymnbooks were expensive and often rare, singing was mainly done by rote. People had to rely on one another to know what to sing.[84] Such waiting and hesitating contributed considerably to slowing down the tempo of singing and, simultaneously, to altering the rhythmic precision in performance.

The progressive slowing down of the singing tempo reached its climax in the nineteenth century. At that time several attempts were made to reinstitute the original rhythms of the Lutheran hymns, though not without encountering strong resistance. In the United States the Lutheran Church—Missouri Synod was very influential in having the original rhythmic versions reinstated in the official North American hymnal, which was achieved in the 1850s.[85] In the 1950s the original rhythmic versions were officially reintroduced worldwide in the German Lutheran hymnals. This, finally, put an end to the issue within the Lutheran Church.

It appears, then, that progressively a direct relationship came to be established, in the minds of the people, between the issue of rhythm and the sacred versus secular character of the hymns. It is, therefore, important to find out whether during the time of Luther this dichotomy was applied to music in general and to the hymns in particular, and how we can draw lessons from this discussion for our situation today.

Sacred Versus Secular in Luther's Time

As we study writings about music and the actual practice of music in the time of Luther and beyond, it appears that reference to sacred and secular, as related to hymn singing, was not established based on elements of the musical language (melodies, rhythms, instruments, etc.), but rather on extramusical criteria. The major factors that determined the sacred character of music were found (1) in the nature of the text underlying the music and (2) in the performance context.

We discussed previously that Luther's alterations to the music were not done out of a desire to make the song more sacred, but exclusively with the concern for a better fit to the words (in terms of rhythm and accentuation). The same approach can be observed with Luther's closest collaborator, Johann Walter. Walter Blankenburg, one of the foremost twentieth-century German musicologists specializing in Protestant church music, comments in the following way about Walter: "The opposition between sacred/secular was of course familiar to Johann Walter; however, it was not used to categorize various musical styles and forms of expression, but rather in consideration of good or bad texts."[86]

In his lecture "*Sakral und Profan in der Musik*" ("The Sacred and Profane in Music"), musicologist Thrasybulos Georgiades reiterates that the distinction between sacred and secular music cannot be made on the basis of the elements of musical language or on its structure. The sacred or secular character of a piece of music is, rather, determined by its *function*,[87] i.e., the circumstances in which it is performed and the spirit in which it is performed or received.

This reality can be illustrated by musical practices in the church in Luther's time and beyond. Most musicians wrote for both the secular and the ecclesiastical worlds. While the performance venues and occasions changed from one work to another, the style of the music remained the same. Later composers, such as Henry Purcell, Johann Sebastian Bach, George Frideric Handel, Wolfgang Amadeus Mozart, Ludwig van Beethoven, Felix Mendelssohn, Johannes Brahms, etc., all fall into this category. We already saw that Johann

Sebastian Bach used identical musical sections for his secular and sacred cantatas, and that Handel wrote his oratorios using the same musical language and style as for his operas. The same was true for composers all the way down to the twentieth century.

To attribute a sacred or secular character to a piece of music based on its musical language and structure is generally seen by scholars in the fields of music history, church music, and the philosophy of music as a narrow, ambiguous, or illinformed approach. Warren Dwight Allen, renowned author in the field of the philosophy of music history, remarked, "Leading historians are no longer so sure of strict and narrow classification of 'sacred' and 'secular.'"[88] A similar view was also expressed by German musicologist Friedrich Blume: "Neither the contrafacta of the sixteenth century nor the parodies of the eighteenth century recognized any boundary lines of a musical nature, and in the oratorios of the nineteenth and twentieth centuries the distinctions between 'sacred' and 'secular' were completely erased."[89]

The origins of the polarized view of music, as sacred and secular, can be traced back to Saint Augustine (fourth and fifth centuries A.D.). Under the influence of Platonic philosophy, Saint Augustine, indeed, had advanced the idea that art was given a right to exist only to the extent that it was put in the service of praise to God. Intellectual activities (i.e., the liberal arts, which included music) were to be consecrated entirely to glorify God and His plan of salvation. Otherwise, they were nothing but "frivolities, deceitful insanity, and windy nonsense."[90] Music not done in a spiritual context came to be considered as "a beguiling service of devils."[91] If the arts were not sacrificed to God, said Saint Augustine, they "served not to my use but rather to my perdition."[92] There were only two categories of music for Saint Augustine: "music among the wise" and "music among the lecherous."[93] Thus, earthly music was perceived as "lower beauty," which "defiles the soul"[94] and could be escaped only with the help of God.[95] Only musical practice limited to the church and its worship was, then, considered worthwhile. *Secular* musicians were relegated to the rank of dishonest citizens. Modern times did inherit the same idea of separation between sacred and secular music. Indeed, Saint Augustine's perspective on music lies at the root of our current separation of music into *serious* classical music (high, sacred practice) and *popular* entertainment music (low, mundane practice).[96]

During the advent of humanism this view of music began to undergo changes, as can be observed in a variety of statements by Luther and his contemporaries with regard to the nature and use of music. Luther understood the harmony between body and soul to be an expression of the universal harmony of the cosmos and the spheres. Therefore, music produced by human beings partook equally of the harmony of the universe. Because of this harmony of body and soul there was, then, no more need to distinguish between sacred and secular music, since both were part of the same structure, and a manifestation of the same unity.[97]

It is, then, not surprising to read several statements by the Reformers that point to their belief that the same musical structures can be used for both secular and sacred purposes. Their explanations went beyond the mere idea of adaptation from the secular to the sacred. Their real concern was the transformation, spiritualization, sublimation and elevation, even conversion, of the same music. Through the process of transformation the music was cleansed and elevated in the Spirit. Through the process of spiritualization music was rooted in a new spiritual experience. Through the process of sublimation and elevation the everyday experience of the believer (including music) was sanctified—the status of the familiar was elevated through the substitution of edifying words. Through the process of conversion the songs now were apt to inform, improve, and shake up. Such concepts transpired repeatedly in writings about music.[98] If the world was God's gift and if music was primarily a gift from God, then one could infer that all music could be used for the benefit of humanity: "Reason sees the world as extremely ungodly, and therefore it murmurs. The Spirit sees nothing else than God's benefits in the world and therefore begins to sing."[99]

In a similar way, the understanding of music as related to the senses now became an acceptable, even desirable, quality. A shift was happening in the world of music. Previously seen as a mathematical and speculative science, music was now recognized as a performing art, a rhetorical art, an art meant to move the heart and the senses.[100] According to this new worldview, secular things could be subjected to intellectual discipline by means of piety, a communal approach to religion, and didactic tools such as propaganda and education. For Luther, the role of religion was to transform the world, like salt penetrates and transforms food. He strongly believed that the secular could be sanctified by creating new, sacred associations. Therefore, referring to 1 Thessalonians 5:21, he said, "We shall try all things, and what is good we shall retain."[101]

The dichotomy between sacred and secular presented no issue for Luther. On one hand, the worldview prevalent in his time did not call for such distinctions and, on the other hand, musical practices moved naturally between the two domains. Only later, during the eighteenth and nineteenth centuries, under the impact of the Enlightenment, did the rift between the sacred and secular begin to open. At that time the ties between the ecclesiastical community and the individual had loosened, and world consciousness would be replaced progressively by self-consciousness. Interestingly, this was also the time when a reverse phenomenon took place in music, namely, the artistic secularization of sacred music. Sacred music was no longer written necessarily for liturgical purposes, but also for the concert hall.[102]

The previous reflections reveal that the issue of Luther's adoption of secular tunes is more complex than it may appear at first view. It is, then, appropriate to ask whether a reference to Luther is justified nowadays and, if yes, how his practices can be applied for today.

Luther's Relevancy for Today

Our times are subject to a number of inherited ideas that do not make the task of the church musician easier. One of these ideas, born out of the spirit of Romanticism, is that anything from the past is of higher value than things of today. Theologian, musician, and philosopher Albert Schweitzer was one among many to notice, with a touch of irony, that "age confers on all music a dignity that gives it a touch of religious elevation. A mystic bond embraces and unites antiquity and religion."[103] This belief can easily develop into an agent of intolerance and become a major obstacle for any effort of renewal. Indeed, the past might be used as an absolute and authoritative model for how things should be done today. It is, then, essential to take an objective view of the past and apply its lessons in an appropriate way to a new context. Changes in approach to worship and music necessarily happen throughout history, and for a variety of reasons new and different ways are adopted, which then become established as firm "truths." It is important to verify whether there is a real foundation to these "truths" or whether, in adopting certain practices from the past, we simply perpetuate customs and ideas that have no relevancy to our times and for which no true biblical foundation can be established.

Among the inherited ideas, two in particular are known to create discussion and dissent in churches in regard to music. The first such inherited idea has to do with a process that took place in the course of the seventeenth and eighteenth centuries. During this time the church at large distanced itself from the joyous and life affirming experiential religion practiced by Luther and moved toward a "spiritualized" understanding of worship, in which piety and solemnity became the predominant, and often exclusive, mark of expression. The second inherited idea is found in the theory that the sacred or secular character of music resides inherently in the language and structure of music itself, rather than in its context and function. As we consider the relevancy of Luther's approach to music for our times, it is important to keep these two issues in mind.

Today's musical context and worldviews have changed drastically. As for the former, we are not only surrounded by a proliferation of musical styles, but music has also gained an incredible power of expressiveness that it did not possess in the time of Luther. A multiplicity of instrumental sounds, greater capacity to produce stronger sound, extreme dynamic levels, enriched harmonic vocabulary, and much greater complexity of the musical language have increased the expressive capacities of music. In contrast, the sixteenth-century melody was of relatively undistinguishable character with regard to expressiveness or emotional content. It could carry any specific expression, so the disparity between secular and sacred did not pose a problem. Moreover, in sixteenth-century aesthetics, music was considered primarily as a learnable craft, and composers were still very much occupied with symbolic or mathematical structures, or intellectual games, when composing. The search for musical means to express emotional content was, then, barely in its primitive steps and found expression mainly in simple musical figures meant to serve as pictorial illustrations of the text.[104] When songs or tunes were borrowed, they could easily be adapted to any new content with slight adjustments to the prosody of the new text.

Today's worldview is marked by a deep gap between religious and secular culture, and moves more and more into a post-Christian, neo-pagan direction. The pervading interaction between religion and culture, as it was known in Luther's time, bridging together the church community and everyday life, has largely vanished. Emphasis on communal structures has given way to exacerbated individualism. Daily life is no longer primarily permeated with the sacred. The secular world has appropriated sacred symbols to mock religion. Absolute truths have been replaced by relativism. Standards of sacredness are most often set individually according to one's personal interpretation of the Scriptures, feelings, or personal perception of things—without an objective reference. There is no more opportunity to sanctify the secular because there is no longer a need for *transformation* in the religious sense of the term. More often than not, religion is not so much a matter of hearing, listening to the voice of God, or, in Luther's terms, of *bettering* or *shaking up* the individual, as it is an ensemble of emotional responses. Art has become the domain of everybody and nobody, and the music of the people has fallen under the control of commercial enterprise. A whole repertoire of music has come about that is so strongly anchored in practices or settings contrary to biblical values and standards that it seems difficult, at first sight, to change their original associations.

In the light of these stark changes in worldview and in matters of musical practice, is it still possible to use Luther as a model for the handling of church music issues? In spite of all appearances and contradictions, I believe it certainly is. Music can be given new and healthy associations—if the process is done carefully and with discernment. Luther acted out of strong principles, not just opinions or local needs, and it is on the level of these principles that we can still learn from him. Here are four principles that were fundamental to Luther's approach to church music and that can still be applied today with good results.

1. The Word of God must be heard *and* proclaimed.

For Luther, hearing and saying/singing the Word of God were of primary importance. His whole effort was centered on the Word of God, how it was understood and proclaimed. One of his major purposes for music was to proclaim the Word of God and make it understandable. It is, then, of primary importance that our music today accompanies the *Word of God* and not some subjective or simplified interpretation of it. This presents a twofold task: to make sure that the Word can actually be heard and understood (not

overpowered by the music or the volume of sound) and to enrich and reinforce the meaning of the Word of God through musical means. Music in
church is always subservient to the Word.

2. Music in the church is an active and participatory experience.

While Luther's primary focus was on the Word of God, this focus was informed by the perspective of making the Word available to the community
of believers. While most of Luther's efforts in music went toward creating
collections of songs for the people as a means for teaching, edification, and
warfare against evil influences, he always did so keeping in mind what
sounded familiar to them. This would assure an active and participatory experience, in church or outside the church. Similarly, our efforts in making
music in church must be done keeping the congregation in mind. The songs
must be apt for community singing. They must be easily singable, quickly
learned, and have a familiar and attractive sound. The choice is determined
by the needs of the congregation rather than by personal preferences.

3. Music is a power for good.

Very seldom do people comment about the power of music for good.
Most of the remarks about music are made against it, focusing on its negative
effects and its power to seduce and entice us to evildoing. When Luther
speaks about it, he praises music for its effects *over* evil and the power music
adds to the Word as it associates with it. After mentioning music as a precious
gift from God, Luther continues: "The devil is a sad spirit and makes people
sad, therefore, he cannot stand rejoicing. And therefore, also, he flees from
music."[105] "We know that to the devils music is something altogether hateful
and unbearable."[106] "For the evil spirit is ill at ease wherever God's Word is
sung or preached in true faith."[107] One of the lessons to learn from Luther
is precisely this attitude: to see music as a gift from God, an instrument of
the Holy Spirit that affirms the goodness of God's creations and has power
to change the world.[108]

4. The professional musician has a distinct role in the church.

Luther was not alone in putting together the new body of hymns. While
he composed a certain number of original chorales, he also surrounded himself by professional poets and musicians.[109] These composers participated in
Luther's task of writing new tunes or adapting numerous borrowed songs.
Time and again Luther appealed for quality poetry and music.[110] The pro-

fessional musicians he worked with handled the songs in a skillful and adequate way in order to ensure that they fitted the rhythm and accentuation of the new words or were given an appropriate form for congregational singing.

Martin Luther saw in music a power for good that benefits all people and the church, and he made extensive use of this gift of creation. Since he considered all music as a gift from God, instead of prohibiting secular elements, Luther advocated their use with the ultimate goal of their *transformation*. Nearer to our times, twentieth-century theologian Paul Tillich formulated the same relationship between culture and religion as he stated that religion as "ultimate concern . . . gives meaning, seriousness, and depth to all culture and creates out of the cultural material a religious culture of its own."[111] Luther was careful to make music fit its various purposes. Both text and music had to correspond to the occasion. While he was open to the new, he never rejected the old and traditional. He never advocated forgoing the past in favor of innovation. On the contrary, he adopted the past generously, making changes only to adapt the language to the new theology. His first concern was to serve the Word of God. Along with this came the concern to reach the people where they were—in the streets, in the workplace, in the home, and in the church. To achieve this goal, Luther understood that different purposes must accommodate different styles. Ultimately, however, it was the people who decided what styles would survive. Thus, the initial intent of music was not always respected. What was meant for the street could end up in the church, and what was meant for the church would sometimes find a new life in the secular realm.

There are, indeed, lessons that modern, postmodern, and millennial believers can draw from Luther's approach to congregational singing. The fundamental mission of the church consists of responding to Jesus' call to "go into all the world" (Mark 16:15). One important condition for reaching the world is to contextualize: be able to speak the world's language, communicate, make sure people understand, and obtain a response. In this sense Luther becomes a model for us with regard to congregational music.

Luther's impact on church music, however, goes beyond his concern for relevant and appropriate congregational singing. To consider only this aspect of his philosophy of music would be equal to using his statement out of context. If we want to apply Luther's principle of borrowing from the secular to today's musical scene, we must also consider what he had to say about art music. The two cannot be dissociated. The *popular* element must be considered and understood in light of Luther's high appreciation of art music, especially in regard to standards of performance. Only then can our reference to Luther be taken seriously.

Luther and Art Music

Through his personal training in art music[112] of his time, Luther was well prepared to impact the musical scene of the Protestant church. Indeed, he saw in art music a possibility for both service and education: "I have always loved music. Those who have mastered this art are made of good stuff, they are fit for any task. It is necessary indeed that music be taught in the schools. A teacher must be able to sing, otherwise I will not look at him. Also we should not ordain young men into the ministry unless they have become well acquainted with music in the schools. We should always make it a point to habituate youth to enjoy the art of music for it produces fine and skillful people."[113]

It is noteworthy that Luther extended the need for education in art music equally to the student in theology, the future pastor-to-be. In doing so, he situated himself within the biblical tradition, indicating again the importance of music and music leadership in the church. Education in art music started at church schools, where children were taught Latin and singing. The primary purpose of this instruction was to help the congregation learn to sing; during worship the children's choir led out in congregational singing.

Service, then, appears as one of the primary goals for the teaching and study of art music. It is important to keep in mind this emphasis as we reflect on the role of art music in today's worship. Often the argument invoked by professional musicians in favor of art music for church is that of raising the level of the congregation in matters of musical taste. This is a didactic argument. Aesthetics is here made equivalent with ethics, a stance that brings about the questions of the purpose and goal of worship. Is worship an educational event, in which we further our knowledge and appreciation of classical music, or is it a communication event, in which the people of God search to get in touch with the Divine and with one another?

The role of art music, as with any music in worship, is to fulfill certain functions. One faculty of art music is its capacity to make worship loftier. The universal character of music overall and, at the same time, its capacity to speak in an individual and personal way to establish the place of music in general in worship. Beyond having these attributes that are common to all music, art music fulfills a particular role by reason of its preoccupation with deep and essential questions concerning the struggles of life, the complexity by which these issues are approached, and the nuanced and subtle ways in which answers are suggested. It is here that art music finds a place as a powerful communicator for values and truths that are difficult to put into words otherwise. There is music to communicate on the horizontal level, to convey the message in a simple and direct way, as a mode of expression in the language of the common worshipper. But there is also music to speak on the vertical level, to bring us in touch with the transcendent, the infinite, to take us beyond the realm of everyday life to a higher plane. Both have their place in worship, and both are needed in tension with each other.

Luther also encouraged youth to study and perform the great polyphonic works of his time to provide an alternative to the prevalent popular songs: "I have brought together some spiritual songs . . . [that] have been arranged into four voices, for no other reason than that I fervently wish that young people, who should and must be trained in music and the other fine arts, had something to make them abandon love tunes and carnal songs and in their place learn something wholesome, and thus fill the good with pleasure, as is best for the young.[114]

In this statement Luther suggested that exposure to art music can cultivate high standards of taste and excellence. In the same way that reading quality literature develops standards of appreciation of language, the experience of art music provides a means to measure tastefulness and quality in other styles of music.[115] As a result, it leads to a better and more just appreciation of musical quality and encourages raised expectations for the use and production of music for worship, in whatever style is desired.

Luther's keen interest in art music and, therefore, in music education, produced a long lasting and strong tradition of quality music in the Lutheran Church that carries right into our times. A great school of choral music and organ playing developed in seventeenth-century northern Germany, culminating in the works of Johann Sebastian Bach in the eighteenth century. Many of the great Lutheran chorales became the basic material on which organ, choral, or instrumental works were built, either to introduce or accompany congregational singing or to embellish the services with great works of art.

The debate over the place of art music in church was started 130 years before Luther by the English reformer John Wycliffe.[116] It is still going strong today, predominantly in evangelical churches. The issue at stake is whether art music should be given a place within a congregational setting or whether music should maintain its rank of servant to the common worshipper through congregational song. Luther made it very plain that he firmly believed in the spiritual role of art music in the church. Beyond the refining influence of the practice of art music, Luther also saw in it a venue to get in touch with the transcendental, divine wisdom: "After all, the gift of language combined with the gift of song was only given to man to let him know that he should praise God with both word and music, namely, by proclaiming the word through music and by providing sweet melodies with words. . . . But when [musical] learning is added to all this, and artistic music, which corrects, develops, and refines the natural music, then at last it is possible to taste with wonder (yet not to comprehend) God's absolute and perfect wisdom in his wondrous work of music."[117]

This was also the opinion of the composer Johann Walter, who closely worked with Luther in bringing about the new hymnody. While describing some of Luther's musical contributions, Walter himself commented on the importance of both art music and music for the people during the worship service: "I do not at all approve of people who want to drive sacred music in Latin[118] entirely out of the church, thinking it not really Evangelical or properly Lutheran. Nor do I think any better of singing nothing but Latin music in church, since in that case the congregation understands nothing. The simple, old Lutheran songs and psalms in German are best for most people; those in Latin, however, are also useful for the benefit of students and scholars."[119]

The effort of contextualization on the part of Luther and his close collaborators did not limit itself to the common people, but also embraced the learned people of the Protestant congregations. Aware of the diversity of educational and cultural backgrounds in the church, Luther refused to favor one group at the expense of the other. The Word in song and music was to be preached to all people, the rural and the urban, the unlearned and the educated, in their respective languages. True to his philosophy, Luther believed that the gospel in song was for everybody.

Luther understood and appreciated the role of music in church on the two levels of folk and art music. For him, both genres were necessary and complementary: high quality sacred folk song and appropriate art music. Thus, he was able to maintain excellence and truth in both genres without sacrificing the spontaneity of the people.

-----

[1] The important role played in the development of Christian hymnody by Jan Hus, from Moravia, is often overlooked. This zealous reformer, who preceded Luther by 100 years and paid with his own life at the stake, actively promoted hymn singing in the vernacular among his followers. Their efforts resulted in the publication, in 1501, of a collection of hymns under the title *kancionál* ("little song book"), containing 87 hymn texts ("The Czech 'kancionál'," *Grove Music Online*, L. Macy, ed., accessed June 18, 2008, http://www.grovemusic.com). The Moravian hymnal was the first major collection of hymns from the Reformation tradition; it was to become a source from which all subsequent Protestant denominations would draw for their own hymn collections.

[2] M. Johann Mathesius, a personal friend of Luther, recorded this statement in *Dr. Martin Luthers Leben* (St. Louis: Druckerei des Lutherischen Concordia Verlags, 1883), p. 227.

[3] The Meistersinger (master singers) were a guild of professional musicians in Germany who set standards for musical quality and excellence during the fifteenth and sixteenth centuries. The hallmark of their compositional output was the *Hoflied* (courtly song), which followed strict patterns of composition with regard to line, form structure, and rhythm. The Meistersinger contributed in various ways to the expansion of the hymn repertoire (see John Wesley Barker, "Sociological Influences upon the Emergence of Lutheran Music," *Miscellanea musicologica, Adelaide Studies in Musicology* 4 [1969]: 164).

[4] See his sketch of a treatise on music in the form of a poem, *Peri tes musikes* (1530), recorded in Oskar Söhngen, *Theologie der Musik* (Kassel, Germany: Johannes Stauda Verlag, 1967), pp. 87, 88; cf. also Martin Luther, *Tischreden*, chap. 68, p. 1541, in vol. 22 of *Sämmtliche Schriften*, Johann Georg Walch, ed. (St. Louis: Concordia Publishing House, 1858-1887). Hereafter all citations from Luther's works in German will be referred to as *SS* (*Sämmtliche Schriften*, ed. Johann Georg Walch [St. Louis: Concordia Publishing House, 1858-1887]); citations from his works in English are taken from *Luther's Works*, Jaroslav Pelikan, ed. (St. Louis: Concordia Publishers, 1958) and will be referred to as *LW*.

[5] Letter to Ludwig Senfl, October 4, 1530, in Luther, *SS*, vol. 21b, *Briefe (1507-1532)*, col. 1575.

[6] "Preface to the Wittenberg Hymnal (1524)," in *LW*, vol. 53, p. 316.

[7] The first hymnal under the supervision of Luther himself was published in Wittenberg in 1529. Cf. Konrad Ameln, "Luthers Kirchenlied und Gesangbuch: Offene Fragen," *Jahrbuch für Liturgik und Hymnologie* 32 (1989): 20.

[8] We will mostly refer to the Lutheran congregational song as a hymn since this expression evokes something more familiar in the mind of most readers. Occasionally, though, chorale will also be used.

[9] For more information, see Rebecca Wagner Oettinger's dissertation "Music as Popular Propaganda in the German Reformation, 1517-1555" (Ph. D. dissertation, University of Wisconsin-Madison, 1999).

[10] Cf. Hans Grüss, "*Martin Luther und die Musik seiner Zeit*," in *Ansichtssachen, Notate, Aufsätze, Collagen*, Hans Grüss, Thomas Schinköth, and H.-J. Schulze, eds. (Altenburg, Germany: K.-J. Kamprad, 1999), p. 56.

[11] See Rebecca Wagner Oettinger, pp. 25, 26; cf. also R. W. Scribner, "Oral Culture and the Transmission of Reformation Ideas," in *The Transmission of Ideas in the Lutheran Reformation*, Helga Robinson-Hammerstein, ed. (Dublin: Irish Academic Press, 1989), pp. 85-93.

[12] The name for such songs was *Zeitlieder* (songs of the time), indicating that they dealt with current issues.

[13] Carnival is a time of reveling that takes place just before Ash Wednesday, which marks the beginning of Lent. Similar revelries are still practiced in New Orleans, Louisiana; Rio de Janeiro, Brazil; and Venice, Italy.

[14] These songs were more of the art song type and were favored among the nobility and the people of the bourgeois and wealthy classes: merchants, lawyers, etc.

[15] Luther's very first hymnal, the *Erfurt Enchiridion* (1524), was intended for such uses rather than for the church services; see John Wesley Barker, "Sociological Influences on the Emergence of Lutheran Music," *Miscellanea musicologica: Adelaide Studies in Musicology* 4 (1969): 178.

[16] John Wesley Barker, "Sociological Influences on the Emergence of Lutheran Music," p. 181.

[17] See, for example, his sermons on 1 Corinthians 15 (1532) and on the Gospel of Saint John (1537) and his preface to the hymnal *Geistliche Lieder*, published by Babst in 1545.

[18] While some trades allowed for ample reading, hearing, and discussion during work hours (e.g., weavers and leather workers), people in other professions found time for such activities during their after work meetings at the guild taverns. Still others, through the mobility required by their trade (as, for example, the weavers), became important factors for spreading the Word. For more detailed information about the various ways the gospel was spread by means of oral tradition during the early times of the Reformation, see R. W. Scribner, *Popular Culture and Popular Movements in Reformation Germany* (London: The Hambledon Press, 1987).

[19] Pictorial representations of the gospel were another tool for reaching this goal, as, for instance, the woodblock pamphlets of Regensburg (1554) and Nuremberg (1624), cf. Gerald Strauss, *Luther's House of Learning: Indoctrination of the Young in the German Reformation* (Baltimore: Johns Hopkins University Press, 1978), pp. 226f.

[20] For that purpose Luther provided solo songs built according to the *Hofweise* or *Gesellschaftslied* of the Meistersinger. Cf. Markus Jenny, *Luthers geistliche Lieder und Kirchengesänge* (Cologne, Germany: Böhlau Verlag, 1985), p. 111.

[21] See, for instance, his catechism hymns.

[22] Cf. Konrad Ameln, "Luthers Kirchenlied und Gesangbuch: Offene Fragen," *Jahrbuch für Liturgik und Hymnologie* 32 (1989): 28; Hans Grüss, "Martin Luther und die Musik seiner Zeit," p. 63.

[23] A number of theses and doctoral dissertations about Luther's chorales have been written during recent years and specifically address the matter of Luther's use of popular culture to spread the cause of the Reformation. See, in particular, Joseph Herl, "Congregational Singing in the German Lutheran Church, 1523-1780" (Ph.D. dissertation, University of Illinois at Urbana-Champaign, 2000); Rebecca Wagner Oettinger, "Music as Popular Propaganda in the

German Reformation, 1517-1555" (Ph.D. dissertation, University of Wisconsin-Madison, 1999); Katherine Joan Sander, "Johann Walter and Martin Luther: Theology and Music in the Early Lutheran Church" (M.A. thesis, University of Alberta, 1998).

[24] Ameln, "Luthers Kirchenlied und Gesangbuch: Offene Fragen," p. 15.

[25] Cf. Kurt Hennig, *Die geistliche Kontrafaktur im Jahrhundert der Reformation* (Halle, Germany: Max Niemeyer, 1909); G. Rietschel, *Die Aufgabe der Orgel im Gottesdienste bis in das 18. Jahrhundert* (Leipzig, Germany: Verlag der Dürr'schen Buchhandlung, 1893), pp. 10, 37.

[26] See "Heirs of the Reformation," pp. 165-170 of this book.

[27] Even though they were well aware that this procedure attracted criticism, the Moravians also embraced this principle with the purpose "to attract the people by means of the familiar sound to grasp the truth" (Letter to Prince Frederick III, October 12, 1574, quoted in Robert A. Skeris and Maria Laach, "Zum Problem der geistlichen Liedkontrafaktur: Überlegungen aus theologisch-hymnologischer Sicht," *Kirchenmusikalisches Jahrbuch* 67 (1983): 29.

[28] In order to get a taste of his style, one should sing the battle hymn of the Reformation, "A Mighty Fortress Is Our God," in its original rhythmic version, as available in more recent versions of the *Lutheran Hymnal*, full of dynamic, rhythmic energy.

[29] Cf. the literary work *The Aeneid*, by Virgil, which is a direct reference to the Greek epic poems *Iliad* and *Odyssey*, by Homer.

[30] Cf. Dufay's *L'homme armé* Mass and the motet *Se la face ay pale*, which became a model for a Mass of the same name. This practice was condemned by the Council of Trent (c. 1562) but continued nonetheless. Composers would simply omit the name of the secular source and give their sacred works the title "Sine nomine" (without name).

[31] For examples of secular songs and their religious contrafacta, see Friedrich Blume, *Protestant Church Music: A History* (New York: W. W. Norton, 1974), pp. 29-35. Cf. also W. Lipphardt, "Kontrafakturen weltlicher Lieder in bisher unbekannten Frankfurter Gesangbüchern vor 1569," in *Festsschrift W. Schmieder*, K. Dorfmüller and G. Von Dadelsen, eds. (Frankfurt am Main, Germany: 1972), pp. 125-135; cf. idem, "Adam Reissners handschriftliches Gesangbuch," in *Jahrbuch für Volksliedforschung* 12 (1967): 42-79.

[32] Christoph Petzsch, "Kontrafaktur und Melodietypus," *Die Musikforschung* 21 (1968): 275; cf. Kurt Hennig, *Die geistliche Kontrafaktur im Jahrhundert der Reformation*, p. 304.

[33] See Hennig, *Die geistliche Kontrafaktur im Jahrundert der Reformation*, pp. 311-313.

[34] See Werner Braun, "*Die evangelische Kontrafaktur*," *Jahrbuch für Liturgik und Hymnologie* 11 (1966): 109.

[35] *New Grove Dictionary of Music and Musicians*, online edition 2000, s.v. "Contrafactum," accessed July 15, 2007.

[36] Cf. Christoph Petzsch, "Kontrafaktur und Melodietypus," p. 274; cf. also *Musik in Geschichte und Gegenwart*, 1997 edition, s.v. "Parodie und Kontrafaktur." The two expressions carry the same meaning.

[37] Often, only some words needed to be changed to adapt the text to its new context. This technique had the twofold advantage of (1) preserving the original rhythm and accentuation, thus maintaining the relationship between music and text, and (2) reinforcing the familiarity factor. An example of such adaptation can be found in the well-known hymn "O Sacred Head Now Wounded," drawn from the familiar love song by Hans Leo Hassler, "*Mein G'müth is mir verwirret*" (*My Peace of Mind Is Shattered by a Tender Maiden's Charms*). See *The Seventh-day Adventist Hymnal*, No. 156; for a side-by-side comparison of the two versions, see Donald Jay Grout and Claude V. Palisca, *A History of Western Music*, 6th ed. (New York: W. W. Norton, 2001), pp. 225, 226.

[38] Werner Braun, "*Die evangelische Kontrafaktur*," p. 89.

[39] Only in subsequent centuries were major alterations made, more specifically with regard

to rhythm, in order to desecularize the music. See "The Derhythmization of the Lutheran Chorale," pp. 147-151 of this book.

[40] Those are "*Wir glauben all an einen Gott*" ("We All Believe in One True God,"), *Lutheran Hymnal*, No. 252; "Ein feste Burg ist unser Gott" ("A Mighty Fortress Is Our God,"), *The Seventh-day Adventist Hymnal*, No. 506; and the Sanctus hymn "*Isaiah dem Propheten das geschah*" ("Isaiah, Mighty Seer,"), *Lutheran Hymnal*, No. 249); cf. Carl F. Schalk, *Luther on Music: Paradigms on Praise* (St. Louis: Concordia Publishing House, 1988), p. 26.

[41] Pamphlet "Against the Heavenly Prophets" (1524), *LW* 40:141.

[42] "Preface to the Burial Hymns" (1542), *LW* 53:327, 328. This reference to the sweetness and charm of secular melodies can also be found in Luther's chapter "On Music" in his *Tischreden*: "Why is it that, for the secular phases of life (carnalibus) we have so many fine poems and beautiful melodies, while for spiritual matters (spiritualibus) we have such poor and cold stuff?" (*SS*, Vol. 22, col. 1539). This is the closest one comes to the legendary saying by Luther that "the devil is not the only one to have beautiful melodies." This statement has never been formally attested to in Luther's writings.

[43] Cf. Blume, *Protestant Church Music*, p. 30. The hymns of the Reformed church feature more than a hundred such borrowings (idem). For a more detailed survey of the practice of contrafacta as related to Luther's hymns, see the chapter "The Contrafacta" in Blume, pp. 29-35.

[44] Later borrowings, by Luther's successors, also included well-known riding songs, mining songs, and even street songs (see Blume, *Protestant Church Music*, p. 33).

[45] For a detailed description of text and music origins for all of Luther's hymns, see Konrad Ameln, *The Roots of German Hymnody of the Reformation Era*, Church Music Pamphlet Series, Hymnology: Number One (St. Louis: Concordia Publishing House, 1964); for musical and textual illustrations and correspondences, see also Markus Jenny, ed., *Luthers geistliche Lieder und Kirchengesänge*, supplement to vol. 35 of the Weimar edition of Luther's works, Gerhard Ebeling, et al., eds. (Cologne, Germany: Böhlau Verlag, 1985).

[46] See Jenny, *Luthers geistliche Lieder und Kirchengesänge*, pp. 57, 154.

[47] *The Lutheran Hymnal*, The Evangelical Lutheran Synodical Conference of North America (St. Louis: Concordia Publishing House, 1941).

[48] See Jenny, *Luthers geistliche Lieder und Kirchengesänge*, pp. 109, 110.

[49] Translations have been kept literal for the purpose of comparison.

[50] See also Luther's chorale "*Sie ist mir lieb, die werte Magd*" ("She Is Dear to Me, the Worthy Maid"), a tribute to Christ's church. This song may also have circulated as a Marian song (see Jenny, *Luthers geistliche Lieder und Kirchengesänge*, pp. 111, 112). Here again, the text serves both a secular and sacred setting very well.

[51] The editors of the hymnals published by Hans Weiss (1528) and Valentin Bapst (1545) used the terms to "better," to "Christianize," and to "Germanize" with reference to the changes made to the texts. Cf. Werner Braun, "*Die evangelische Kontrafaktur*," p. 94.

[52] Thus, for example, in his Trinity hymn, "Gott der Vater wohn bei uns" ("God, Father, Dwell Among Us"), Luther reworked the text of a traditional Marian song, "Holy Mary, Assist Us." He kept the beginning lines of the first stanza of this well-known, beloved song and reworked the text from the middle of the stanza on (Markus Jenny, *Luthers geistliche Lieder und Kirchengesänge*, pp. 79-83).

[53] Cf. Konrad Ameln, *The Roots of German Hymnody of the Reformation Era*, in which he discusses several types of adaptations made to the original texts; see especially pp. 15-26.

[54] The practice of *Umtextierung* (the rewording of an existing text to the same melody), did not end with Luther. It continued in later times as new political situations emerged and created new needs. Cf. Bernhard H. Bonkhoff, "*Umdichtung, Nachdichtung und zeitgenössis-*

che Aktualisierung:Das Schicksal des Lutherliedes im deutschen Protestantismus," Luther 77 (2006): 141–163.

[55] "Letter to Georg Spalatin, 1523" (No. 140), *LW* 49, *Letters* 2:68–70. Cf. also Edward Foley, Capuchin, "Martin Luther: A Model Pastoral Musician," *Currents in Theology and Music* 14 (1987): 405–418. Cf. Markus Jenny, *"Luthers Gesangbuch,"* in *Leben und Werk Martin Luthers von 1526 bis 1546. Festgabe zu seinem 500. Geburtstag,* Helmar Junghaus, ed. (Göttingen, Germany: Vandenhoek and Ruprecht, 1983), p. 315.

[56] Luther, *Tischreden,* chap. 68 "Von der Musica" ("Of Music"), in *SS,* vol. 22, col. 1537.

[57] Cf. Luther's pamphlet "Against the Heavenly Prophets," in which he associates the text, notes, accentuation, tune, and mood of a song, *LW* 40:141. See also Wichmann von Meding, *Luthers Gesangbuch: Die gesungene Theologie eines christlichen Psalters,* Theos: Studienreihe Theologischer Forschungsergebnisse, 24 (Hamburg, Germany: Kovac, 1998), p. 310.

[58] Cf. Werner Braun, *"Die evangelische Kontrafaktur,"* p. 90, referring to W. Blankenburg, *"Geschichte der Melodien des Evangelischen Kirchengesangs,"* in *Handbuch zum EKG* II:2 (Göttingen, Germany: 1957), p. 73. Cf. also Jenny, *Luthers geistliche Lieder und Kirchengesänge,* p. 15.

[59] See Helmut Huchzermeyer, *"Luther und die Musik," Luther: Mitteilungen der Luthergesellschaft* 39, No. 1 (1968): 21; Wichmann von Meding, *Luthers Gesangbuch,* p. 310. A similar technique was applied to the metrical psalms of the Reformation, especially in the English tradition, in which a handful of melodies accommodated the singing of the whole book of Psalms. See the *Scottish Psalter, 1929: Metrical Version and Scripture Paraphrases with Tunes* (London: Oxford University Press, Humphrey Milford, 1929).

[60] See, for example, the hymn *"Vater unser im Himmelreich"* ("Our Father in Heaven"), for which Luther rejected his first melodic version. His second melody fit the text much better. It was found later that his second version was probably based on an old melody from the hymnal of the Bohemian Brethren (1531). Cf. Ameln, *The Roots of German Hymnody of the Reformation Era,* pp. 21, 22.

[61] See "Against the Heavenly Prophets," *LW,* vol. 40, p. 141; cf. also Wichmann von Meding, *Luthers Gesangbuch,* pp. 305–312.

[62] Cf. Jenny, *"Luthers Gesangbuch,"* pp. 317, 318.

[63] Luther, "Preface to the Burial Hymns," in *LW,* vol. 53, p. 328. It is interesting to note how Luther, in this quote, emphasizes again the necessity to change the text, but not the music.

[64] See Edward Foley, "Martin Luther: A Model Pastoral Musician," p. 412.

[65] The term *melismatic* refers to a musical setting that uses several or many notes for one syllable of the text. This results in a highly ornamented and complex style, as was customary for certain types of plainchant. Cf. Ameln, *The Roots of German Hymnody of the Reformation Era,* pp. 17–26.

[66] See Jenny, *"Luthers Gesangbuch,"* p. 315.

[67] See von Meding, *Luthers Gesangbuch,* p. 305, 307; cf. also Ameln, *The Roots of German Hymnody of the Reformation Era,* pp. 25, 26.

[68] See Ameln, *The Roots of German Hymnody of the Reformation Era,* pp. 25, 26.

[69] In musical language, syncopation is defined as "a rhythmic displacement created by articulating weaker beats or metrical positions that do not fall on any of the main beats" (see "Syncopation," pp. 25–28 of this book).

[70] Contrary to widespread misunderstanding of this term, the bar form used by Luther has nothing to do with bars in the sense of taverns or pubs. The term refers to a particular formal pattern predominantly found in the art song of the Renaissance. Even today, the bar form is present in many hymns and chorales in our hymnbooks. It consists of three sections (AAB), the second being a repetition of the first, the third and longest one forming the ending section. Ed-

ward Foley mentions that this was the most frequent formal pattern used by Luther throughout his contributions to the Protestant hymn: "Only six out of thirty-seven chorales (15%) ... either do not employ the bar form or do not employ pre-existent material" (p. 410). The bar form also features the seven to eight syllable line that was equally favored by Luther. In his translations or adaptations of texts, he predominantly adjusted the text to this syllable pattern, sometimes at the expense of correct accentuation of the text in relationship to the musical accents. Cf. Foley, "Martin Luther: A Model Pastoral Musician," pp. 408-410, 414.

[71] Cf. Jenny, *Luthers geistliche Lieder und Kirchengesänge*, p. 15. Luther had, indeed, earned the title "the greatest of all Meistersinger," given to him by the seventeenth century historian Wolfhart Spangenberg in his *Geschichte des Meistergesangs* (approx. 1614). Cf. Ernst Sommer, "*Die Metrik in Luthers Liedern*," *Jahrbuch für Liturgik und Hymnologie* 9 (1964): 70. Syncopation technique was featured by Johann Walter in his own version of the hymn, "*Vom Himmel hoch*," in which he used the rhythmic device to underline the words "the good news" (for a musical example, see Melody C in Jenny, *Luthers geistliche Lieder und Kirchengesänge*, p. 288).

[72] For the musical examples of these songs, see Jenny, *Luthers geistliche Lieder und Kirchengesänge*, pp. 194, 206, 217, 299.

[73] During the nineteenth century the Lutheran Church reverted to the old rhythmic style. Lutheran hymnals today feature the chorales in their original rhythmic versions (see, *The Lutheran Hymnal*, The Evangelical Lutheran Synodical Conference of North America, 1941). In evangelical circles, however, the modified isorhythmic version is still predominantly in use.

[74] See Christian Gerber's comment (1732) on the use of instruments for the singing of Passion chorales during Palm Sunday ("'Theatrical' Passion Music," quoted in H. David and A. Mendel, eds., *The Bach Reader: A Life of Johann Sebastian Bach in Letters and Documents*, rev. ed. [New York: W. W. Norton, 1966], pp. 229, 230).

[75] The most striking examples of Bach's borrowing from the secular for the sacred can indeed be seen in his *Christmas Oratorio*, BWV 248. Movements One to Four feature several borrowings from his secular birthday cantatas BWV 213 ("*Lasst uns sorgen*") and BWV 214 ("*Tönet, ihr Pauken*"), and from the *dramma per musica* "*Preise dein Glücke*" (BWV 215) (see *The Bach Reader*, pp. 21, 22, 43). The aria "Crown and glory of crowned ladies, Queen" from BWV 214, which praises the charms of the queen, was set in the oratorio to the text "Great Lord, powerful King, beloved Savior" to sing praises to the God incarnate (J. A. Westrup, *Bach Cantatas*, BBC Music Guides, Gerald Abraham, ed. [London: British Broadcasting Corporation, 1966], p. 43).

The adoption, by J. S. Bach, of characteristic features of opera, such as the recitative and the da capo aria, as well as the style of instrumental music—reminiscent of dance pieces or concerto movements (Westrup, *Bach Cantatas*, p. 39)—placed his church cantatas into the genre of operatic music. This was clearly expressed by Neumeister, a Lutheran pastor, theologian, and librettist contemporary of J. S. Bach, some of whose texts were used by Bach for his church cantatas (*ibid.*, p. 6). As in opera, choruses in the cantatas were assigned only a minor role and were relegated most often to the first and last movements; some of Bach's Leipzig cantatas feature no chorus at all (*ibid.*, pp. 27, 32, 33, 47). Instrumental accompaniment of the cantatas was considered standard, and the use of the organ represented only a last resort (*ibid.*, p. 51).

One choral section of cantata BWV 215 was also used by J. S. Bach as the "Osanna" for his Mass in B Minor (Wolfang Schmieder, ed., *Theamtisch-systematisches Verzeichnis der musikalischen Werke von Johann Sebastian Bach: Bach-Werke-Verzeichnis* (BWV), 2nd ed. [Wiesbaden, Germany: Breitkopf and Härtel, 1990], pp. 353, 355, 357.

J. A. Westrup pointed out that "there cannot be two ways of writing a recitative: the same formulas have to serve for joy in God and the praises of a prince, for a sinner's repentance and despair in love.…There is no material difference between the recitatives in Bach's secular works and those in his church cantatas, oratorios and Passions. The same is true of his arias and choruses. Hence it was perfectly easy for him to adapt new words to music which originally had served quite a different purpose" (*Bach Cantatas*, pp. 6, 17).

[76] See, for instance, some of his choruses in the *Messiah* that are based on earlier Italian duets. But Handel also borrowed from other composers, i.e., from a serenata by Stradella for his oratorio *Joseph*, and from a canzone by J. K. Kerll for his oratorio *Israel in Egypt* (*The New Grove Dictionary of Music and Musicians*, 2001, s.v. "Handel, George Frideric," par. 15: "Borrowing," vol. 10, p. 768).

[77] His earlier oratorios were written "in the well-established form of the Italian vernacular oratorio, very similar in style to the aria-dominated opera of the period" (*The New Grove Dictionary of Music and Musicians*, 2001, s.v. "Handel, George Frideric," par. 22: "Oratorio Forms," vol. 10, p. 775).

[78] *Ibid.*, pp. 775, 776.

[79] Cf. Joseph Herl, "Congregational Singing in the German Lutheran Church 1523-1780," p. 190.

[80] See Michael Praetorius, *Syntagma musicum*, vol. 3: *Termini musici* (Wolfenbüttel, Germany: J. Richter, 1615; reprint edition Kassel, Germany: Bärenreiter, 1958), pp. 87, 88.

[81] Blume, *Protestant Church Music*, p. 71.

[82] Heinrich Georg Neuss, in his 1712 preface to the hymnal for Wernigerode, quoted in Joseph Herl, "Congregational Singing in the German Lutheran Church," p. 187.

[83] Quoted in Johann Daniel von der Heydt, *Geschichte der Evangelischen Kirchenmusik in Deutschland* (Berlin: Trowitzsch and Son, 1926), p. 195.

[84] See Nicholas Temperley, *The Music of the English Parish Church* (New York: Cambridge University Press, 1979), vol. 1, pp. 92, 93.

[85] For more details, see the booklet by Carl Schalk, *The Roots of Hymnody in the Lutheran Church-Missouri Synod*, Church Music Pamphlet Series, Hymnology, No. 2 (St. Louis: Concordia Publishing House, 1965). Schalk gives an interesting description of the five types of arguments that were, at that time, advanced against the reinstatement of the original rhythms of the Lutheran chorale: (1) the rhythmic chorale is a manifestation of the secular; (2) its use developed from the "Union" movement; (3) it constitutes an unwarranted change in the "good old tradition;" (4) the rhythmic chorales are difficult to learn; and finally, (5) the whole undertaking is too new and untried a venture (p. 30).

[86] Walter Blankenburg, *Johann Walter: Leben und Werk* (Tutzing, Germany: Beacon Press, 1952), p. 373. A similar approach can be observed within the Catholic Church during the same time period. See Karl Gustav Fellerer, "*Beziehungen zwischen geistlicher und weltlicher Musik im 16. Jahrhundert*," *Report of the 8th Congress New York*, 1961, p. 207.

[87] Thrasybulos Georgiades, *Sakral und Profan in der Musik* (Munich: Max Hueber Verlag, 1960), p. 3.

[88] Warren Dwight Allen, *Philosophies of Music History: A Study of General Histories of Music 1600-1960* (New York: Dover Publications, 1962), p. 146.

[89] Blume, *Protestant Church Music*, p. xiii. See also Albert Schweitzer, *J. S. Bach* (New York: Dover Publications, 1966), vol. 1, p. 20; Harold Best, *Music Through the Eyes of Faith*, p. 42; J. Nathan Corbitt, *The Sound of the Harvest: Music's Mission in Church and Culture* (Grand Rapids: Baker Books, 1998), pp. 36, 40, 41, 245-255. Nearly 200 years after Luther the same idea was echoed by New England minister Thomas Symmes as he was trying to reform the manner of singing in churches: "If any would suppose there is a relative holiness in some psalm tunes, I affirm, there is no more real holiness in the most elaborated Psalm tune, than in the tune of, Pepper is black. And if people have taken up any other notion, it's high time they should

be better informed, and convicted of their error. Psalm tunes and song tunes are all made by the same rule and those that made the psalm tunes were not divinely inspired, nor had they authority to consecrate any tune to the worship of God" (Thomas Symmes, *Utile dulci, or a Joco-Serious Dialogue Concerning Regular Singing* (Boston: B. Green for Samuel Gerrish, 1723), p. 44.

[90] Saint Augustine, "Letter 101," in *Letters 100-155 (Epistulae)*, transl. Roland Teske, S. J., Boniface Ramsey, ed., *The Works of Saint Augustine, A Translation for the 21ˢᵗ Century*, part 2, vol. 3 (Hyde Park, N.Y.: New City Press, 2003), p. 18.

[91] *The Confessions of St. Augustine*, David Otis Fuller, ed., A Christian Life Library Selection (Grand Rapids: Zondervan, 1947), chap. 3, p. 37.

[92] Saint Augustine, *Confessions*, book 4, chap. 30, Great Books of the Western World, No. 18: Augustine (Chicago: Encyclopaedia Britannica, 1952), p. 26.

[93] Saint Augustine, *On Christian Doctrine*, book 4, chap. 7, par. 19, The Library of Liberal Arts, Oskar Piest, ed., No. 80 (New York: The Liberal Arts Press, 1958), p. 131.

[94] Saint Augustine, *De Musica*, book 6, chap. 46, in W. F. Jackson Knight, ed., *St. Augustine's De Musica: A Synopsis* (Westport, Conn.: Hyperion Press, 1949), p. 118.

[95] Saint Augustine, *De Musica*, book 6, chap. 50, in *St. Augustine's De Musica: A Synopsis*, p. 120.

[96] This hierarchical concept of music is a reflection of the ancient and medieval (scholastic) worldviews, wherein music belonged to the realm of philosophical speculation and was understood as part of the great harmony of the cosmos (cf. the Platonic doctrine of the "harmony of the spheres"). Music was subdivided into a three-tiered hierarchical system. *Musica mundana* was representative of the metaphysical order of the universe. The numerical proportions characteristic of musical intervals corresponded to the numerical proportions that expressed the distances between the planets of the solar system. It was believed that the original musical sound was produced by the revolution of the various planets around the sun, each planet producing its own particular pitch. Music was, then, the only language capable of translating the harmony of the universe into humanly understandable language, and thus took on a particular place within the speculative world. Next in rank was *musica humana*, representing the harmony of the human body and soul. Last and lowest came *musica instrumentalis*, seen as the "craft" of musical practice, "wholly destitute of speculation" and, therefore, little respected, except when used within the church. (Boethius, *De institutione musica*, book 1, sec. 33, quoted in Oliver Strunk, *Source Readings in Music History: From Classical Antiquity through the Romantic Era*, [New York: W. W. Norton, 1950], p. 86). *Musica instrumentalis* could even reach much lower regions when its purpose became to function as pure entertainment for the human senses. It was, therefore, easily dismissed as something destined to damnation.

The two approaches, by Saint Augustine and the scholastic world, share a common disdain for music happening outside of the realm of the church or the philosophical domain.

[97] Cf. Luther's reference to the theories of Pythagoras in his "Lectures on Genesis, chapters 1-5," Jaroslav Pelikan, ed., *LW* 1:126. See also his emphasis on the rhetorical function of music, namely, to touch and speak to the emotions, in "Preface to Georg Rhau's *Symphoniae Iucundae* (1838)," in *LW* 53, *Liturgy and Hymns*, U. Leupold, ed. (Philadelphia: Fortress Press, 1965), p. 323.

[98] See, for instance, these words from the preface to the 1535 collection of contrafacta entitled *Street Songs, Cavalier Songs, and Miner Songs*: "transformed into Christian and moral songs, for the abolishing in course of time of the bad and vexatious practice of singing idle and shameful songs in the streets, in fields, and at home, by substituting for them good, sacred, honest words" (quoted by Blume, *Protestant Church Music*, p. 33).

[99] Luther, "Lectures on Isaiah," chaps. 40-66 (1527-1530), *LW*, vol. 17, p. 356. The concept

of music as God's gift is so essential to Luther that he mentions it in many of his writings. Cf. his "Treatise on the Last Words of David," *LW*, vol. 15, pp. 273, 274; his "Preface to Rhau's *Symphoniae iucundae*, *LW*, vol. 53, p. 321; *Tischreden*, chap. 68, "On Music," *SS*, vol. 22, col. 1536; and his "Preface to Harmonias de passione Christi," *SS*, vol. 14, pp. 428-430.

[100] Luther himself, taking the stance opposite Saint Augustine's, subscribed to this new role of music: "Music is a beautiful and lovely gift of God which has often moved and inspired me to preach with joy. Saint Augustine was afflicted with scruples of conscience whenever he discovered that he had derived pleasure from music and had been happy thereby; he was of the opinion that such joy is unrighteous and sinful" (*Tischreden*, No. 2641: "*Passions-Gesang*," in *Dr. Martin Luthers Sämtliche Werke*, vol. 62, part 4: *Vermischte Deutsche Schriften*, vol. 10 (Erlangen, Germany: Heyder und Zimmer, 1854), p. 111.

[101] Luther, "*Formula missae*" ("An Order of Mass and Communion for the Church at Wittenberg"), *LW*, vol. 53, p. 22.

[102] See, for instance, Handel's *Messiah*, Beethoven's *Missa solemnis*, Mendelssohn's and Brahms's oratorios, etc.

[103] Albert Schweitzer, *J. S. Bach*, transl. Ernest Newman (New York: Dover Publications, 1966), vol. 1, p. 18. With humor, he goes on in his quote, saying: "One clever writer maintains, not without reason, that we could mislead all the purists of church music by putting before them an old secular motet with an accompanying sacred text" (*ibid.*).

[104] For instance, an ascending melodic line was used to express joy, and a descending melodic line meant sadness or mourning. Such rhetorical musical figures were still in use during the baroque period. J. S. Bach used them profusely, especially in his "Little Organ Preludes" (*Orgelbüchlein*).

[105] Luther, *Tischreden*, *SS*, vol. 22, p. 770.

[106] Luther, "Letter to Ludwig Senfl" (1712), *SS*, vol. 21a, col. 1575.

[107] Luther, "Treatise on the Last Words of David," in *LW*, vol. 15, p. 274.

[108] Luther, "Preface to Georg Rhau's *Symphoniae iucundae*, 1538," in *LW*, vol. 53, p. 323.

[109] See especially Johann Walter (1496-1580), Georg Rhau (1488-1548), Ludwig Senfl (1486-1543), and Martin Agricola (1486-1556).

[110] See, among others, his letter to Georg Spalatin, in *D. Martin Luther's Werke. Briefwechsel* (Weimar, Germany: Hermann Böhlau, 1930-1985), vol. 3, p. 220; and his preface to Johann Walter's *Gesangbüchlein*, in *D. Martin Luther's Werke* (Weimar: Hermann Böhlau, 1883-1990), vol. 35, p. 474.

[111] Paul Tillich, *The Protestant Era*, transl. James Luther Adams (Chicago: University of Chicago Press, 1984), p. 59.

[112] The term *art music* is used here as contrasted with popular music and traditional (ethnic, folk music).

[113] Luther, *Tischreden*, chap. 68, "On Music," *SS*, vol. 22, col. 1538.

[114] Luther, Preface to Johann Walter's *Gesangbüchlein* (1524), in *LW*, vol. 35, pp. 474, 475.

[115] The comparison between popular and art music should not be made on the level of "low" versus "high" music. Popular music and art music belong to two different domains with different criteria of composition and listening, i.e., they serve different purposes. The common factor between these two styles must be found on the level of excellence in design and performance.

[116] The late fourteenth-century reformer John Wycliffe preceded Luther in advocating congregational singing in the vernacular. He had, however, expressed great skepticism as to the use and role of art music in church, characterized by "flourishes so that no-one can hear the words, and all the others are dumb and watch them like fools" (John Wycliffe, *Sermon on the Feigned Contemplative Life*, quoted in E. Routley, *The Church and Music* [London: Duckworth, 1978], p. 105).

[117] Luther, "Preface to Georg Rhau's *Symphoniae iucundae*" (1538), *LW*, vol. 53, p. 324.

[118] In speaking of "Latin" music, Walter refers to what we call today "learned" music, i.e., art music (classical music).

[119] Recorded by Michael Praetorius in his *Syntagma musicum*, vol. 1: *Musicae artis Analecta* (Wolfenbüttel, Germany: 1615; reprint Kassel, Germany: Bärenreiter, 1959), pp. 451-53, quoted in Piero Weiss and Richard Taruskin, eds., *Music in the Western World: A History in Documents* (New York: Schirmer Books, 1984), p. 105.

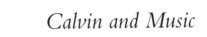

CHAPTER 12

Calvin and Music

W hat Luther represented to the German Reformation in terms of congregational singing, John Calvin (1509-1564) represented to the
French-speaking Reformation, which mainly took place in Geneva, Switzerland. Contrary to Luther, who saw the church's mission within the world,
Calvin considered the role of the church not to be of the world. He had a
deep suspicion of society that resulted in the development of his theology
of the "elect," and he took a disciplined approach to church life.[1]

Calvin was not a trained musician, but he appreciated the role of music in
the church as an aid to piety and worship. He too worked with professional
musicians—Louis Bourgeois and Claude Goudimel—to bring about a whole
body of melodies to accompany the psalms translated into metrical verse in
French by the Parisian court poet Clément Marot.[2] Bourgeois especially was
active in arranging already existing tunes to fit the prosody of the new texts.
A number of these tunes had originally been taken from the traditional or
popular religious heritage or from secular repertoire and were adapted for
ease of singing in the sturdy and straightforward manner characteristic of the
French Psalter, better known as the Genevan Psalter.[3] Some tunes from the
Genevan Psalter later found their way into the hymns of Isaac Watts.[4]

Calvin's suspicion of the world found an echo in his mistrust of music.
His disciplined approach to church life was reflected in the music he prescribed: it was characterized by simplicity, modesty, and majesty.[5] Only
syllabic style and straightforward rhythms,[6] unison singing in a cappella
style, and scriptural texts—the psalms and a small number of other biblical
texts[7]—were allowed for congregational song. Instrumental music was
"not now to be used in public thanksgiving," as Calvin explained in his

commentary on Psalm 71:22.[8] The use of instruments was labeled as an "outward service" and "silly delight,"[9] "no more suitable in celebrating the praises of God than the burning of incense."[10] To demonstrate his opposition to the use of instruments during worship, Calvin had all the organs in Genevan churches destroyed and thrown into Lake Geneva.[11] The metrical versions of the new psalms translations were done in an objective and universal language and featured stanzas of equal length, with same meter and rhyme. The tunes were strict and straightforward, yet not without a certain lyrical beauty. At this point the psalm had moved away from the free and flexible manner typical of the traditional psalmody style and came to resemble the hymn.

The elements of joy and celebration of salvation, as found with Luther, are not predominant in Calvin's approach to church music. Here, the accent is, rather, on gravity and reverence: "As for the melody it has seemed best to moderate it in the way we have done, so as to lend it the gravity and majesty that befits its subject, and as might even be suitable for singing in Church, according to what has been said."[12]

As we compare the hymns these Reformers brought about, we can observe that the principle of music as a conveyer of theology holds true. A comparison of parallels and divergences will underline this fact even more.

Both Reformers strongly believed in the value and necessity of music for church and worship. Their differences were, however, essential. While Luther affirmed the role of the church within the world, Calvin preached suspicion and separation from the world, and Zwingli, separation from the flesh. For Luther, life was to be affirmed joyfully; Calvin saw life from an austere and disciplined perspective. While Luther embraced both the old and the new, Calvin dwelled primarily on the old. To Luther, music had to be both appropriate and relevant; Calvin put the emphasis on appropriateness. Luther borrowed freely from the secular and maintained the original and lively qualities of the tunes; Calvin also used existing tunes but had their characters completely transformed into rigid metrical patterns that could be fitted to any text featuring the same poetic meter.

To put it in a nutshell, Luther's approach could be summarized by two key traits: *affirmation of life* and *renewal*. Calvin's approach could also be described by two key traits: *restraint* and *separation*.

As Seventh-day Adventists we like to consider ourselves as heirs of the Reformation. The questions, then, arise naturally: To which side of this picture do we see ourselves belonging in our music making in church? Do we partake of the tradition of Luther, which embraces the world in order to transform it, or are we part of Calvin's tradition, which retracts from the world into separation? Do we seek to be "the salt of the earth" (Matthew 5:13), or do we strive to "come out of her [Babylon]" (Revelation 18:4)?

The biblical message actually calls us to do both: to be *in* the world sharing the gospel, but not to be *of* the world (see John 17:14-18). This makes the task much more difficult. Again, we are confronted by the tension between the vertical and the horizontal, challenged to find a just balance between being in the world so as to transform it but also being separate from it. This is a task that demands discernment, wisdom, love, tolerance, and grace. If we want to be true to our theology, we have to do so with our music making in the church. Our singing and playing speaks to the people and conveys our theology whether we are aware of it or not. It is time to embrace our music and intentionally shape it so that it clearly and fully states what we believe.

---

[1] Cf. John Calvin, *Oeuvres choisies* (Geneva, Switzerland: Chouet, 1909), pp. 173-76, quoted in Piero Weiss and Richard Taruskin, *Music in the Western World,* pp. 107-109.

[2] Like Calvin, Marot had to flee from the French court in Paris for reasons of heresy, on behalf of his metrical translations of the psalms. After Marot's death Theodore of Beza continued the translation process to include all the psalms of the Bible.

[3] See William J. Reynolds, *A Survey of Christian Hymnody* (Carol Stream, Ill.: Hope Publishing Co., 1987), pp. 30, 31. See also Edith Weber, *La musique protestante de langue française* (Paris: Honoré Champion, 1979), pp. 80, 81. Some of these psalms can still be found in *The Seventh-day Adventist Hymnal,* e.g., No. 13 by Goudimel, No. 16 by Bourgeois (the latter is known as "Old Hundredth," or "Doxology"). The Genevan Psalter was the first collection of all 150 psalms in the French language, with musical settings by Louis Bourgeois.

[4] See William J. Reynolds, *A Survey of Christian Hymnody,* p. 47. Many of Watts's hymns were actually sung to the already familiar tunes from the Psalters. The tunes from the Genevan Psalter reached England via the 1561 Anglo-Genevan Psalter (*ibid.,* p. 32).

[5] John Calvin, "Epistle to the Reader," from *Cinquante Pseaumes en françois par Clem. Marot* (1543), quoted by David W. Music, *Hymnology: A Collection of Source Readings,* pp. 65-68. The Swiss reformer Huldrych Zwingli (1484-1531) was even more radical in his approach to singing in the church. Though a highly educated musician, he did not promote singing or instrumental music in corporate worship. To Zwingli, singing was like prayer, and prayer was a personal and private matter with God. Public singing, as well as public prayer, was considered by Zwingli as hypocritical (see David W. Music, pp. 51-53). He made this

point in his interpretation of Colossians 3:16: "Paul . . . indicates the true song that is pleasing to God, that we sing the praise and glory of God not with the voice . . . but with the hearts. . . . Hypocrites do their work that they may be seen of men, thus having the reward in their life" (forty-fifth article from "*Auslegungen und Gründe der Schlossreden*," in Emil Egli and Georg Finsler, eds., *Sämtliche Werke* vol. 89 of *Corpus Reformatorum* [Munich: Kraus, reprint edition, no date] vol. 2, pp. 348-350, quoted in David W. Music, p. 53).

[6] Syllabic style consists in singing one syllable only per note. The tunes from the Genevan Psalter feature only two rhythmic values, long and short. There is a total absence of dotted rhythms or triple meter, and only very few melismatic passages, to avoid a light and vulgar character (see Markus Jenny, *Luther, Zwingli, Calvin in ihren Liedern* [Zurich: Theologischer Verlag, 1983], p. 229).

[7] These included the Ten Commandments and the song of Simeon (*Nunc dimittis*) (see Reynolds, *A Survey of Christian Hymnody*, p. 31).

[8] John Calvin, "Commentary upon Psalm 71," *Commentary on the Book of Psalms*, transl. Rev. James Anderson (Grand Rapids: Wm. B. Eerdmans, 1949), vol. 3, p. 98.

[9] Calvin, "Commentary upon Psalm 92," *Commentary on the Book of Psalms*, vol. 3, p. 495.

[10] Calvin, "Commentary on Psalm 33," *Commentary on the Book of Psalms*, vol. 1, p. 539. Calvin echoed the church fathers' explanations that instrumental music in the Old Testament was tolerated by God in those times "to help forward a people as yet weak and rude in knowledge in the spiritual worship of God" ("Commentary upon Psalm 92:1," *Commentary on the Book of Psalms*, vol. 3, p. 495). Calvin was not opposed, though, to the use of musical instruments for private use (see "Commentary upon Psalm 71," *Commentary on the Book of Psalms*, vol. 3, p. 98).

[11] In doing so, he contributed to the destruction of a number of fine historical instruments (see Pierre Meylan and Andrew Clark, "Geneva," *Grove Music Online*, L. Macey, ed., http://www.grovemusic.com, accessed July 15, 2007).

[12] John Calvin, *Oeuvres choisies* (Geneva, Switzerland: La Compagnie des pasteurs de Genève, 1909), p. 176, quoted in *Strunk's Source Readings in Music History*, rev. ed., ed. Leo Treitler, vol. 3: *The Renaissance*, ed. Gary Tomlinson, transl. Oliver Strunk (New York: W. W. Norton, 1998), p. 89.

CHAPTER 13

The Council of Trent

I n an effort to emulate the changes brought about in congregational singing and worship by the Reformation churches, the Catholic Church undertook its own reform during the Council of Trent (1545-1563). Criticism was voiced against the adorned and elaborate ways of the liturgy. Indeed, increasing complexity in the musical language had resulted in a style whose subtleties could be appreciated only by the elite. The great humanist Erasmus (c. 1466-1536) had already complained about this: "Modern music is so constructed that the congregation cannot hear one distinct word. The choristers themselves do not understand what they are singing, yet according to priests and monks it constitutes the whole of religion. . . . In college or monastery it is still the same: music, nothing but music."[1]

The issue of secular borrowing again became a major topic of discussion. Secular tunes, in the form of love songs or battle songs,[2] provided the compositional basis for most Masses composed during the late fifteenth and the sixteenth centuries. In addition, the intricacy of the polyphonic musical language was perceived as a hindrance to the intelligibility of the text—the music had become more important than the words.

For the second time in history, then, the Catholic Church issued rules to govern musical writing for sacred services. These rules dealt with the lack of intelligibility of the text, the mingling of the "profane, lascivious, impure"[3] with the sacred, and the loss of the functional character of the music, which was to serve the Word: "Let nothing profane be intermingled, but only hymns and divine praises. The whole plan of singing . . . should be constituted not to give empty pleasure to the ear but in such a way that the words may be clearly understood by all . . . and thus the hearts of the listeners may be drawn to the desire of heavenly harmonies, in the contemplation of the joy of the blessed."[4]

These decisions were introduced as general recommendations, and their practical realization was left up to national and local instances.[5] As a result, composers continued to use secular models for their Masses but took care not to reveal the music's original identity in the new titles—they were simply called *Missa sine nomine* (*Mass Without a Name*).

The example of the Council of Trent is still another illustration of how the imagination and creativity of the people dictated what music would be used in the churches. This force gained strength over the coming centuries as new reformers worked to bring religion closer to the people and as the people were given a voice of their own with the advent of the French Revolution and the ensuing democratic and popular movements.

[1] Erasmus, "Annotations to the First Epistle of Corinthians, chapter 14," in Anna Reeve and M.A. Screech, eds., *Erasmus' Annotations of the New Testament: Acts-Romans-I and II Corinthians* (Leiden, Holland: Brill, 1990), p. 507.

[2] Cf. Dufay's secular song "Se la face ay pale" and his popular battle song "L'homme armé" ("The Armed Man"), which became basic melodic materials for Mass composition. The latter song's influence lasted more than a century.

[3] Abbé Chanut, *Le saint concile de Trente*, transl. from Latin by Pierre Thened, 3rd ed. (Paris, 1696), p. 251.

[4] R. F. Hayburn, *Papal Legislation on Sacred Music* (Collegeville, Minn.: Liturgical Press, 1979), pp. 25-31, quoted in Andrew Wilson-Dickson, *The Story of Christian Music From Gregorian Chant to Black Gospel: An Illustrated Guide to all the Major Traditions of Music in Worship* (Minneapolis: Fortress Press, 1996), p. 74.

[5] See Edith Weber, *Le concile de Trente et la musique: De la Réforme à la Contre-Réforme* (Paris: Honoré Champion, 1982), p. 95.

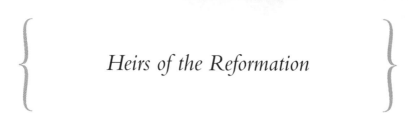

CHAPTER 14

Heirs of the Reformation

In the course of the four centuries following the Reformation, the principles established by the sixteenth-century Reformers were adopted and further exploited by several religious leaders.[1] The hymn, from the years of the Reformation until today, continued to rely on secular popular models for the setting of new texts. Then the nineteenth century, the Romantic era, ushered in the time of the people's voice, i.e., the beginnings of the reign of popular music, in Europe as well as in the United States.

During the seventeenth century the epicenter of the Reformation moved from Germany and Switzerland to England. Both the Church of England and the Protestant churches practiced psalm singing inspired by the Genevan Psalter. The hymn, properly speaking, came into its own only little by little and with great difficulties. The main problem for acceptance of the hymns came from the texts, which were not scriptural (as were the psalms) but, typically for hymns, paraphrases of Scripture. Because of the general decline in psalm singing, as a result of the low quality of singing in churches, the acceptance of hymn singing became more of a possibility. With Isaac Watts (1674-1748), a nonconformist pastor and hymn writer, known as the "father of English hymnody," the hymn had its first great breakthrough. On the musical side, though, it was still predominantly set to the old Psalter tunes.

The real break for the hymn came with John Wesley (1703-1791), founder of Methodism. Wesley was part of the Great Awakening in the eighteenth century. He had a deep compassion for those who were needy and poor in his country, and his evangelistic efforts were directed toward this group of the population. By the time of Wesley, Lutheranism had become a dry and formal religion. In an effort for renewal and reform Wesley advocated a practical religion, a religion of the heart and of personal experience. He became convinced of the importance and benefits of hymn singing as he was crossing the Atlantic together with a group of Moravians, whose habit was to sing hymns with great enthusiasm.[2] Henceforth, Wesley became an active promoter and publisher of hymns. The hymns he published covered the whole gamut of Christian experience. Wesley's efforts in favor of hymn singing were driven by a twofold motivation: spiritual renewal and artistic renewal. He saw in hymn singing an important ally to preaching. He also emphasized how important it was for hymns to be relevant to present times. Thus, he freely borrowed tunes from Lutheran chorales, from classical music, and from operatic airs.[3] The artistic qualities of the hymns, both in text and tune, were paramount to him. Out of a concern for improved hymn singing, Wesley published a list of directions for singing.[4]

One century later another revivalist, General William Booth (1829-1912)—who was also the founder of the Salvation Army—reproduced Wesley's experience. As part of the Revivalist Reform Movement in England, which spread to the United States as the Second Great Awakening movement, General Booth was also burdened by the suffering of those who were poor. He dedicated his ministry to the outcasts of society and to people living in the slums. The singing of hymns was then, as it still is today, an essential part of the Salvation Army's ministry. Booth understood how important it was for the people to be able to join in the singing immediately. In his recommendations for good singing, he comments on the importance of a good tune: "Let it be a good *tune* to begin with. I don't care much whether you call it secular or sacred. I rather enjoy robbing the devil of his choice tunes. . . . Let us have a real tune, that is, a melody with some distinct air in it, that one can take hold of, which people can learn, nay, which makes them learn it, which takes hold of them and goes on humming in the mind until they have mastered it. That is the sort of tune to help you; it will preach to you, and bring you believers and converts."[5]

As did so many before him, Booth also borrowed from or imitated the popular tunes of his time. While this was offensive for many ears, as it had been in the past, he followed closely in Luther's footsteps. In his Christmas address to the readers of the *War Cry*, he writes: "Music is to the soul what wind is to the ship, blowing her onwards in the direction in which she is steered. . . . Not allowed to sing *that* tune or *this* tune? Indeed! Secular music, do you say? Belongs to the devil. Does it? Well, if it did I would plunder him of it. . . . Every note, and every strain, and every harmony is divine and belongs to us."[6]

The same attitude may be observed in the nineteenth-century revival movements that produced what were to become the greatest contributions of North America to Christian hymnody, along with the Black spirituals: the camp meeting songs and gospel songs. Pressed by the necessity to effectively reach frontier people, that is, the unchurched and often uneducated and illiterate, hymns had to be simple and easy to memorize. Emotionalism was not seen as negative, but, on the contrary, as an important means by which to reach the hearts of the people.[7] The words of these songs came in the simplest language. The tunes were simple and folklike, easy to teach by rote, and contagious. Catchy refrains became a staple element because they allowed everyone to join in wholeheartedly.

The camp meeting era contributed greatly to breaking down the barriers between Black and White America. The result was cross-fertilization between the camp meeting songs and the Black spirituals and gospel songs, the traditional African-American folk repertoire. This influence was ultimately to reach beyond the borders of North America and affect hymn singing in Christian churches all around the world.

The mounting increase of popular and folk elements in nineteenth-century hymnody is a striking phenomenon. A look at the political and cultural backgrounds will help to obtain a better understanding of the sweeping success and influence of popular music during the twentieth century and today, in both secular and sacred settings.

The Romantic era (nineteenth century) was ushered in by the French Revolution in 1789. The impact of the French Revolution went far beyond the political realm to encompass the social and cultural aspects of life. The *people* were now given a voice to speak, and that voice was indeed listened to. This resulted in a wealth of output of hymns and songs by the people and for the people. Matters of worship and music were no longer the exclusive privilege of the professionals. Worship and music were now in the hands of the common people, who drew their melodies from the rich repertoire of their own heritage, namely, folk and popular music. At the same time, there was a movement away from corporate expression in religion and toward a more individual expression of the *true self.* Subjectivity triumphed over objectivity, emotion and imagination over intellect and judgment. This trend can easily be observed in the texts of the nineteenth-century hymns, camp meeting songs, and gospel songs. These times and circumstances mark the beginnings of the popular music trend.

Yet the emancipation of the popular element was not the only characteristic in church music during the nineteenth century. Romanticism, with its emphasis on all things natural and organic, stimulated a renewed interest in the past. The things of the past were seen as representative of anything original, pure, and unaltered. Things of the past also appeared as shrouded in an atmosphere of mystery and were often associated with spiritual qualities. From there, it took only one step to declare the superior nature of the past over the present, glorify it, and lift it above the present. The trend to unearth music from the past[8] and reintroduce it to the masses can be observed for the first time during the Romantic era. Before the nineteenth century, concerts and musical events featured works by contemporary composers. With the exception of plainchant and performances given in the papal chapel, it would not have occurred to a musician to think of performing a work by a past musician for a concert or church service. Johann Sebastian Bach labored his whole life to produce a new cantata for every Sunday morning, allowing himself only occasionally to borrow parts from his own previous works.

This new interest in past music fostered an initiative of church music reform. It not only brought about the unearthing of past masterworks but was, at the same time, a reaction to the growing influence of popular styles in church services. Several reform efforts sprang up over Europe: the Cecilian movement in Germany, the Oxford movement in England, and, in France, the revival of plainchant at the abbey of Solesmes. A common feature of all these reform movements was their interest in the music of the past. This was the time of revival of the music of the great past masters, especially Palestrina, Johann Sebastian Bach, and George Frideric Handel. There was also a return to the medieval Roman Breviary and the old hymns of the past, from the Middle Ages to more modern times. Old hymns were being translated from Greek, Latin, and German and were made available to churches.[9] In reaction to the trend toward a popular or folk music style, found among contemporary evangelical groups, these reformers advocated a *high church* spirit, rein-troducing rituals and vestments, anthems and canticles. The reform move-ment was, in particular, associated with the official churches, such as the Roman Catholic Church in continental Europe and the Anglican Church in England. Its influence, however, soon reached other denominations, in-cluding some evangelical ones. The situation was comparable to a feud be-tween the *established* church and the *evangelical* church. The established church emphasized musical tradition and tried to ensure the respect and at-tention of the educated public. The evangelical church favored emotions and persuasion, and adopted popular culture in order to be close to the people.

The consequences of this were far-reaching. The development of two sep-arate strands of church music created a rift that kept widening as time went by. This rift is still with us today in a remarkable manner, and very much re-sponsible for the disagreements and disputes over music in our churches. The same issues are at stake now as were at stake during the church's early experiences with music: the ignorance of the principle of balance between the vertical and the horizontal and a reticence to accept the challenge of this tension. While the so-called high church adepts invoke the holiness of the moment of worship, the protagonists of popular music emphasize the importance of the people in worship. It is the age-old dispute about appro-priateness and relevancy. They are seen as two separate, unreconcilable ele-ments for worship rather than as two complementary factors in the process of adoration. One side sacrifices the people to the cause; the other side opts for the people at the expense of the cause.

This was the state of church music and congregational singing around the middle of the twentieth century. That time was also witness to the awakening of contemporary Christian music, which was to have a revolutionary impact in Christian denominations all around the globe.

---

[1] For a comprehensive survey of the history of Christian music and the Christian hymn, see Andrew Wilson-Dickson, The Story of Christian Music From Gregorian Chant to Black Gospel: An Illustrated Guide to all the Major Traditions of Music in Worship (Minneapolis: Fortress Press, 1996).

[2] The Moravians were the spiritual descendants of Jan Hus, the Czech reformer, and had contributed a large number of hymns and hymnals to Christian hymnody; cf. Nola Reed Knouse, "Moravians, music of," Sec. 2: "The Renewed Moravian Church," *Grove Music*

Online, L. Macy, ed., http://grovemusic.com, accessed July 15, 2007.

[3] See, for instance, No. 122 in *The Seventh-day Adventist Hymnal,* "Hark! the Herald Angels Sing." This is a melody taken from Felix Mendelssohn's choral work *"Festgesang,"* written for the 1840 Gutenberg festival commemorating the invention of the printing press. For a discussion of the origin of Wesley's hymn tunes, see William J. Reynolds and Milburn Price, *A Survey of Christian Hymnody* (Carol Stream, Ill.: Hope Publishing Co., 1987), p. 50; Donald P. Hustad, *Jubilate! Church Music in the Evangelical Tradition* (Carol Stream, Ill.: Hope Publishing Co., 1981), p. 127; Andrew Wilson-Dickson, *The Story of Christian Music,* p. 117; Harry Eskew and Hugh T. McElrath, *Sing With Understanding: An Introduction to Christian Hymnology,* 2nd ed., rev. and expanded (Nashville: Church Street Press, 1995), pp. 139, 140.

[4] See his preface to the 1761 collection *Select Hymns,* quoted in David W. Music, pp. 138, 139. In comparing Wesley's recommendations for singing with those given later by Ellen G. White, we find many parallels and correspondences, an indication of Ellen G. White's early association with the Methodist Church.

[5] General William Booth, "Good Singing," *The Christian Mission Magazine,* 9 (August 1877): 205.

[6] Booth, "A Merry Christmas," *War Cry,* No. 53, London, December 23, 1880.

[7] This was also true for the early Seventh-day Adventist Church. See Ronald D. Graybill, "Enthusiasm in Early Adventist Worship," *Ministry,* October 1991, pp. 10-12. Early Seventh-day Adventist hymnody also has its examples of borrowing tunes from the secular scene or of adopting secular style. The hymn "Land of Light," with a text by Uriah Smith, was set to the tune "Old Folks at Home," by Stephen Foster, included in the 1858 *Supplement* to the 1855 hymnal (see James R. Nix, *Early Advent Singing* [Hagerstown, Md.: Review and Herald Publishing Assn., 1994], p. 99).

[8] This is the time of the first historical editions of complete works of composers. First among them were the works of Palestrina, Johann Sebastian Bach, and George Frideric Handel.

[9] See especially the 1859-1861 collection *Hymns Ancient and Modern for Use in the Services of the Church: With Accompanying Tunes,* William Henry Monk, ed. (London: Novello and Co., 1861), put together with the collaboration of John Henry Newman, John Mason Neale, and Catherine Winckworth. For a more recent edition of this collection of hymns, see *Hymns Ancient and Modern Revised* (London: William Clowes and Sons, 1950).

PART FOUR
The Contemporary Challenge

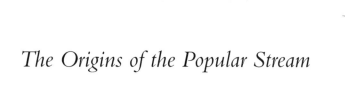

CHAPTER 15

{ *The Origins of the Popular Stream* }

I n many churches contemporary worship music is either tolerated as a nuisance and plague of our time or ignored, if not outright prohibited as an agent of Satan to lead the church to perdition. Some, though, welcome it as a refreshing, enriching part of the service. The controversy is certainly present, to varying degrees of intensity or loudness. One fact is true: contemporary worship music is here to stay. It is spreading more and more into churches, getting a stronghold in many of them and sometimes even becoming the exclusive style of music used during worship.

People react in different ways to such a situation. Some reject its reality and fool themselves into believing that one just has to live through it and it will disappear with the next generation. Others try to understand the phenomenon in its context, find out where it comes from and how it functions, and then, eventually, propose answers and attitudes that will help deal with the situation from a biblical standpoint.

We have seen that the issues the church struggles with today are not new. We have also discovered how theology has shaped musical understanding and practice throughout the ages and how music actually became an expression of theology. The question, then, should be asked about the relationship between theology and music today: How does contemporary worship music reflect theology, and how can theology impact Christian worship music?

The origins of the popular stream

One of the events that opened the path to popular music in the church was the liturgical reform introduced by Vatican Council II on December 4, 1963, with the document called "The Constitution on the Sacred Liturgy."[1]

The reform continued according to the examples of past reformers and moved away from the uses of Latin language and Gregorian chant during liturgical services, encouraging the use of vernacular language, popular melodies, and instruments.[2] What happened here was a grassroots movement in which music was made by the people and for the people. The new way to make music in the church spread like fire, not only through the Catholic Church but also into other mainstream denominations. The advent of a number of religious and/or spiritual movements characteristic of the 1970s and beyond contributed to the strengthening of the new trend.

Under the impact of both the Jesus movement and the Charismatic movement in the 1960s and 1970s, a shift in emphasis happened in matters of spiritual authority, from church and Scripture to an increased role of the Holy Spirit.[3] This trend intensified in subsequent years with a strong interest in mysticism and spirituality. Personal expression and experience became an essential characteristic of one's faith.

Moreover, the influence of evangelicalism and postmodernism can be observed in many churches today.[4] Evangelicalism brought with it a certain shift in emphasis from spiritual transformation to spiritual encouragement, from a rational approach to religion to a predominantly emotional one, and from collective faith to personal faith, accompanied by a simplification of truth that comes with a domesticated, user-friendly God.

Postmodernism shapes us as believers, though we might not even be aware of it. Postmodernism puts the emphasis on the individual and, as such, emphasizes the individual character of religion. Spirituality may be seen as separate from institutional and moral entities. Established values are challenged on the observation that they fall short of contributing to a true and authentic way of life and to a just and equitable society. The failure to see the traditional values shape the lives of those who preach them results in relativism, cynicism, and deconstructionism. Rational knowledge is now acquired under the control of personal intuition and experience, and communication happens best through narrative that moves the whole being rather than through abstract universal principles. What counts is that the message comes through, a message that touches the core of the individual and becomes a real experience. Tradition, authority, or anything else is irrelevant. But does this necessarily mean that the postmodern generation is sentimental and superficial, and relies only on subjective values?

Contemporary worship music (CWM) is often dismissed as superficial and sentimental, and seen as an expression of the postmodern spirit. Here again, a number of misconceptions and inconsistencies need to be dispelled before we can make any statements on the *value* of CWM. Indeed, heart searching and desire for an informed approach must happen on both sides of the fence. Too much mutual contempt or ignorance has created mistrust and misuse in churches with regard to CWM. What is needed is an objective assessment of the style of music—its strengths and challenges, as well as its role and appropriateness in the context of worship.

---

[1] *The Constitution on the Sacred Liturgy of the Second Vatican Council and The Motu Proprio of Pope Paul VI* (Glen Rock, N.J.: Paulist Press, 1964).

[2] *Ibid.*, see especially pp. 43, 49, and chapter 6, "Sacred Music," pp. 67-70.

[3] See James F. White, *Protestant Worship: Traditions in Transition* (Louisville, Ky.: Westminster/John Knox Press, 1989), p. 192.

[4] It is not the purpose of this study to provide an in-depth look at these two currents. We will limit ourselves to a number of key concepts necessary for a better understanding of the following discussion, being fully aware, though, that such an approach must, by necessity, remain schematic.

CHAPTER 16

{ *Dissipating the Misunderstandings* }

One of the greatest misunderstandings in the discussion of contemporary worship music is the belief that today's youth want to hear exclusively the contemporary style of music in the church. A recent survey
among the college-age attendees of Pioneer Memorial Church, on the campus of Andrews University in Michigan, revealed a great eclecticism in matters of musical tastes and preferences.[1] While there was a strong desire for
the presence of contemporary components in the worship service, the great
majority of students still wanted to maintain the traditional hymns, organ,
and choir music.

A similar reaction was observed during a popular Seventh-day Adventist
Christian rock band's tour in California a few years ago. In some places
where the band offered church services in the contemporary style, the youth
came up at the end and said: "We don't want this kind of music for worship."[2]

In the minds of the younger generation there is no desire to throw out
the past completely and feed only on the present. There is, however, a need
for something they can identify with, something that is not entirely remote
from their daily musical experiences—something that will enable them to
infuse their everyday with the sacred, and something that closes the wide
gap between the secular and the sacred. By excluding the contemporary musical style from church, one creates the misconception that there is music
for Sabbath (sacred) and then there is music for the rest of the days of the
week (secular). Doing so contributes to the rift between the secular and the
sacred instead of encouraging the musicians to infuse the secular with the
sacred and transform the secular for appropriate use in church.

The desire for and openness to a plurality of styles is very characteristic of today's culture. There is a range of interests that reaches from pop/rock to folk, classical, and world music. This trend stretches, as well, into the highest circles of the world of classical music.[3] Musical interest today is *global*. This newly understood value of diversity has also found a voice in church music. A number of hymnals published nowadays combine a selection of both the best and most popular traditional hymns with new contemporary worship songs that were carefully selected.[4]

Maintaining the historical role of hymn singing is indeed an essential component of a healthy congregation. The believers' faith does not function within a historical void, but is shaped and formed by the past experiences of the church. If we ignore this past, we cut ourselves off from our roots. In order to grow into a beautiful plant, we need to be connected to our roots. The old hymns tell us about the joys and struggles of our forefathers and serve as a link between the believers of today and the believers throughout the church's history. On the other hand, being steeped in the musical language of one's own times is just as essential to a meaningful worship experience. A healthy religious experience looks to both the past and the present as it becomes a dynamic experience. This is also the lesson learned from Scripture.[5]

A second step, when approaching contemporary style, is to distinguish between contemporary Christian music (CCM) and contemporary worship music.[6] Contemporary Christian music is music that happens primarily in extraliturgical situations. It is meant for personal listening and enjoyment or for evangelistic outreach through concert venues. Contemporary worship music, on the other hand, refers to music with a particular function within a liturgical setting. The two genres fulfill roles that are essentially distinct from each other. One is primarily oriented toward personal enrichment and enjoyment, while the other is primarily worship oriented. The use of CCM songs during worship can add a problem of a practical nature. CCM songs are primarily written for solo performance during concert settings and often feature more complex melodic contour and direction, greater rhythmic intricacies, an overall irregular structure, and elaborate instrumental interludes. These do not respond to the basic criteria of group singing, in which one expects a song with a melody that shows enough regularity to be easy to follow or remember, and sufficient returns to previous materials in order to create familiarity. When CCM songs are used for congregational worship, a sudden drop in the participation and enthusiasm of the singing can easily be observed. This is mainly caused by a feeling of insecurity on the part of the worshippers as to the direction the melody is going to take. Such songs must undergo a substantial adaptation process before they become effective for congregational worship.

A final step in introducing our study of contemporary style is to establish the difference between the traditional hymn and the contemporary praise song. Criticism directed against contemporary praise songs often mentions their lack of theological depth, even though many of them are indeed using scriptural texts. There is a time to learn in church and to remember biblical teachings through song—this is traditionally the role of the hymn. But there is also a time to give praise and pour out our hearts in worship—this is done through the praise song.

Diversity in church song is as old as the Bible. Paul advised the church to sing psalms, hymns, and spiritual songs (Ephesians 5:19). The hymn has been recognized, from its earliest times, as a didactic tool, a means of teaching and spreading doctrine and truth.[7] This was also the purpose of the "teaching" psalms. Some other psalms, however, illustrate the more personal and emotional character of adoration and present early examples of praise songs, expressions of the heart and soul of the poet.[8] Closer to our time, the camp meeting and gospel songs were a pure expression of the soul, meant to touch, primarily, the hearts of the sinners. There is, then, no valid reason to belittle praise songs with the excuse that they do not teach theology. Both hymns and praise songs are needed in worship, and both have their raison d'être.

All musical ages and musical styles have real geniuses, as well as those who pretend to be geniuses. There is shallowness to be found in praise songs. There is also shallowness to be found in certain hymns which, nevertheless, enjoy great popularity among congregations. Let us not forget that the hymns in traditional hymnals have already passed the test of time. At one point, though, additional hymns existed that—poetically and musically speaking—were found to be on the cheap, shallow side and, therefore, did not survive to be in publication today. CWM style deserves to be granted the same trial of time before we throw the baby out with the bathwater.

While there are cheap texts and poor musical style within CWM, there are also a great number of gems to be found.

---

[1] The last of such surveys was conducted in April 2007.

[2] This statement was received by the author on the occasion of a personal conversation with the band leader during the late 1990s.

[3] See, for instance, the latest musical concerts and recordings by Itzhak Perlman, Yo-Yo Ma, Luciano Pavarotti, Joshua Bell, and many others.

[4] Cf., for instance, the hymnals *Renew! Songs and Hymns for Blended Worship* (Carol Stream, Ill.: Hope Publishing, 1995), and *Sing! a New Creation* (Grand Rapids: Calvin Institute of Christian Worship and CRC Publication; New York: Reformed Church Press, 2001), which combine songs from the traditional hymn repertoire, worship songs from various cultures in several languages, and praise songs.

If a church chooses to use contemporary worship songs outside of a hymnal, permission must be obtained from Christian Copyright Licensing International (CCLI). Their Internet site can be accessed at www.ccli.com. Licensing is available for four regions: Africa, Asia-Pacific, Europe, and North America. For a relatively small yearly license fee, churches can download songs (lyrics and music with chords) that are ready in PowerPoint format.

[5] See "The Old and the New," pp. 103, 104 of this book. See also Ephesians 5:19, in which Paul enjoins the believers to sing not only hymns (the new), but also psalms and spiritual songs (the old).

[6] The term was coined by John Frame in the title of his book *Contemporary Worship Music: A Biblical Defense* (Phillipsburg, N.J.: P&R Publishing, 1997).

[7] See final paragraph of "The New Testament Church," p. 147 of this book.

[8] See "The Psalms as a Model for Worship Music," pp. 101, 102 of this book.

CHAPTER 17

The Strengths of Contemporary Worship Music (CWM)

O ne of the great strengths of CWM lies in its lyrics. Often, the lyrics were taken directly from the Scriptures,[1] either literally or slightly paraphrased. Singing them has brought back the old and forgotten practice of memorizing Scripture, this time not in a mechanical way, but through the fibers of the heart, renewing a love for the Word of God. Other songs address age-old human needs in a fresh and modern language. Modern language for church song has moved away from the often heroic, military, pompous, and triumphalist language of the nineteenth century. What characterizes today's language is its simplicity and directness, its straightforwardness and intelligibility to everybody.

The same qualities of simplicity and directness can be found in the musical language of CWM. Our "traditional" ears are trained to respond to the traditional sounds of melodies from the seventeenth, eighteenth, and nineteenth centuries. Most traditional tunes have one common quality: they are very predictable! You hear the beginning, and you can almost guess the ending.[2] Twentieth-century music, especially classical music, has contributed in manifold ways to changing and expanding the melodic style, as well as rhythmic invention and diversity. These elements, in their updated forms, are found in the melodies of CWM. Unusual turns and a joyful, fresh, colorful character that moves away from the established formal and harmonic patterns are some of the elements that characterize modern melodies. One term very well summarizes the new musical style: *unpredictability*.[3] This creates surprise and a challenge, and eventually fosters more attention in participation.

Contemporary songs are often criticized for their repetitiveness. However, the principle of repetition is a very old and proven principle of teaching.

When used with good taste and moderation, repetition fulfills its original purpose well, making it easier to learn the song and to involve everybody. The technique is especially useful for singing in larger groups of people. But repetition is also an expression—ever so subtle—of our desperate yearning for something we desire with all our hearts. Repeated expression intensifies and heightens the vividness and urgency of the plea or statement. In traditional worship this is known as a litany. A litany is a prayer that is repeated again and again because it flows out of a desperate heart: it seems that the only relief this heart can obtain is through constant repetition of the petition. The principle of repetition is present in the refrains we sing in certain hymns. There are biblical examples of such repetition in song, especially in the psalms. The basic poetic structure of the psalms is built on the principle of repetition, namely, parallelism.[4] Psalm 136 is, perhaps, the most typical and extreme example.[5] This was one of the psalms sung at the inauguration of the Temple of Solomon (see 2 Chronicles 5:13). In Psalm 136, after each half verse of the psalm is delivered by the solo singer, the congregation is called to repeat the same phrase again and again: "His love endures forever." On the other hand, the technique of repetition can also be abused. It should never be used in a mechanical way, as a means to manipulate worshippers into a certain emotional or spiritual state. Repetition is meant to enrich, not to dumb down. Here again, appropriate application is necessary, and balance rules.

Contemporary melodies are also characterized by a very flexible rhythm. Often, the rhythm of the songs is dictated by the natural rhythm of speech, thus coming much closer to the ideal of simplicity and directness. In addition, contemporary songs feature a flexibility of phrase structure that pertains more to prose than to poetry. This does not mean they lose poetic quality. There is more to poetry than metric feet and rhyme. The irregular phrase lengths of these songs contribute, again, to their unpredictable and, therefore, fresh and new character.

The instruments associated with CWM make it possible for many a young musician to use his/her talent to the glory of God. Most of these instruments are affordable; they can actually be bought without spending a fortune (which is not the case for a piano or an organ). The instruments used in CWM are also accessible in terms of learning to play, and they can be carried around easily. In other words, they correspond to the economic and social possibilities of this generation of musicians. In addition, these instruments reflect practices found in today's mainstream music making.

I believe it is important to consider these aspects of CWM, because they represent a reality that enables young musicians to contribute to the service of God with their own tools—the instruments belonging to this generation. The young people should be able to worship God through their own languages, both verbal and musical. The youth desire, and need to have, a place and role to fulfill in the church, so that they can bring the gift of themselves—who they are and where they stand—and of their talents, in whichever venue they excel.

Finally, another strength of CWM is musical creativity. It is true that this can become one of CWM's major challenges as well. Musical creativity is also often overlooked because it mostly happens behind the scenes. Many pastors and people in the congregation are not aware of the fact that the major part of the music they hear is actually the product of individual and collective creativity. The scores for contemporary worship music usually come with just the melody line and very basic chord symbols. Choice of instruments, orchestration, harmonization, accompaniment patterns, descants (embellishing parts) for additional instruments, and segues (musical bridges) between the songs are all the product of musicianship and creativity on the part of the music team. This is also the reason instrumentalists and singers are so vulnerable to criticism. Playing, singing, and leading out in contemporary worship require more than just playing or singing from a preexisting score. They demand musical imagination, excellent musicianship, discriminating taste, familiarity with a wide range of musical styles, high instrumental skills, trained voices, and leadership abilities in order to create a meaningful musical texture from a simple melodic line. When those abilities are present, worship through music will draw the congregation into a meaningful, inspired, wholesome, and lasting experience.

---

[1] Cf. "Seek Ye First the Kingdom of God" (Matthew 6:33; Deuteronomy 8:3; Matthew 7:7); "As the Deer" (Psalm 42:1, 2); "Behold, What Manner of Love" (1 John 3:1); etc.

[2] This is the result of a long practice of melodic and harmonic writing in symmetric fashion, with antecedent and consequent musical phrases.

[3] There is a limit, though, to the efficiency of unpredictability. Congregational songs, in

order to function well, require a patterned structure that allows for returns or allusions to previous musical phrases. The unpredictability factor should not prevent people from sensing or remembering where the melody is going. If the song is structured so freely that it never returns to familiar phrases (principle of familiarity), but constantly meanders in a new direction, people will hesitate to join the singing or will be prevented from investing themselves fully in the experience. After all, singing is meant to be done with full heart and voice!

[4] See "The New Testament Church," p. 147 of this book, for an explanation of parallelism in Psalms and its impact on singing.

[5] See also Psalms 67 and 107.

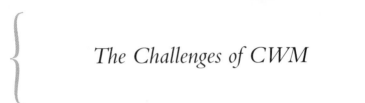

CHAPTER 18

The Challenges of CWM

The challenges presented in this section are the same as for any other style of music used in church, including classical or traditional style. Many of the criticisms actually address basic rules to be observed in any style of church music. It is true, though, that CWM styles are more prone to certain challenges because of their close connection to commercial popular genres.

The youth generation is willing and eager to bring its talents to the church. The youth come the way they are, at the present stages of their musical abilities, with a great deal of enthusiasm and conviction. Too often, they have not yet had the opportunity, or even the idea, to reflect about the purpose of their music making in church or the nature of worship. On the other hand, the church often does not fulfill its role of modeling worship to the young people as they attend the service every week. For many youth, church means fellowship and meeting and spending time with friends. For them, the focus in worship is on the human aspect rather than on the divine element. In addition, most are not informed about the musician's duty and responsibility to convey the message of worship to the congregation faithfully, truthfully, and specifically through the musical language he or she chooses. Moreover, not every young musician is well trained and understands the need for high musical standards. In the majority of cases his or her training took place in a very informal and casual manner through observation and emulation of secular music performances or of the CCM concert scene. Their music making, then, needs to be adapted and transformed for the new occasion, equipped with truth in order to reflect a correspondence and harmony between the principles that govern worship and the way worship actions or expressions are shaped.

In dealing with CWM, the challenge of *truth* can be found on several levels of the musical offering in church: truth in theology, truth in music, truth in performance, and truth in attitude.

Truth in Theology

In the context of worship the song lyrics are of paramount importance. In a religious setting the purpose of singing has always been to teach, to remember, or to express various moods or emotions. The purpose of the music of these songs or hymns is to drive the teachings even deeper into the hearts, minds, and memories of the worshippers. Lyrics must, therefore, be probed not only for their theological correctness but also for their depth, meaningfulness, directness, and poetic quality. Content cannot be separated from form—beautiful and well structured form conveys the message in a more effective and powerful way.

One of the great criticisms expressed against CWM by its adversaries is the shallowness and emptiness of its textual content, religious sentimentality, and I-centeredness. As happens with every movement of renewal—popular as well as traditional—a great number of new songs are composed, and one needs to go through the natural process of weeding through this forest of materials in search of only the best, trying to separate the grain from the chaff, the substantial and rich texts from the shallow and empty ones.

The problem is one not only of depth versus shallowness. Several voices among the contemporary Christian musicians have also raised the issue of specificity or distinctiveness of the gospel message: "The lyrics of a good number of the songs don't betray anything specifically Christian—they may have some moral message, but not a lot of the big songs are identifiably Christian. . . . There is an essential part of the gospel that's not ever going to sell. The gospel is good news, but it is also bad news"[1] (Michael Card, singer, songwriter). "What's critically important about Christian music is its distinctiveness. If it loses the Cross, if it loses Christ, if it becomes just 'positive pop,' then I'd rather be cut off from it. I just can't imagine anything more insipid"[2] (Steve Taylor, alternative rock musician). "I look at the majority of the [contemporary Christian] music I hear today and think it's virtually meaningless"[3] (Stan Moser, former CEO of Word Records). "If I have one criticism of contemporary Christian music, it is this: The life of the mind is gasping for breath. If anything, Christians should be about the life of the mind. We should be the most thinking people in the world. I'm disturbed that CCM lyric content does not reflect that"[4] (Charlie Peacock, singer, songwriter, producer).

These various reflections and opinions about the lyrics of CCM shed light upon a crucial challenge that exists within the contemporary scene—the specificity and depth of the message carried by the songs. They underline how important it is to make theologically informed and artistically sound decisions with regard to the choice of song lyrics. This issue needs to be addressed seriously by contemporary worship musicians in order for contemporary church music to find a respectable place within the repertoire of the church. The choice of songs is more than a matter of personal preference or approximate general agreement with the church's beliefs. The theological truth of the church is at stake here, as is the spiritual well-being and growth of the congregation. This reality challenges the musician to reach beyond his/her musical or poetic skills and to become informed and proficient in matters of biblical and theological truth as well as worship in general, in order to be able to make sound decisions from the perspective of a true and meaningful worship.[5]

Truth in Music

In today's culture, when there is music, it is often playing in the background. Very rarely do we concentrate exclusively on *listening to* and *hearing* the music. Music surrounds us at every moment of the day. We hear music in stores, at the doctor's or dentist's office, at airports, in restaurants, when waiting on the phone, as we are driving, when we are studying or working at our computers, etc. Music has lost its meaning and message and has become a mere "wrapping" for all sorts of activities. In order to find truth in music, we need to redeem the consistency between the message carried by the text and the message carried by the musical style. We need to rediscover and understand that music speaks a language of its own, independently of the words, and that the listener interprets this language according to conventions that have been taught formally or informally. As was shown earlier when discussing Ezra Pound's reflections on art, truth in music is perfect harmony between the message carried by the text and the message carried by the music. In a time when distortion of truth is commonplace in the media and elsewhere, this is not an easy task. Truth in music starts with the musician's personal striving for authenticity regarding the nature of his or her faith. Truth in music has to do with the nature and quality with which the musician presents music in worship. And finally, truth in music concerns the way our music genuinely (faithfully) translates and expresses our beliefs in an artistically truthful way.

In a first step toward true music in worship, then, it becomes important to remember the worship values: to be aware of the special character of the occasion (the focus on God), of the particular mood of the worship moment (adoration, praise, confession, thanksgiving), and of the group of people who will participate in this musical offering (the congregation). Then comes the issue of appropriate musical expression. I am purposely avoiding here the term *musical style*, because the quest for appropriateness should happen *within* every musical style—it is not a matter of choice *between* musical styles.

But there is more. When dealing with art—church music is art, too—authenticity passes through aesthetic quality. In order to convey truth, art must be good art, that is, well articulated, flowing freely, and able to carry a message clearly. Translated into practical terms, this means, for the singer, a good mastery of the voice as an instrument and the ability to carry a tune and to project and sustain sound. It also means clear intonation, a sense for nuance and expressiveness, and the competence to communicate with a congregation. For the instrumentalist, it means drawing on a variety of playing styles, knowing the rules of composition or improvisation, and expressing every nuance of the moods of the text. Aesthetic quality also implies clearly articulating the various stages of the musical speech and addressing and communicating with the congregation through one's instrument. A good musician will broaden his/her exposure to include a variety of styles in order to develop high taste and standards and a sense for adequacy.

Only when these three factors concur—genuine faith, appropriate music, and high aesthetic standards—will the musician achieve truth in music and bring a musical offering "pleasing to him [God]" (Psalm 104:34).

Truth in Performance

Any worship experience implies a live offering on the part of the worshipper (Romans 12:1); the worshipper offers his/her heart, mind, and soul. It is because of this very personal aspect of the worship experience that people still come physically to the worship service instead of merely watching it from their living room or bedroom on television. Similarly, a musical performance during worship is more than just delivering music. It is a gift of the whole person that, in the context of worship, takes on the character of an *offering* of oneself and of one's talents. The true personal, individual, and live character of this offering remains an important factor in relationship to worship.

As we consider music in worship as an offering from a perspective that accounts for modern technology, we need to be aware of a certain number of philosophical issues that surround this situation.

Technological Enhancement

The use of technology has become a hallmark of popular music culture. It is hard to imagine a popular musical performance without amplification and mixing. These techniques have also found their way into the church. Electronic enhancement is necessary for two reasons: to amplify sound in a large building so that everybody can hear and understand, and to create balance between the singers and instrumentalists. The purpose of these electronic tools is not to "overdrive" the production and blow it up to larger dimensions with throbbing basses and dominating rhythmic sections. It is not to favor one instrumental group over another or over the singers. It is, rather, to ensure a clear and prominent perception of the human voices that carry the text, leaving the instruments to their role of surrounding, enhancing, and commenting expressively on the message of the text. We should never lose sight of the central place of the Word in the worship service.

As a result of modern technology, talent has become almost superfluous in music. Stage presence and attitude are often mistaken for talent, and mixing and amplification take over where talent is missing, covering up lack of talent or preparation, and magnifying the performance to unnatural levels. Technological enhancement cannot replace talent, though. Without a naturally beautiful and well trained voice, good taste, and artistic sensitivity, even the best technological enhancement available will leave the performance sounding poor and devoid of beauty and artistry. Of course, natural talent and artistic sensitivity will not always be present in the occasional programs presented by children's Sabbath School groups or in the spontaneous musical contribution of a church member at special, more intimate occasions. What we are dealing with here is a carefully planned and organized divine service for which the musicians are asked to prepare the music so that it fits the occasion or the theme of the sermon—a service for which the musicians are called upon to *lead* a whole congregation into a spiritual experience through song and music. How often has a congregation literally been forced to listen to poor and tasteless performances from ill equipped and/or ill prepared singers and musicians? The same question should be applied, of course, to performances of classical music. How can you possibly create and sustain a worship experience with such a casual approach to what should be one of the highest moments in life? Truth in performance implies the offering of an authentic gift to God's glory, not a performance for personal glorification.

Sound Tracks

The use of sound tracks, or canned music, to accompany singers is related to the same issue of truth in performance. Sound tracks have become an ever more popular way of doing special music. It is true that they are handy when it comes to making up for the lack of instrumentalists and/or avoiding time-consuming rehearsals. And these are certainly good arguments from a practical point of view. I wonder, however, if practicality can or should become an argument in matters of worship and art. If we go for practicality, we buy ourselves a compact disk or watch the worship service on television, from the comfort of our living rooms. What makes worship so special is, precisely, the live human connection we encounter on Sabbath morning. Worship is meant to happen among physically present individuals. What makes art so special is the same human factor, the transmission or conveyance of the human soul, of a particular understanding of truth through the avenue of music enhanced by voices, facial expressions, eye contact, and other physical gestures. Without this live human dimension, there would be no more concerts and live performances. The fact that people still go to live performances shows how much the human connection still counts.

I will always remember the disappointment and anger of the audience at a performance of Tchaikovsky's ballet *Swan Lake* when it was found that the music was not performed by a live orchestra, but came from a recording instead. And I wonder, in the same way, about the possible reaction of an audience at a pop concert if the singer put on a tape to accompany him or her rather than having the band play! Everybody in the audience would feel cheated.

Even in this age of cyberculture, with its partial loss of the sense for real-life human relationships, worship is still an event—maybe one of the few left—in which we render ourselves physically and in person because we expect to enter into relationships, to connect with God and other human beings. We physically go to worship as an expression of the offering of ourselves to God, and we can expect to hear the Word of God preached by an actual human being whose physical expressions translate a very personal experience with God and His Word. Worship is still a time when we look forward to connecting personally with our fellow worshippers and to engaging in human relationships, enriching one another with our presence and experiences, witnessing our faith through our gestures, expressions, and live voices. Music making in worship enters into the same framework of a personal experience and a human relationship. If we take away the personal and live aspect of music making in worship, we destroy the human and relational aspect of music making.

But there is a still deeper reason to ponder when considering the use of sound tracks. As we compare the mechanism of worship and the mechanism of entertainment, the two procedures appear to be at opposite poles. In worship we *offer ourselves* as gifts to God in order *to please God*. In entertainment the attention is drawn *to the performer*. Because of certain musical effects and behavioral attitudes produced when using sound tracks in worship—attitudes and effects similar to the entertainment scene—there is a possibility of sending mixed messages and creating an ambiguous situation similar to the entertainment scene. The use of sound tracks is like a fine line that must be walked very carefully.

Questions, then, need to be asked. Does technological replacement of the human musical offering have the ability to lead a congregation into worship? Is there a reason to use sound tracks as long as we have the human potential to offer our music to the Lord? Is there a possibility that, because of the particular performance tools we choose, and through association with circumstances from a nonworship context, the congregation actually misinterprets our offering as a performance? Could the worshippers be led to adopt the passive attitude of spectators being entertained? How can the talents of new singers and instrumentalists be stimulated—and new vocations for them created—in the absence of live role models who, beyond musical skills, also teach worship values and worship attitudes?

I am not saying here that the use of sound tracks is inappropriate for church or that the use of sound tracks in church should stop. I think that, under certain circumstances, there is a place for them, particularly in situations in which there are no instrumentalists or singers available—and such churches do exist. A number of congregations actually use the compact disks available for hymn singing when no pianist/organist is available.[6] And these groups know very well about the artificial character of such a singing experience. The situation is not exactly the same when dealing with CWM. The use of sound tracks generally happens within the context of special music. The problem here lies not so much in the lack of available musicians, but rather in the choice of songs that come straight from the CCM concert scene. Some musicians feel pressed, as they present special music, to reproduce the same grandiose style of orchestral accompaniment as in the original performance setting. A simple performance of the song with live musicians would be perceived as poor and unartistic. Here also, tasteful and well-balanced decisions must be made. Any musician, music team, or congregation confronted with the use of sound tracks should take some time to ponder the implications of their use from the perspective of a truthful worship and a faithful character in musical performance.

Harold Best, in his book *Music Through the Eyes of Faith*,[7] refers to the use of sound tracks in church in terms of "excellence in absentia." He discusses the philosophical aspect of the bigger-than-life approach that lurks behind the use of sound tracks, as well as all the implications with regard to unethical and deceptive behavior—for instance, a sound track being used to cover up lack of talent or to create a bigger-than-life situation. Such effects carry the potential to create an impression of performance or show that can distract from a genuine worshipful atmosphere. If this reality is not always recognized as such on the part of the performer, it often is perceived this way by the congregation. Adding to the challenges, technicians sometimes fail to start a sound track at the right time, or they choose the wrong track or volume level, which causes multiple attempts at starting the piece. These situations quickly lead to the breakdown of the worship atmosphere. If, in addition, the skill of the singer is not up to the artistic quality of the sound track, the result may be a pitiful performance that ruins the worship experience not only for the singer but also for the rest of the congregation.

Could it be that we have become so used to the commercial standards of sound production that we now are looking for similar sounds during worship? Is the use of sound tracks driven by consumer needs? If this is so, then the secular is invading the sacred, because we have lost a sense for, and can no longer appreciate, the simple and natural sounds of our music making.

The use of sound tracks is certainly to be considered with much discernment and moderation. Keep in mind the essential worship principle of the musical offering—that music in worship is a live expression of the individual, meant to draw the rest of the congregation into an experience of offering *themselves*, by way of a personal communication and a relationship between the participants in worship and God.

The truth thus conveyed in live music might sound less impressive, but it will be illuminated by the live presence of the artist, carried and magnified by the conviction, emotions, and gestures that accompany the musical presentation—similar to the rays of sunshine that illuminate and animate the inert material of a stained glass window. When this happens, truth is again achieved through a harmonious blending of the faith experience and the artistic experience.

Emotional Manipulation

Congregations often express their uneasiness about emotional manipulation through music. What is in question here is the truthfulness with which the musicians lead the congregation into a spiritual journey and experience.

A popular concept in music leadership today is the repetitive use of a short musical and textual phrase in order to bring people to an emotional mood or state of surrender in which they can completely open up to the influence of the Spirit. Repetition is a basic musical technique necessary to create feelings of pleasure or comfort through familiarity. It can be found in any type of music, including the biblical psalms, at any level of complexity. However, using sustained repetition of a simple phrase with the express purpose of creating moods or emotional states is equivalent to emotional manipulation. With emotional manipulation, instead of letting the Holy Spirit act, external mechanisms are put to work to bring people to a state in which decisions are made without their full cognitive consent or control. It is part of the nature of emotions to be unstable and shifting, because they depend on external circumstances and moods. Decisions pertaining to religion should not be built upon feelings—they must take their roots deeper. Worship has always been a matter of the heart *and* the mind, the whole human being. If we purposefully shut off one or the other, our worship becomes suspicious. When we exclude the *minds* of those in our congregation from the worship experience, with the willful purpose of leading the people in a specific direction, we open avenues of deceit. Only the Holy Spirit should lead our hearts. Attempting to do so through human means, especially using such an ambiguous tool as music, would come close to dishonesty.

Truth in Attitude

Major complaints about CWM, both from within the world of CWM (musicians, producers, etc.) and from without, deal with issues of performance attitudes. Such attitudes are shown through inappropriate dress, exaggerated behavior and deportment, and/or singing and playing styles that have more to do with sentimentalism, seduction, despair, anger, and rebellion than with worship and adoration. While these questions are not exclusively related to the contemporary style and can certainly be found in performances of traditional worship music as well, they seem to be more prominent in CWM settings.

A look into the mechanism of popular music helps us understand where the problems come from. Two particularities govern popular art: (1) it is *commercial*, that is, made to sell; and (2) it is *mass mediated*, that is, advertised on a large scale through common media.[8] Moreover, today's pop culture is predominantly about people and, more specifically, about celebrity and celebrities. Fame can come from admirable achievements, as in sports or music, involving effort, discipline, and excellence. It can also come—as illustrated by the great number of talk shows, reality TV shows, or media coverage of crimes and other news—from indulgence in debasing acts and attitudes or self-glorification, such as when people expose themselves and revel in the most degrading, lewd, and antisocial behaviors, encouraging exhibitionism and narcissism. In the face of these cultural attitudes, worship values, focusing on God rather than the self, are essentially countercultural.

The cultural values that surround and shape individuals on a daily basis will naturally tend to be carried over into the church. As we discuss performance attitudes in church, we will better understand where they come from if we place them in their general cultural context. On the other hand, to consider these attitudes in the context of true worship values will help to correct and transform them.

High principled contemporary artists find it more and more difficult to resist the requirements of producers for a more commercial production style. Even when dealing with religious music, recording companies need and want to sell. As a result, a series of internal criticisms have been voiced on the part of a number of contemporary Christian artists and others who function as pastors to these artists.

In an interview in the May 20, 1996, issue of *Christianity Today,* Michael Card and Steve Taylor expressed concerns about the celebrity-driven, competitive, and commercial trends happening on the contemporary Christian music scene: "Now, the industry is celebrity-driven. The song is almost irrelevant. The focus is on the person. . . . There's no community in Christian music, but instead there's competition, commercialism, and individualism"[9] (Michael Card). "The artist drives a lot of what we see. I've been busy for the past couple of weeks and have noticed how easy it is to start thinking that the people around me exist to serve me, and they've got no other life. We can develop this huge sense of self-importance"[10] (Steve Taylor). Scotty Smith, pastor to many Nashville musicians, supported the same view: "One of the curses of contemporary Christian music is 'celebrityism.' This has created an environment that feeds the very things against which the Scripture warns us. . . . The church must also be willing to raise a prophetic voice against 'celebrityism.'"[11]

Beyond the influence of the cultural context, the way people were trained in the musical art also plays a role in the way their music making is carried out in church. A great number of contemporary Christian musicians are self-trained, learning through observation of artists in concert settings, in super-churches, on TV shows, or from books and magazines. It is, then, only natural that beyond the music, instrumental skills, and vocal skills, these musicians also adopt and imitate the commercial attitudes of entertainment and show business, featuring spectacular theatrical, show driven, and consumer oriented techniques, attitudes, and expressions. Such attitudes have great audience appeal, and musicians feel encouraged by listeners to practice them, learning to put themselves into the spotlight. Particularities of behavior become one of the major stumbling blocks in the field of special music when the solo performer, instrumentalist or singer, is particularly vulnerable to inappropriate attitudes.

Classical musicians are as vulnerable to these excesses as contemporary Christian artists. Anyone "performing" for an audience (including preachers!) needs a good dose of self-awareness, at least out of respect for the listeners. A healthy sense of drama and expression is also in order if one is to be able to capture the attention of the audience and carry it through the many moods of a piece of music. The danger of self-exaltation always lurks right around the corner though. In worship, on the contrary, the paradigm is entirely reversed, and that is why difficulties and problems arise.

In worship the music is God-centered, and the musician becomes a servant of God and of the community. In worship the music becomes an offering, a gift presented through surrender of one's talent to the One who bestowed it upon him or her in the beginning. Dramatic attitude changes into humility and a spirit of service. Self-awareness is translated into God-awareness, and a performance is turned into an offering.

Musicians must be changed into church musicians. As long as musicians are asked to participate in worship in the role of musician, they will do music in the spirit in which they have been trained, namely, as professional musicians or as popular musicians. There is, then, a need to train and make musicians—traditional as well as contemporary ones—aware of the particular setting and occasion of worship and the ways worship music's purpose is set apart from ordinary music making's goal, namely, audience enjoyment or entertainment. Part of the responsibility for the present state of matters lies on the shoulders of pastors who may not have conveyed—through their ways of conducting worship—a genuine understanding of worship. The first duty of the church musician, traditional or contemporary, is to learn about worship and about his or her function and role as a musician within the congregation. As the musician grows in his/her own spiritual journey, the inner transformation that takes place, as well as the coming to a full understanding of the particular character of the occasion, naturally leads to a reconsideration of one's attitudes, gestures, and styles of playing and singing.[12] The musician becomes, then, a church musician. The eventual result is an adaptation and transformation of the mainstream musical practices into true worship music. It is this transformation of the heart of the musician that will guide him or her in finding the appropriate expression *within* a given style.

Associations

Issues related to the ideas of truth in performance and truth in attitude are sensitive points because of associations. The elements of any performance style used in worship, including those of the classical style, are inevitably associated with a secular counterpart. Performance manners in CWM—attitude, playing style, and instruments—are even more vulnerable to a comparison because of their association with secular pop culture. Additional care and attention are in order, then, when using contemporary style in worship.

There is no need to enter again into a lengthy discussion on associations.[13] One should be aware, though, that the impact of associations in the context of worship cannot be emphasized enough. Music's purpose is to *lead* people into worship, and no one should be hindered or prevented from worshipping because of inappropriate associations. Associations should be given careful examination and consideration by worship leaders, musicians, and worship committees. Most of the issues that churches have with contemporary style are directly related to associations with popular music culture. For this reason, too, the most vulnerable part of the praise experience is the special music, since it is more prone to be presented with secular performance attitudes and behaviors. A sensitive, considerate, and prayerful approach to these issues is the best advocate for the place of CWM in Seventh-day Adventist churches.

Concluding Remarks

As we contemplate the use of contemporary style in church and consider its various strengths and challenges, it becomes clear that the introduction of contemporary style must be governed by an informed and responsible attitude. Wisdom, prayer, and discernment are needed in order to make the right decisions with regard to words and music, the adoption of an appropriate attitude and playing style, and the handling of the style's elements that are controversial and need to be adapted or given up.

In the final analysis the debate over CWM comes down to an issue of spiritual and aesthetic maturity on the part of the worship leader and the church musicians. It is the quality of the personal relationship with God, cultivated on a day-to-day basis, and the inner disposition that grows out of this relationship that enables the worship leader and musicians to draw the congregation into a meaningful and deep journey during the worship service. This experience cannot be achieved through some magical effect of the music. On the contrary, the music serves only as a channel to convey conviction and experience. Without this personal preparation on the part of the worship team, the music sounds shallow and artificial and is seen as a *performance*. Ellen G. White underlined the importance of the preparation of the heart as she spoke about the use of music in general. Her words still apply to today's music scene: "Music is acceptable to God only when the heart is sanctified and made soft and holy by its facilities. . . . Men and women will not then depend upon their instrumental music but on the power and grace of God, which will give fullness of joy."[14]

Too often, it is believed that our joy is the result of our music making. There is a classic strategy applied by song leaders in which praise singing starts out softly, builds up to enthusiastic singing, then fades out in preparation for the Word of God. Such strategies consider the role of music to be that of creating a spirit of rejoicing. If joy is only the result of a stimulation of senses through music, it will not be long lasting. In reality, joy and celebration should already be present in the hearts of the worshippers as they come to the house of God. The music making is simply a channel for worshippers to express their joy.

The relationship of cause and effect that the Scriptures establish between joy and the power and grace of God should be of particular importance to every artist and musician. In his description of the ceremonies dedicating the new wall at Jerusalem, Nehemiah attributes, in a significant way, the people's rejoicing to God's action: "God had given them great joy" (Nehemiah 12:43). Joyfulness in worship is from God and, as Paul puts it, a "fruit of the Spirit" (Galatians 5:22). Joy in worship comes from "what we have seen and heard" (1 John 1:3, 4) and from our awareness that "we belong to the Lord" (Romans 14:8). Ellen G. White adds that joy in worship is the result of our personal experience of the "love and tender compassion of our Heavenly Father."[15]

Spiritual integrity, knowledge and adoption of biblical worship values, an understanding of the emotional impact of music as well as the potential for psychological manipulation, and an awareness of the role music can play in favor of truth are all prerequisites for qualifying a musician to become a church musician. As "youth . . . take a higher stand and make the word of God the man of their counsel and their guide,"[16] they will come ever closer to reaching this goal.

Aesthetic maturity and the search for excellence require the contemporary church musician to be informed about the validity and roles of musical styles other than contemporary for worship, and to embrace those in the worship experience as well. This should happen not only for the sake of the older generations but also for the sake and spiritual growth of the youth. Our church is not a self-sufficient entity suspended in a void apart from any roots or ties to history. The contemporary artist and musician, in church, needs to understand the historical role of congregational singing. Congregational singing connects the worshipping community to its forefathers and allows it a glimpse into the theological world and faith experience of the church throughout the ages. The songs reveal the spiritual path and journey of a different group of worshippers in their community.

Today's youth bring eclectic expectations to worship. They enjoy the praise songs and instrumental sounds of the worship band. They also enjoy the traditional hymns led out by the organ, and appreciate the singing of a choir or the sound of an instrumental ensemble. This eclectic approach to worship has been understood in a number of churches that, as a consequence, have adopted a *blended* style of worship. Blended style does not limit itself to a moment of praise singing at the beginning of the service. Blended style means a blending of traditional and contemporary music and worship elements throughout the whole service. There are many ways of implementing blended service: the singing of one or several hymns in the middle of the praise service; the accompaniment of hymns by contemporary instruments; the singing of praise songs to the sound of the organ; the choir's invitation to the congregation to join in the singing of a contemporary selection or a contemporary arrangement of a traditional hymn at specific times of the song. Traditional instruments, such as trumpet, flute, clarinet, violin, etc., can play together or alternate with guitars, synthesizers, keyboards, saxophone, and percussion. A contemporary song in the middle of the sermon has the power to drive home the truth in a unique manner. The only limit to a blended service is the degree of creativity of its leaders. Blended style touches the hearts of many worshippers, who find themselves in familiar territory throughout the worship service. The juxtaposition of contemporary and traditional selections safeguards the quality and relevance of worship music. It also stands as an affirmation of the corporate character of worship and as a witness to the esteem and consideration we bear toward one another in worship.

The idea of a blended style of worship reflects the essential principle that what is important is not so much to be able to choose *between* styles, but to make appropriate choices *within* a style, drawing on a multiplicity of musical possibilities. Rather than debating *what style should be used*, we must find out *whether and how a style can be adapted and transformed* to become appropriate for the occasion. A number of questions formulated by Marvin Robertson,[17] former chair of Southern Adventist University's Department of Music, may help us in our pursuit of appropriate contemporary music in our church services. The answers that we, as a group representative of our community, give to these questions can guide us in making informed and adequate decisions:

1. What is the message of this music?
2. What is its emotional and behavioral impact?
3. What is its cultural context?
4. What is its worship value?
5. What is its aesthetic value?

As we pursue the *ideal* worship music in our church, let us remember that when Jesus comes back in glory, there will be people from every nation who will sing to Him (Revelation 7:9, 10), and they will all sing in their own languages. There is a place for many songs in the kingdom of the Father, and the songs all have one quality in common: they reflect His character and speak of His many deeds of love.

---

[1] Interview of Michael Card, in "Who's the Leader of This Band?" *Christianity Today*, May 20, 1996, pp. 22, 23.

[2] Interview of Steve Taylor, in "Who's the Leader of This Band?" *Christianity Today*, May 20, 1996, p. 23.

[3] Stan Moser, "We Have Created a Monster," *Christianity Today,* May 20, 1996, p. 27.

[4] Quote by Charlie Peacock, in Stan Moser, "We Have Created a Monster," *Christianity Today*, May 20, 1996, p. 27.

[5] Terri Bocklund McLean has devoted a whole book to this issue, in which she not only gives excellent advice on the importance of sound choices in matters of song texts but also demonstrates how to achieve this goal. In addition, she considers musical matters as they relate to an appropriate rendering of the text. See *New Harmonies: Choosing Contemporary Music for Worship* (Herndon, Va.: The Alban Institute, 1998).

[6] *"Hymns Alive"—A Compilation of 700 Christian Hymns (organ, piano), to sing along with and glorify God*, recorded by Susan Maehre, 33 compact discs, PAVE Records.

[7] Harold M. Best, *Music Through the Eyes of Faith*, p. 130.

[8] Cf. Donald P. Hustad, *True Worship: Reclaiming the Wonder and the Majesty* (Wheaton, Ill.: Hope Publishing Co., 1998), p. 197. It would, then, be absurd to speak about pop culture or pop music before the nineteenth century, since during the nineteenth century, mass dissemination became possible for the first time. Before that time music was predominantly written for, and aimed at, elite groups in society. With the advent of the nineteenth century and a general trend toward democracy, however, music started being aimed at the common people, the large masses, not only through the simplification of the music's content but also in the ways it was advertised to the masses. Folk music cannot be included in the category of pop because, by its essence, it was never meant to become commercial, nor was it mass mediated. It must instead be seen as a genuine expression of everyday life themes and events, to be shared or joined in performance with a well-defined social group.

[9] Interview of Michael Card, in "Who's the Leader of This Band?" *Christianity Today*, May 20, 1996, p. 22.

[10] Interview of Steve Taylor, in "Who's the Leader of This Band?" *Christianity Today*, May 20, 1996, p. 25.

[11] Interview of Scotty Smith, in "Shepherding the Stars," *Christianity Today*, May 20, 1996, p. 28.

[12] It is good practice to let musicians know about performance manners and dress style in church before their first participation in worship. Pioneer Memorial Church's Worship Commission has put together a sheet of guidelines that is handed out to each worship participant at the moment he/she is contacted for the first time. Informing participants ahead of time puts things straight from the very beginning and helps to avoid sensitive situations after the fact. For a sample of "Worship-leading Guidelines," see Appendix 1.

[13] See Part One, "Associations," pp. 61-65 of this book.

[14] Ellen G. White, *Evangelism*, p. 512.

[15] See E. G. White, *Messages to Young People*, p. 363.

[16] E. G. White, *Testimonies for the Church*, vol. 1, p. 497.

[17] Marvin Robertson, "Are Music Choices Really Important?" *Dialogue* 6/1 (1994), on-line version. Available at http://dialogue.adventist.org. Accessed July 15, 2008.

Excursus: The Case of Rock Music

One cannot deal with the issue of contemporary worship music without considering the question of rock music. Though in the majority of Seventh-day Adventist churches that feature contemporary worship services the issue of hard rock has not come up yet, it is important to include this topic in a discussion of church music. Full-blown rock music concerts have become a standard practice among young Seventh-day Adventist believers—for youth gatherings or outreach reasons—and bring about concern on the part of the church.

The major difficulty when speaking about rock music is finding a common denominator for discussion. There are many different styles of rock music, from pleasantly soft rock played in elevators or the upbeat rock that accompanies, for instance, news broadcasts on television, to the earsplitting types of heavy metal, punk, etc., and all the intermediary stages and cross genres in between. Often, time or care is not taken to clarify or distinguish between the various genres of rock music, and anything that features rhythm and/or electric guitars ends up in the same bag, labeled as rock music. The result is a series of pointless monologues, without the possibility of ever finding a point of intersection or encounter that would make the discussion really fruitful and worthwhile.

The difficulty stems from the fact that we speak about rock music in terms of a musical *style* rather than considering it as a music *culture*.[1] There are several distinct rock cultures that share common musical components but are defined or differentiated by characteristic cultural components. Rock, like other types of popular music, such as rap, country, or jazz, is a combination of musical style, playing or singing styles, stage deportment and dress styles, visual effects, subject matter, and ideological presuppositions.[2] These extramusical elements have more to do with culture than with music.

Rock music started as a cultural phenomenon in the 1960s when it was adopted as an icon of youth culture—a music the youth could call their own, a stylized representation of their *real world* and how they dealt with it rather than a dreamworld of entertainment. The *content* of rock music was, then, from its very beginnings an expression of the values behind the music. Rock music was soon to become a privileged place for the expression of the individual and collective social experiences of youth culture. While it first started out as an expression of social protest against middle-class materialism and prejudice, rock music, throughout the decades, became the voice for various social and political agendas: protest against the Vietnam War; alienation from, and frustration with, society because of poverty; protest against sexism, racism, and the political Right; protest against society for destroying and deforming the human being; accusation of the loss of human relationships; proclamation of nihilism as an expression of rejection of all received values; and declaration of abandonment of respect and decency.

Behind every style and genre of rock one can find a particular social or cultural agenda that shapes the characteristic style of music or musical performance. A few of these performance styles and "sound forms" are folk rock, art rock, jazz rock, Latin rock, country rock, Christian rock, electronic rock, hard rock or heavy metal, punk rock, grunge rock, new wave, industrial rock, new romantics, techno, etc.

Some of these forms of rock are characterized by specific deportment, dress codes and hairstyles, "body cults" such as piercing, and body movements during performance or on the dance floor. In addition, a rich array of commercial products provides a multimedia framework and creates a consumer oriented structure, catering to the desires and aspirations of the targeted cultural group through recordings, magazines, movies, and radio and television programs. It is impossible to imagine the rock music scene without those cultural expressions—they are an integral part of rock music.

The musical elements of rock can be classified into two basic categories: (1) meter and rhythm characterized by a constant tension relationship and (2) electronic enhancement and manipulation of instrumental and vocal sounds. Sound is manipulated through amplification, mixing, and distortion. Sound distortion is applied to both vocal and instrumental parts. In instrumental distortion the instruments basically imitate vocal sounds such as screaming, screeching, howling, sobbing, breaking or flexing the voice, guttural sounds, etc. Synthetic manufacturing of acoustical effects—such as reverberation or virtual distance effects—are often produced in the studio before the actual live performance and then combined with onstage performance.

The experience that characterizes most genres and styles of rock music, from the simple text oriented ballad by Bob Dylan to the sonic orgies of heavy metal, can be summarized under one concept: the pursuit of a sound experience. Sound as a phenomenon per se is the central aesthetic category of rock, the common denominator that connects all the various genres of rock. In many forms of rock, what creates this experience is the driving rhythmic section, the electronically produced acoustic effects, the sheer volume, and the metallic quality of sound.[3]

It is on the level of the sonic experience that the effects of rock music should be considered. Some of the musical elements of rock, taken separately in isolation or in alternation, can also be found in other genres of music, particularly classical music. Pulsing rhythm and beat, loud volume, and electronically created acoustic effects are core components of twentieth-century classical music. As such, they may be considered and discussed as general constituents of the musical language. However, when these separate elements are combined and placed within a highly emotional and collective cultural setting with specific meaning (as understood and interpreted by a given social group), the complexity of the resultant musical event produces an experience of such intensity that the emotions are stimulated to their extreme.

Consider the combined effects of the driving rhythm and beat, the volume of sound carried to its extreme, the complex interaction of highly active instruments "speaking" the language of the human voice stretched to its physiological and emotional limits, the visual effect of the facial expressions and suggestive deportment of the artists, and the explicit video clips and electrifying light effects. Imagine all of these elements placed within the social context of a mass event in which the individual is carried by the general excitement and euphoria or stimulated by his or her own imagination. Add the possible mental and somatic effects of drug consumption or other stimulants, and the emotional outcome is heightened exponentially. The physical, mental, and psychological experiences are pushed to their limits. This is all about losing oneself in obliviousness, in mass phenomena, and in the hopes of discovering new regions of consciousness and expanding the limits of human knowledge.

The experience of letting go and losing oneself is precisely one of the goals sought in rock music. It was explicitly expressed for the first time in the 1960s with psychedelic rock, when the rock artists demonstrated their desire to explore new areas of experience and to explode the limits of the human psyche through the use of drugs combined with the sheer effects of sound, in conjunction with highly stimulating visual effects (strobe lights, etc.). At that time one of the major pursuits of rock music, though not for all of its forms, was to expand the regions of emotional range, human consciousness, and knowledge. The realm of music was, then, broadened beyond the sensorial, sensuous, and mental domain to become a powerful tool in the pursuit of a somatic experience, an experience that acted on the deepest level of human consciousness, transforming and modifying the human soul. The aim of this music was to lead the listener into an experience enabling him or her to pursue regions of the soul and mind that had, thus far, been out of reach.

This is the point at which we should start to be concerned about rock music—when it tinkers with the very essence and limits of human nature. In trying to push the limits of human consciousness and knowledge and unveil and penetrate the mysteries of the mind and existence, we place ourselves above the Creator and take the place of God. This attitude reminds me of the tale about the sorcerer's apprentice, which was so fittingly put to music by Paul Dukas. One day, during his master's absence, and in spite of explicit instructions not to try his hand at the dangerous art of sorcery, the apprentice could not resist the temptation. But once he had unleashed the magical forces, he was unable to stop them and as a result was almost destroyed by them. In the same way, when we try to unleash the powerful and unknown forces of the human psyche, there is a danger of not being able to control them anymore. We become their victims, and they may destroy us.

When referring to extreme settings such as these, the rock experience presents us with values that are difficult to reconcile with a Christian lifestyle and the responsibility we carry for our bodies and souls in terms of affirmation of life, self-control, functional human relationships, etc. Many of the values represented by rock cultures are in blatant contradiction with the worship values of reverent acceptance of God as the eternal Creator of all living beings, as we recognize our own limitations and finiteness in His presence, remaining humble and seeking repentance for our shortcomings, respecting our bodies and other human beings, etc.

Not all rock music makes use of such excessive expressions. The recognition of different rock cultures calls for a balanced approach to rock music.

Take off one or several of the radical components of rock music, recast the setting, and the situation and results change radically. There are still the same instruments, the same chords, and the use of technological enhancement. The presence of these elements classifies the music as still belonging to the category of rock music. But if the attitudes of the performers have changed, the purpose of the music is different, and the sonic experience respects the primacy of the message—by not overpowering it, a positive message can be conveyed by people who have a real burden for a real cause.

Rock music still has a voice in society at large. It does not necessarily work against society, and can even be well used in favor of great societal causes. On July 7, 2007, the Live Earth concert sponsored by Al Gore, organized in New York and all around the world to create awareness in favor of protecting our environment, featured a performance by rock singer Melissa Etheridge. Her message was clear, strong, and positive, and her demeanor and dress normal, without any eccentricities. The music of her band, though energetic and driven, did not overpower or drown out her words (this would have been counterproductive). The tone was one of protest, urging, and engagement. The music fit her song perfectly.

Many Christian rock concerts or praise events embrace this music with a comparable spirit: to celebrate life and friendship, to thank God for the gifts He has given, to convey the urgency for change in people's lives. The character of the music fits the energy and excitement of youth.

In so many ways the musical component of rock culture is a fitting representation of today's culture: driven, fast, loud, high-powered, and aggressive. These words summarize the very reality of everyday life, especially in urban settings. Rock music is also a global event, a language spoken on every continent that unites youth in a distinctive way. Before the Internet, before Facebook and MySpace, rock music already epitomized the global character of youth culture. Rock music surrounds every aspect of our lives, from news broadcasts to dentist's offices to supermarkets to cafeterias—many individuals do not even realize the fact that they are, indeed, listening to rock music. And sometimes, possibly without being aware, they even enjoy what they hear.

But rock music no longer exclusively dominates the popular music scene. It shares popularity with several new trends featuring the same global character. World music, in particular, has transformed the realm of pop music, especially by associating with a variety of music genres. The world of classical music itself has eagerly embraced crossover procedures, so that today's market presents an array of music simultaneously incorporating popular, classical, and world music elements. The eclectic interests of many young people have taken away the exclusive edge that rock held for the past decades.

But what about rock music in worship? Are the two compatible?[4] Because of the strong impact rock music still exerts in society on many levels, and because of the particular nature of its multiple associations, great caution is needed in considering its use for worship. On close examination some of the values commonly embodied by secular rock music are far removed from, even in blatant contradiction with, worship values. The typical musical attributes of rock music per se—with their overpowering, self-affirming, and driving character—are not naturally suited to make room for the hearing of the Word of God or to create distinctive worship moods. It takes a special caliber of musician to *transform* traditional rock style into a worshipful event.

Today's musical language, at large, borrows a number of its elements from the rock scene: instruments, playing techniques, chords, rhythm, etc. This is the musical idiom of the younger generation, and it would be very difficult, if not impossible, to turn back the clock in terms of instruments and styles. Similarly, nobody today would even think of going to work in a horse cart or on the back of a donkey. The tools today are different, but the spirit must remain the same. If used with skill and balance, in a way appropriate to a circumstance, today's tools can enrich certain musical experiences and give the people a voice to praise and sing in their own idiom. If it is not possible to realize this purpose, if there is "greater fear of loss than hope of gain,"[5] then one should be able to recognize the limitations of a style, or one's own limits, and renounce its use. After all, this is not about us or about music. This is about worship, about being true children of God. What is at stake here is, first and foremost, the kingdom of God and the spiritual well-being of those individuals who were entrusted to us.

---

[1] For an in-depth analysis of rock music, see the article "Rockmusik," in Musik in Geschichte und Gegenwart, Ludwig Finscher, ed. (Kassel, Germany: Bärenreiter Verlag, 1998), Sachteil, vol. 8.

[2] The same can also be said, to a certain extent, about classical music. Classical music cer-

tainly comes with its own cultural baggage. However, this cultural baggage remains more or less the same across all the classical music styles. Typically, concert goers will wear similar dress and show similar attitudes at a concert of baroque music as they do for a concert of nineteenth- or twentieth-century music. The various popular music styles, however, are clearly identified and differentiated by their particular extramusical elements. Consider, for instance, the differences in dress or behavior associated with rap, jazz, or punk rock, etc.

[3] Infrasound is one of the aspects of the sonic experience. Infrasound is produced by frequencies lower than 20 Hz and is not audible to the human ear. Infrasound is a natural phenomenon encountered during volcanic eruptions, earthquakes, or tsunamis, and it is used by certain animals to communicate among themselves, but it can also be produced by engines or aircraft, or be generated electronically. Since infrasound is inaudible, most of the time we are not aware that we live with it.

Infrasound has been used in medicine, in which it brought about results such as relaxation of the muscles and the nervous system ("Infrasound and Its Effects on Humans," sec. 3.4. "Other uses of infrasound," online paper published by Diana Carolina Fernandez Valencia, Faculty of Architecture, Design and Planning, University of Sydney, Australia, 2007, available at http://web.arch.usyd.edu.au/~densil/DESC9137/Fernandez.pdf, [accessed July 16, 2008]).

The use of infrasound adds a new dimension to the musical experience, namely, physical immersion. With infrasound a tone is felt rather than heard. Deep bass sounds are sought after for their capacity to create strong vibrations in our bodies. Human organs have resonant frequencies in the lower range and start vibrating when exposed to very low frequencies.

The use of infrasound in music is not a recent phenomenon. Infrasound has been used by a number of classical composers. Indeed, a few acoustic instruments are capable of producing infrasound, namely, bass instruments, the trombone, and especially the organ. (A list of recordings of classical music featuring infrasound can be found in the above mentioned paper by Diana Carolina Fernandez Valencia, "Infrasound and Its Effects on Humans," sec. 3.2. "Arts and music.")

A study based on a clinical experiment and reported on in 2003 by BBC NEWS relates how infrasound of a frequency of 17 Hz at levels of 6–8 decibels, produced by a seven meter long organ pipe during a regular concert, was added sporadically to the music being performed. The (inaudible) infrasound created in the audience sensations of "an odd feeling in [the] stomach," "increased heart rate," "feelings of sorrow, coldness, anxiety, and even shivers down the spine." This effect of deep basses also seems to lie at the core of the religious feelings (often physically perceived as goose bumps) instilled in many individuals when listening to the sound of the organ in church (Jonathan Amos, "Organ music 'instills religious feelings,'" online article, BBC NEWS, September 8, 2003, available at http://news.bbc.co.uk/2/hi/science/nature/3087674.stm, [accessed October 22, 2009]; see also the description of the experiment in the online paper by Diana Carolina Fernandez Valencia, "Infrasound and Its Effects on Humans," sec. 5.1. "Silent music").

The results of a similar experiment have shown, though, that the effects perceived can vary from one individual to another, and even be contradictory. One listener may be overwhelmed by an impression of the transcendent, while another may very well feel uncomfortable, uneasy, or even ill, during the same musical event. It has also been shown that the various impacts cease when the infrasound stops, that the results can be suggestive once the subject is aware of the possibility of the stimulus, and that the symptoms decrease or cease with repeated exposure (Diana Carolina Fernandez Valencia, "Infrasound and Its Effects on Humans," sec.. 5.2. "Comparable experiment").

Infrasound can become audible when high sound pressure levels are applied to it. Under those circumstances it was possible for subjects to feel annoyance, resentment, displeasure, irritation, or nausea, or undergo changes in blood pressure levels (lower or higher, depending on the individual). The intensity of the symptoms was proportional to the sound pressure level and the duration of exposure to the infrasound. With high sound pressure levels (above 100 decibels), the effects of infrasound were felt as "noise intrusions" or "acoustic attacks," and brought about more severe and stressful symptoms. But even in this experiment, results varied and were contradictory (Diana Carolina Fernandez Valencia, "Infrasound and Its Effects on Humans," sec. 4.1. "Effects of exposure to infrasonic sound").

Infrasound has been part of traditional music for a long time. It is a natural component of the music phenomenon. Its effects depend on the manner in which it is used: as an accent within a broader context, or as a pronounced and sustained core element of the musical experience. The impact of infrasound also depends on the frequency and the intensity with which it is used. While infrasound may cause some individuals to feel uneasy or ill, this does not mean that it changes them morally, that it necessarily will have an impact on their behavior. An individual affected by infrasound certainly needs to address the problem and eliminate it from his or her life. But not everybody is affected in the same way. The example of infrasound illustrates once again the principle we discussed earlier: different people react in different ways to external influences. To one, a deep bass experience can have a debilitating effect; to another, barely any effect.

I would like to illustrate this point with an example from the world of dietetics. It has been shown that the consumption of high quantities of milk played a role in the aggressive and violent behavior of juveniles—to the point of criminal offense (Barbara Reed Stitt, *Food and Behavior: A Natural Connection* [Manitowoc, Wis.: Natural Press, 1997], pp. 92, 93). What normally is seen as a healthy and constructive food may in other cases exacerbate already existing behavior problems. The issue is not the milk; it is instead the physiological background of the individual and his or her more or less stable psychological condition. The fact that some people have allergic reactions to milk does not mean that the product has to be withdrawn totally from the market.

It is certainly important to be informed about these musical phenomena. It is as important, though, to understand how they function so as not to attribute to them some obscure supernatural or evil powers. As we mentioned before, Satan uses every possible venue to cause us to fall; this fact does not give these venues magic power over us. Every individual carries a personal responsibility for his or her use or abuse of musical phenomena, and must exercise careful judgment regarding the effect the music exerts on his or her physical well-being.

[4] For a discussion of these questions, see L. Doukhan, "Christian Rock in Worship?" *Student Movement* (Andrews University, Berrien Springs, Mich.), October 15, 1997, pp. 8, 10.

[5] This is a play on words on Saint Augustine's expression from "Letter No. 55," chap. 18, in J.-P. Migne, ed. *Patrologie Cursus Completus*, Series Latina, vol. 33, pp. 220, 221, quoted in David W. Music, *Hymnology: A Collection of Source Readings*, p. 11. Saint Augustine's original phrasing is: "If there is greater hope of gain than fear of loss, they should be performed without question, especially when they can be strongly defended from the Scriptures" (see p. 105 of this book for the complete quote).

PART FIVE
Music Ministry
in the Church

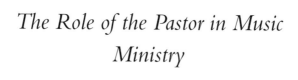

CHAPTER 19

The Role of the Pastor in Music Ministry

Music in the life of the church is often taken for granted, both in inside practices (worship, weddings, etc.) and in outreach activities (evangelism). The rule of thumb is to make do with what you have. Responsibility for the music presented generally rests on the shoulders of the musician or the pastor. Any criticism of the music falls on these individuals, who are then left to carry the blame personally. This frequently results in heartache, frustration, and bitterness on the part of those in service, and sometimes a volunteer abandons his/her work with music ministry. On the other hand, some pastors or church musicians deliberately choose to make all decisions about music by themselves, according to their personal convictions or preferences.

Neither approach to music in the church is ideal. One individual should not have to take all criticism or single-handedly make all decisions that affect an entire congregation. As churches become more and more vocal in regard to what they expect to happen up front, it is important to take the burden/privilege of musical decision making, and the bearing of its consequences, off the shoulders of one individual and instead entrust it to a group of people. More and more churches today are moving in the direction of making decisions about the worship service together as a community.

I have personally been able to observe the fruits of a collective approach to music ministry in the church. A number of individuals work together as a team toward an appropriate and relevant worship experience. This team is made up of the pastor, the musician, and the worship commission. Each individual within the team carries his/her own level of responsibility and field of action.

THE ROLE OF THE PASTOR IN MUSIC MINISTRY

The pastor, as guardian of his or her flock, remains the person who stands at the beginning and end of any reflection or discussion about music in the church. Important decisions as to the role of music and the musicians in worship remain the responsibility of the pastor since he is in charge of the spiritual well-being of his congregation. Even if the pastor has not received any musical training, there are enough indicators in the way music is done during worship and in how people respond to the music to help him assess the situation. As his impressions are then shared with the other members of the worship commission, he will soon learn to become more confident in his own judgment.

On the basis of the principles we have already laid out in the previous sections of this book, I would like to suggest a number of spiritual and ethical guidelines for the pastor in matters of music in worship. The following thoughts are meant to offer some reference points for the pastoral assessment of the musical experience in the church.

Provide an Understanding of Worship to the Congregation and the Musicians

This task is fundamental to authentic worship and music practices in the church; it is the spiritual responsibility of the pastor. Music is only one of the expressions of worship. As such, it is not a mere aesthetic experience. It also expresses and supports the values of worship. Before a healthy discussion of music can be undertaken, there must be a solid understanding of what worship is and what it means. Once the pastor has educated himself/herself about true worship, he/she needs to educate not only the congregation but also the church musician(s) about biblical worship. This goal can be achieved in a variety of ways: preaching a series of sermons on worship, organizing study sessions about worship for worship leaders, elaborating on worship principles with the worship committee or the church musicians, etc.

Safeguard the Worship Values

The *principles* of worship presented in the Scriptures are universal and immutable—they apply to all times and places. As worship *expressions* change over time and place, it is essential to safeguard worship values.

Worship values deal with standards of content and quality observed in all worship actions. These values determine when change is brought about and how it is brought about. They are the values that make a worship service appropriate or inappropriate, relevant or irrelevant. Worship values are not communicated to us through our own ideas or feelings, but come from sources outside of ourselves: the Holy Scriptures and the Spirit of Prophecy. The role of music in worship is to reflect these values. The spiritual responsibility of the pastor is to observe and ensure that these values are respected and maintained in the church's musical practices. Both the quality of the music and the manner of performance play a significant role in this undertaking. The following questions and reflections are meant as guidelines as we strive to safeguard the worship values through our music—on the level of the message it carries and also in the way it impacts our emotions and behavior.

The Message Behind the Music

Is there a clear correspondence between the message that is conveyed through the musical style and the message delivered through the Word? Is the musical message clear and strong? Does the congregation understand this musical language, and how does the congregation understand it? Does this language contribute positively to the worship experience? Is the musical message appropriate to the worship mood it is supposed to sustain or reinforce? It would not be suitable, for instance, to feature bold rhythms and loud volume to accompany a song of repentance and humility; a quiet and meditative mood would better fit this particular experience. Does the music have "beauty, pathos, and power"[1] to help the worshipper progress in his or her spiritual journey? Is the language of the music congenial to spiritual growth, to an authentic experience of transformation? Does the music lead the worshipper beyond a mere aesthetic appreciation and religious emotionalism into a true religious experience, an encounter with God? An aesthetic experience can be an event of spiritual order, but it is not necessarily a religious experience. To admire beauty and harmony may bring one closer to God. When I admire a beautiful sunset, I may feel uplifted and inspired, but such an experience will not necessarily lead to change in my life or to a transformation of my character. A religious experience is about growth, change, transformation of the character. Are there conflicting messages sent through the music, or is there ambiguity as to the message conveyed? It may be that the attitudes of the musicians or the styles in which particular instruments are played pertain more to a secular concert performance than to the spirit of worship.

Contemporary Christian music shares a number of characteristics with secular contemporary music. Both types of music are governed by marketing rules; they are consumer oriented, commercial, and meant to be sold in large quantities. Such music must have quick appeal, provide immediate gratification, and satisfy and please the senses easily, without too much effort. Often this type of music comes across as trivial or commonplace, especially in a worship setting. Because of this close connection with secular music styles, contemporary songs in church may come with associations undesirable for a context of adoration. It is essential to take those associations into consideration and to address the issue in cooperation with the worship commission. Not all CCM merits this criticism. However, should a musical selection fall into this category—by its lyrics, its musical style, or its mode of performance—it is not fit to be used in worship. It is important to distinguish between music that carries worship values and music that is of a commercial character, meant to entertain.

The Emotional and Behavioral Impact of the Music

Is the amount of emotionalism and/or excitement brought about by the music appropriate to a worship setting? Is the behavior fostered by the music in harmony with biblical worship principles? Biblical worship embraces a wholistic experience including the heart, body, and mind. All are needed, and they keep one another in check in order to avoid extreme attitudes in worship, such as dry rationalism or excessive emotionalism. Ellen G. White speaks about music making that is "cheerful, yet solemn."[2] Balanced worship music, then, equally addresses the mind, heart, and body. It brings the worshippers to reflect and meditate on the truth and, at the same time, fills their hearts with joy that is expressed through physical manifestations (body gestures, facial expressions, movement, etc.).

The Role of Music in Worship: Educational?

Contrary to what some believe, worship is not the place to educate people in matters of music. Worship is the place to connect with God, to replenish one's soul in the presence of the Lord. If we want to educate our congregations in the arts, we can do so in separate events, e.g., concerts on special occasions such as Christmas or Easter. These concerts can very easily become moments for evangelistic outreach, as well. The ideal place to educate people about music quality, however, is the church school. In the church school the minds and hearts of young people can be impressed with standards of beauty and excellence. Music education, indeed, provides a framework of reference for the music done in church. Time and again we observe that the best musicians on praise teams are those who received some degree of classical training. Classical training not only gives musicians high standards of practice and performance but also makes them familiar with a wide range of musical styles and genres, and shapes their tastes in musical matters. These remarks are not meant to discourage those who have not received any classical music training. On the contrary, they should inspire them to seek such training to enrich and deepen their own musical experiences and practices.

The delivery of strong worship values through our music making ensures a meaningful service that upholds the truth, keeps the message unambiguous, and establishes a clear difference between the secular and the sacred. It breeds strong values rather than sentimentality and fosters the spiritual growth of the community. On the parts of the musicians, it encourages the search for excellence in text, music, performance, and attitude. Strong worship values create an environment in which people can relate to the music and use it as a channel to respond to God's invitation to worship. The practice of strong worship values in music enables a church to feature several styles of music— as long as these styles are intimately connected to the worship values.

Safeguard the Unity of the Church

An essential task of the shepherd is to keep his/her flock together. This is an ethical responsibility and should form one of the main concerns of the pastor/elder. Originally, music was meant to create harmony and unity. Unfortunately, during recent years it has become a force that drives churches apart into separate factions and leads people away from attending worship.

Often, the pastor himself/herself contributes to this split in the church, a reality that is many times overlooked and ignored. Pastors are encouraged to adopt a very careful attitude in matters of music as related to the church. There is a need to leave behind politics or cultural elitism and to search for a unified language. As representative of the whole community, the pastor/elder cannot afford to let his/her own musical preferences or biases govern the decisions of the church. A pastor should relate equally to all constituencies of the church and must be open to enter into dialogue with every member of his/her church. He or she needs to sit down personally with musicians and church members of all generations and ways of life, listen to them, and sometimes put aside his or her own tastes or opinions. The pastor/elder should be ready to learn from his/her constituencies, but also to instruct and educate whenever necessary, especially in the field of worship and worship values. This is something that cannot be achieved by delegating responsibilities. The traditional debate of high church music versus popular or contemporary church music should be shifted to objective discussions about what is appropriate for worship in a given cultural setting. These dialogues can then be expanded into study groups about worship, the role of music and the musician (music minister), and the history of worship in one's own church. However, such exchanges are fruitful only if all sides agree to explain their own points of view and also listen to—and really hear—the other points of view.

At this juncture the role of the pastor/elder shifts from leader to mediator. This is far from an easy role. First comes the challenge of giving up one's own preferences; then comes the requirement of wisdom, discernment, common sense, and a good sense of humor! While the role of the minister is often seen as that of guarding tradition and truth, a church is not a static entity, but a living organism that grows and goes through changes. Looking to the past and preserving the truth is important and should be done, but it must also be complemented by acknowledging present needs and a vision for the future.

In order for every pastor to function effectively as mediator, it is desirable for him/her to have a wide understanding of musical styles. Before entering into dialogue with a member whose musical language is contemporary, a pastor needs to have some idea of what the church member is talking about. It is necessary to have a certain degree of familiarity with the kind of music that is spoken about. There are plenty of musical examples surrounding everyday life by which it is possible to learn about different styles. Instead of looking down on this music, listen and try to discover what there is about it that makes so many people appreciate it. Speak to those who listen to this music and ask how they are enriched by it and what it contributes to the quality of their lives. Then take your partner in dialogue seriously and believe him or her! Do not dismiss his/her experience as immature and shallow. Try, rather, to find out what they gain from the music that they do not receive in church.

The same is true for entering into dialogue with individuals whose musical experience happens entirely in the realm of classical music. How can the pastor communicate with these members and understand where they are coming from if he/she has never listened to classical music or if he/she thinks of it as something uninteresting, boring, and out of fashion? Any pastor who wants to see his/her church grow in the worship experience must make it a personal duty to educate himself/herself in a variety of musical styles. Understanding comes with practice. Nobody is asking the pastor to change his/her preferences, but it is important that he/she be informed about styles different from the one(s) he/she naturally prefers, in order to be able to relate to the various constituencies of the church and entertain a meaningful dialogue.

Safeguard the Relevancy of the Music

Seventh-day Adventist churches are becoming more and more multicultural and multilingual. They are no longer tight cultural entities in which a single style of worship dominates. Today, when people move, they bring with them their cultural expressions. This is true not only on the intercultural level but also on the intergenerational level. If we want our worship to be relevant, we must address the matter of speaking in the language of the people, that is, the musical language of the people. This is yet another ethical duty of the pastor. Worship happens not only on the level of rational understanding but also very much on the level of the understanding of the heart. Music speaks directly to our hearts and touches us deep inside. It is important to acknowledge the involvement of the total beings of our members. Music helps the message to reach deep into the worshippers' hearts, and enables them to respond to it with heart and soul. This is what relevancy is all about.

Some people unfamiliar with the classical style may not be able to relate to, or be touched by, certain selections of worship music in the classical style (organ, choirs, etc.); the music comes across as too complex or too boring.

Others feel uncomfortable with contemporary songs, either because of their difficulties in following the new rhythms or because of associations that form in their minds. This is where the concept of worship value comes in. Music in church is meant to facilitate worship, to be relevant. Worship value is not an intrinsic quality of a musical style or selection. In a given cultural context, a certain type of music will be more readily understood and experienced as carrying worship value than it might in another context. It is not an easy matter to deal with tensions such as these, and they need to be approached prayerfully and in a spirit of love and discernment.[3] Even though the issue of relevancy is a complicated one, it is critical for the pastor to consider it in all its complexity. Solutions to this problem are best worked out, again, within the framework of a worship commission.

Safeguard the Unity of Theme

One quality of a meaningful worship service that is often overlooked is the unity between the theme of the service/sermon and the worship activities, especially the music. A well-structured, unified service hits home with the truth in a much stronger way than a patchwork variety show. In a unified service, with each new, related element, the message is driven one step deeper into the heart and soul of the believer. When the worshipper leaves the church, the message accompanies him/her during the week and comes back to his/her mind and heart in a variety of ways, each one reinforcing and confirming the others.

Careful and early planning are necessary to achieve this goal of a unified worship service, especially since music is involved in the process. Any musical offering requires solid preparation and practice. This is true for solo performances and group presentations, such as by a choir, but even more so for praise team bands that function mainly on the basis of arrangement and improvisation. The larger the group, the more time that must be set aside for preparation. The same rules apply to those who accompany congregational singing on the piano or the organ; here also, preparation and practice are necessary. This means, for the pastor, that the sermon title or worship theme must be planned well ahead of time. In order to obtain solid unity of theme during worship, a pastor should know his/her theme or sermon title at least one month ahead. This will enable the choir director to choose, prepare, and rehearse a song in such a manner that the choir feels comfortable on the Sabbath of the performance. Feeling ready for and comfortable about the performance helps the singers to put into practice the principle of *singing to God* rather than being self-conscious about a good or bad performance. Special music is generally performed just before the sermon and is meant to open the hearts of the listeners to the message to follow. Thus it is particularly important that unity between the theme of the day and this piece of music be achieved. Special music illustrates in a very distinct way that the purpose of music is to serve the Word.

A specific comment is in order concerning the accompaniment of congregational singing. While the professional church musician has intensive training in this genre of music, playing hymns presents a real challenge for the average keyboard player because of the continuous four part harmony. I have seen so many keyboard players leave the church service unhappy and humiliated because of the many mistakes they made in accompanying the hymn singing. The reason is not that they are bad musicians, but that nobody took pains to let them know in advance which hymns would be sung during the service. The general practice for a minister is to walk in on Sabbath morning and hand the hymn numbers to the deacon, who then posts them on the board. If the organist/pianist is lucky, he/she will get the hymns before they are announced and will have a chance to look them over before playing them.

I have always wondered how a minister would feel if asked to deliver a sermon and handed the required theme just before walking up to the pulpit. Any honest preacher finds it normal to prepare the sermon ahead of time, so as to be able to think about it and develop his or her thoughts and ideas. The musician's situation is similar: any honest musician has the right to be informed about the hymns to be sung ahead of time so that he/she can look over the music, acknowledge possible difficulties, and think of some embellishments and variations for the different stanzas. There are, of course, a number to whom this comes easily. But there are many others who have nonmusical full-time jobs during the week and who offer their musical services week after week for the benefit of the whole church. They are happy to receive the hymns a week ahead of time (or at least in the middle of the week) so that they can practice their musical contribution and lead the congregation in a well-prepared manner. A musician's poor public performance on Sabbath morning is a searing experience capable of ruining the worship experience for that individual. And musicians have the right to worship too.

Ellen G. White emphasized the importance of well-made plans for the worship of God: "Is it not your duty to put some skill and study and planning into the matter of conducting religious meetings—how they shall be conducted so as to do the greatest amount of good, and leave the very best impression upon all who attend?"[4]

Pursuing the unity of the message not only brings about the benefit of a well-planned service but also adds beauty and deeper meaning to the worship experience.

---

[1] Ellen G. White, *Testimonies for the Church*, vol. 4, p. 71.

[2] E. G. White, *Evangelism*, p. 508.

[3] For more thoughts on how to handle such a situation, see "Handle disagreement in a Christian manner," pp. 280-282 of this book.

[4] E. G. White, "The New Heart," *The Advent Review and Sabbath Herald*, April 14, 1885, p. 1.

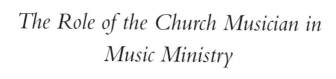

CHAPTER 20

{ *The Role of the Church Musician in Music Ministry* }

M any attributes of the church musician grow naturally out of the propositions mentioned above. Although both the pastor and the musician minister to the church in their respective ways, they fulfill separate and slightly different roles. Their communion of mind and action, however, is fundamental to a congregation's meaningful worship experience.

Understand the Nature of Worship

The first thing for a church musician to understand in the context of worship is that his/her contribution is more than just lending the church his/her talents. Being a church musician represents a *ministry*. This is where the musician's path crosses that of the pastor's. In addition to making thorough artistic preparation, the church musician should undertake an in-depth study of the meaning of worship. Pastor and musician then work out and share a basic understanding of what worship is all about, and decisions regarding music in worship will reflect this mutual understanding.

Understand the Relationship Between the Pastor and His/Her Congregation

Musicians must also gain an understanding of the pastor's concerns for his/her congregation. Church musicians like to educate their congregations in matters of music; it is a very natural desire to share what is cherished most in an effort to bring people to a similar understanding and appreciation. The primary concern of the pastor for his/her congregation, however, is not their growth in matters of the arts, but their spiritual well-being and their connectedness to the community. The pastor's aim is to provide his congregation with an authentic encounter with the Lord through worship, bring them to see their lives and the world from the perspective of God, and awaken in them the desire for profound changes in their lives.

The musician should be careful not to interfere with these goals or tear them down, but to understand and respect these goals and, through his/her music, to assist the pastor in reaching them. The musician's own contribution to these goals is fulfilled by creating *meaningful* music, music filled with a message rather than entertainment, music through which he/she offers his/her own "sacrifice of praise" (Hebrews 13:15), unblemished and beautiful.

Understand the Role of the Musician and Music in Worship

The task of music ministry is closely connected to the Greek concept of *leitourgia,* from which comes our modern word "liturgy." The original meaning of the verb form is "to perform a service on behalf of," "to minister to."[1] The church musician is actively involved in creating the liturgical event of music during the worship service. This idea of being in the service of or ministering to characterizes the work of every church musician. First, he/she is in the service of God and intent on pleasing God—and doing so in a modest and humble manner, resisting any personal display or temptation to entertain. In his/her ministry function, the church musician is a spiritual leader, a coagent with the pastor, delivering spiritual values through music and his/her own person. Second, the church musician is in the service of the congregation, acting as a servant to the whole community. This implies responding to the needs of the congregation in terms of providing music that fulfills a functional role by assisting the various worship moods, as well as presenting venues through which the community can express their response to God's calling. It also implies that he/she is sensitive to the musical language of the congregation, and assists the worshippers in their expression by providing quality music that responds to their cultural language. In short, the musician needs to create avenues of worship on a wholistic level.

There are a number of technical considerations that pertain to the responsibilities of the church musician. A thorough understanding of worship shapes the way the musician interacts with the congregation. The musician ensures that he/she can easily communicate with the congregation in order to lead out in the singing. At the same time, he/she wants to be able to communicate equally well with the pastor, worship leader, elder. These two concerns have an impact on the placement of the instruments in relationship to the pastor and the congregation, who both should benefit from the services of the musician.

I remember a discussion that took place within a committee deciding on the placement of a new pipe organ in the church. The church organist, seconded by a handful of other individuals who had a burden for authentic worship, suggested that the organ console be placed in such a way that the organist would have easy eye contact with both the pastor and the congregation, and that the pipes be placed against the front wall of the church in full sight of everybody. He was then offered the counterargument that people would really be very much interested in seeing the organist sitting up front in order to be able to watch his/her feet on the pedal board. The motivation for this proposition did not grow out of worship concerns, but out of the desire to showcase the musician's talent and to entertain the audience!

Improvement of the acoustic qualities of the church is another duty of the church musician. In their architectural shape, most of the churches resemble the ancient basilicas, with a front stage where all the action takes place. Congregations are aligned in ranks in the manner of spectators. Add to this our modern taste for comfort, and the ideal environment for slumbering and/or comfortably enjoying the show is created! Too many churches, especially those built or remodeled during the recent decades, are equipped with materials that take away from a good sound quality. The churches have wonderful drapes, thick carpets, and comfortable cushions. While these make for a nice, quiet environment, they also take away from the effect of the music, especially congregational singing. Too many drapes and too much carpet swallow the sound and create a dull atmosphere. It has been observed that a congregation that sings in an optimal acoustical environment is encouraged by the hearing of its own sound to sing with even more enthusiasm.[2] Unfortunately, the contrary is also true: dead acoustics produce dull singing. This does not mean, though, that all the walls and floors should remain bare, as this would create the opposite problem, a sound that bounces back from walls and ceilings and is too bright and lively. If a musician is not sufficiently informed about the rules of acoustics, he/she can consult a professional who deals with acoustics.[3]

---

[1] See G. Abbott-Smith, A Manual Greek Lexicon of the New Testament, 3rd ed. (Edinburgh: T. and T. Clark, 1937), p. 266.

[2] See Donald P. Hustad, *Jubilate! Church Music in the Evangelical Tradition*, pp. 193, 263.

[3] Church architecture in itself is an important liturgical factor that can enhance or take away from an interactive worship service. Many newer church buildings, through their very architecture—based on models of ancient synagogues or early Lutheran churches—illustrate principles of an interactive community. For more information on aspects of church architecture, see James F. White, *Protestant Worship and Church Architecture* (New York: Oxford University Press, 1964).

CHAPTER 21

The Pastor/Musician Relationship

I t is important that the pastor acknowledges the spiritual role of the musician in worship. In many churches the musician is not really considered as part of the platform team. He/she becomes some kind of accessory to the service, somebody who, from time to time, comes in to accompany singing, then drops out again. It is almost as if the musician is an object like the instrument itself. In my personal experience as a church musician (I have been active as such for almost 35 years), it was rare that the platform party invited me to participate in the prayer said before the elders went onto the platform. Likewise, during the Lord's Supper the musician is often busy playing and is neglected when the emblems are passed out, as if he/she does not need to worship. In smaller or average-size churches the musician provides the background music for the footwashing ceremony and thus has no chance to participate in this spiritual activity. If, in addition, the emblems are taken away, the musician is completely deprived of participating in the community experience. Such incidents speak volumes about how little the church musician is seen, in the eyes of the pastors and elders, as a ministering participant in the worship experience. Even though the musician is ministering to God and the community, he/she needs, at the same time, to be ministered to also.

Both the pastor and musician must learn to respect each other's roles in worship. While the musician learns and comes to understand the concerns of the pastor for the spiritual health of his congregation and the unity of his community, the pastor should acknowledge the ministering role of the church musician and learn to respect his/her musical decisions. This is, of course, possible only after a common working ground has been established in regard to worship. Strong, meaningful worship results when a pastor and musician function as a team, each one respecting and furthering the ministry of the other. This teamwork is, then, sustained and carried on by the worship commission.

CHAPTER 22

The Role of the Worship Commission

A worship commission brings together a group of people who have a burden for worship in their church and who are willing to work with one another, the pastor, and the church musician to ensure a meaningful, appropriate, and relevant worship experience. Commission members must be chosen carefully to guarantee the success and efficiency of the group.

The Choice of the Worship Commission Members

The members of the worship commission must represent all constituencies of the church. The worship commission is one of the avenues that enables the church as a whole to become more active and involved in its mission. The congregation, not the pastor or the church board, owns the worship service. For this reason it is important that every major people group within the congregation be represented in the worship commission. Members of this group should be chosen according to specific criteria that ensure true dialogue. The pastor may recommend to the nominating committee names of individuals that fulfill the criteria. Because of the particular way this group is put together, the worship commission is sometimes seen as a task force that puts the emphasis primarily on the *mission* character of this group. A representative from every age group, gender group, and/or ethnic group in the church should be chosen to become part of the worship commission. Worship leaders and church musicians are then added to this group.

Each church has its own requirements, based on its unique situation, in regard to its worship commission members. A college or university church considers students, faculty, and people from the wider community in addition to the above mentioned people groups. An urban church works with a wider ethnic spectrum and different educational levels among its members. It is the duty of each congregation to take a good look at itself and decide what groups need to be represented in order to have all concerns brought to the table and heard. The next step is to make sure that the chosen members possess the necessary qualities to make this enterprise work.

The Qualities of the Worship Commission Members

An essential characteristic for worship members is an *interest in worship* that has already been demonstrated in one way or another. An existing interest in worship, though, does not necessarily mean a good *understanding of worship*. Working toward this understanding is one of the early and primary responsibilities of the worship commission. We might think that it is enough if the pastor has a good understanding of worship (which very often is not the case); why should the church know about worship too? If worship is the task of the whole church, then the responsibility of knowing about worship also belongs to the whole church. Seventh-day Adventist worship heavily involves the participation of lay members. Elders, deacons, musicians, and sometimes even the preacher are laypeople committed to making the worship service happen. Congregations spontaneously react to what is happening (or not happening) in church, indicating that they consider the worship service to be their own. For this reason the whole church—but especially those members involved in the worship commission—should be instructed in matters of worship.

Some worship commissions organize a yearly retreat, bringing their members together for one or two days for the purpose of an intensive study of worship from both biblical and historical perspectives. During this time members can also discuss and learn about practical aspects of worship and the dynamics that govern the worship service. Preretreat readings about worship can be assigned[1] to different members of the commission, who then at the retreat take turns presenting their readings and understandings about worship. The goal of these training sessions is not only to achieve a common understanding of worship and its principles but also to create the sense of fellowship and partnership among commission members that is established during these moments of study and interaction. This lays the groundwork for the tasks to come in making decisions about the worship service.

Coming together as a group to study and discuss worship adds another benefit for the worship commission: an *understanding of the different constituencies* of the church. As the members of the commission get to know one another better, they are able to relate to one another on a more personal level. Thus they more readily understand and respect differences in approaches to worship. It is not unusual for the older generations, as they come to appreciate the younger generation through a common experience of study and relationship, to comprehend where the youth are coming from and what their needs and yearnings for worship are. The reverse experience is also true, of course. The more that young people get to know the other generations, the more they come to appreciate and love their elders and to understand their needs. In order to reach this goal, potential members of the worship commission must show the ability to relate to different age, gender, and ethnic groups so as to facilitate and ensure true communication between the different groups who work together in the commission.

In one of my classes a student shared an experience he had in one of the larger Seventh-day Adventist churches on the East Coast. The congregation was going through the typical experience of splitting the worship service into two separate events, one following the traditional style, the other adopting the contemporary style. As the discussions got hotter, the hearts became filled with more and more antagonism, and the gap between the older and younger generations seemed to become only larger. One day an older member made the suggestion to start praying for the younger people in the church, their needs, their spiritual and physical well-being, their aspirations, etc. An incredible thing then happened: the animosity that had characterized the older people's attitude toward the younger generation was transformed into a caring disposition. The older church members showed an interest in the younger ones as individuals, as people in need of relationships, love, and understanding. In turn, this brought about a positive reaction on the part of the youth. Dialogue opened up, and a mutual understanding of, and respect for, each group's concerns and needs facilitated a worship experience marked by more openness, tolerance, and genuine regard. The gap between the two generations was bridged, and worship was again happening together.

The secret to the success of this congregation resided in the prayerful and mutual character of their experience. This is the result of individuals being *willing to dialogue* and wanting to reach the other side. I have often noticed during committee situations that it is more difficult for the older ones to listen and learn from the younger ones than vice versa. While the younger generation is expected to do this by default, the capacity and readiness to listen to others and hear them is still an essential quality to be practiced in old age. The Bible is full of recommendations to *listen* and *hear*: wisdom and intelligence are indeed defined in Scripture as the capacity to listen and hear (Isaiah 50:5; Jeremiah 6:10; Revelation 3:22).[2] We need to relearn the skill of listening and bring it with us when we sit together as a group to work out the worship event of our church. The worship commission is not a battlefield, a place for zealots or crusaders to demonstrate their passion. It is, instead, a place to create positive things *together*.

The Responsibilities of the Worship Commission

On the basis of this common foundation of worship and understanding, the action of the commission can begin to take place. It would be senseless to start to work before this twofold foundation is achieved; such work would be plagued by endless discussions governed by personal bias and preference.

The worship commission's responsibilities encompass all aspects of worship, from the establishment of principles governing worship to the implementation of these principles on a practical level. The worship commission, then, touches all the various expressions of worship, including prayers, Scripture readings, offerings, length of the service, even the announcements. But special attention must be given to music. Music, more than any of the other worship expressions, has the power to draw people into worship or, on the contrary, to distract them from worship. Since music plays such a major part in worship, speaking about worship also means speaking about music. While music is not equivalent to worship, it is intimately connected to it and obeys the same principles. In the following section I propose seven tasks of the worship commission that deal with worship and music matters. While some of the paragraphs are more generally related to worship, the same principles can be applied, of course, in a specific manner to the practice of music in worship.

1. Set Standards for Worship

The first task of the worship commission is to set the standards for worship in its church. These standards should be guided by the universal and timeless principles of worship as uncovered and gathered in the common study about worship. These concepts govern all worship activities and become a point of reference in case of crisis or ambiguity.

Ellen G. White encouraged us to set our standards high: "Never bring the truth down to a low level in order to obtain converts, but seek to bring the sinful and corrupted up to the high standard of the law of God."[3] Speaking more specifically about the young people, she advised that "youth must take a higher stand and make the word of God the man of their counsel and their guide."[4] She saw in music "a precious gift of God, designed to uplift the thoughts to high and noble themes, to inspire and elevate the soul."[5]

2. Work Out a Worship Program

Once the standards for worship are formulated, the commission begins to work out a worship program. While the concept of a worship program can be limited to the order of service, it *should* be understood from a wider perspective—as a general vision for worship and music, for example, or as a master plan for renewal or change. Speaking about music, Ellen G. White insisted on the importance of organization in worship: "Well-matured plans are needed in the service of God."[6] She challenged us: "Is it not your duty to put some skill and study and planning into the matter of conducting religious meetings—how they shall be conducted so as to do the greatest amount of good, and leave the very best impression upon all who attend? You plan in regard to your temporal labors. If you learn a trade, you seek to improve year by year in experience, executing plans that shall show progression in your work. Is your temporal business of as much consequence as the service of God? ... God is displeased with your lifeless manner in His house, your sleepy, indifferent ways of conducting religious worship."[7]

Creativity and variety are fundamental qualities in life, and they also belong to the planning of worship. The search for creative ways to worship is one of the responsibilities of the worship commission. Often worship leaders are reluctant to introduce creativity for fear of offending the congregation or upsetting the order of things that people are used to. They forget that God as Creator introduced the principles of variety and creativity into nature from its very beginning. Creating us in His image also means that He endowed us with creative power.

Recently, as I watched the wonderful movie *Winged Migration* and marveled at the infinite variety of species and the beauty of the birds, I was reminded of the principle that God created things not only beautiful but also rich in variety. Why wouldn't it, then, be appropriate to introduce creativity and variety into the very event that celebrates God as the Creator? This should not be done, though, for the sole sake of variety, but rather as an offering of our own creative gifts that were bestowed on us by the same Creator.

3. Make Sure That Things Happen

Making plans is one thing. Making sure that things happen is another thing. It is the role of the worship commission to ensure that their decisions are followed through on and implemented. Often churches become very discouraged after wonderful plans for worship renewal are made but then none of the promised and expected changes actually take place. Implementing new ideas is more difficult than offering new ideas; it takes effort, perseverance, and enthusiasm to overcome the lethargy of the larger group. Teamwork helps in reaching this goal.

4. Choose the Worship and Music Leader(s)

The most important task of the worship commission is, perhaps, to choose the worship and music leader(s). Once this choice is made, the commission's work is not finished, though. The candidates must be informed of the principles of worship and the directions for worship that the commission has adopted. Too often musicians or worship leaders are selected to lead out in the church because of their skills as artists or communicators. Earlier we learned how the choice of a worship musician was made in biblical times. While it was certainly based on the skills of the individual, the musician also needed to show an adequate and true spirit of worship. An important task of the worship commission is, then, to instruct and mentor its worship and music leaders in matters of worship. Many misunderstandings or mishaps in matters of worship styles or musical styles can be avoided if the chosen leaders are informed ahead of time about the spirit and direction of worship that a church has adopted for its services!

Another experience shared by one of my students illustrates how important it is that the musician be informed about the worship spirit a church is looking for before he/she enters this ministry. The student's church was small and had no one who could provide the music for the service, so the decision was made to hire a woman from a neighboring non-Adventist church. Trying to do and be her best, she came Sabbath after Sabbath wearing her best jewelry. You can imagine the agitation created within the congregation! Finally, under heavy pressure from his members, the pastor approached the woman and mentioned the problem caused by her wearing jewelry. She was, of course, very sorry and wished somebody had told her about this from the beginning. Not wearing jewelry would not have been a problem for her. But this is not the end of the story. In fact, this brave woman was very much hurt by the way the issue had been handled. And even worse, during her time as musician in this particular Seventh-day Adventist church, she had come to appreciate the spirit and message, and had started to become more and more interested in the Adventist truth. Ill-prepared and inattentive handling of the situation had not only deeply hurt this woman but also prevented her from becoming a member of this congregation. While this is an extreme example, one that brings up other issues with regard to worship participants, it shows clearly how easy it is to create an unfortunate situation by simply neglecting to inform and prepare a musician before he/she enters into this function.

In our Andrews University church we have adopted a process for selecting the music and worship leaders that has proven to be fruitful time and again. It is true that in such an educational setting there are many people to choose from, mostly from groups in the process of training as ministers and/or musicians. Not every church has such a palette of choices. Still, the principles behind our procedure should always be the same: to assure that the candidate has the right spirit for worship or the right disposition to learn about worship and, in the case of the musician, a broad acquaintance with more than one musical style.

We start by interviewing/auditioning the candidates who have indicated an interest in the position and those who have been recommended by members of the worship commission. As we contact the candidates initially, we let them know that we would like them to share in a few words their understanding of worship and their view on the role of worship leader/musician. This is our way of communicating to them, from the very start, the importance of relating their activities to a reflection on worship. At the same time, we help them start the process of thinking about worship and their role in leading the congregation into the presence of God through word and music.

Once the selection process is finished, the work continues with mentoring the newly chosen leaders, both on the spiritual level and in technical matters (communication and music skills). Retreats for worship teams are organized, in which the pastor, musicians, and worship leaders spend one day together studying, praying, and communicating.[8] In addition to spiritual mentoring, training sessions can be provided for the musicians and singers to help them reach greater skill levels and attain higher artistic quality and excellence in their areas.[9] This mentoring process is an ongoing effort, Sabbath after Sabbath, as the team chooses the songs, works out the arrangements, prepares for the service, and delivers the message.

5. Provide Encouragement

Another role of the worship commission is to provide encouragement to its worship and music leaders. Every congregation has individuals who take it upon themselves to criticize the service. While constructive criticism and feedback are essential for growth and betterment, some types of criticism are difficult to take, especially after working so long and hard to be sure that the best efforts are put into the worship service. It is much fairer when criticisms are addressed to the worship commission, which then can evaluate whether they are justified, and propose and implement changes when there is reason to do so. But through all of this the commission is to encourage the worship team's efforts, help the team overcome discouragement or bitterness, and spur them on to new and still more appropriate ways of leadership. Discouragement can very quickly lead to abandonment of duties. Especially our young people need to see and hear that they have a place in the church and that the congregation is willing to walk with them on the long path of growth and learning.

6. Evaluate the Worship Service for Its Strengths and Weaknesses

The worship commission needs to take time, on a regular basis, to evaluate the worship service. It is important to share comments and to look at what is being done during worship, how things are being done, and how the service is received by the church. The following questions are samples of what needs to be asked in the process of evaluation:

- Is our worship service appropriate to the occasion in the light of biblical principles?
- Does the worship service reflect our specific theology and beliefs?
- Is the worship service relevant, i.e., does it reach out and speak to all the constituencies of the church?
- Is the worship service participatory?
- Is the form of the service (order of service,[10] style of service, characteristic elements of the service, such as the length of prayers and the sermon) appropriate and meaningful to the congregation?

- Are there creative elements that renew the worship service and make it fresh again?
- Does the worship service reach out to visitors?

Evaluation can happen at the level of the worship commission, but it should also, from time to time, involve the opinions of the whole congregation. This can be done by a simple questionnaire[11] that addresses some of the questions mentioned above. An evaluation process is conducted not simply to gather personal opinions but also to gain well-informed and thoughtful feedback on the topic. Such large scale surveys can become, at the same time, valuable tools to create congregational awareness about worship, its nature, and its purpose.

Evaluation is an essential procedure for growth. When things are done out of habit, it is easy to fall into a rut and no longer question the validity of what is being done. From there it is but a small step to think that because something has been done for so long, because it has become a tradition, it must be good. But life is not following a rut. Life is ever changing. Just think of a child, how he/she grows and changes, and how watching this change happen affects us as adults, renews and refreshes us. Just observe our eating habits: if we eat the same things every day, we will soon stop eating because the food will become tasteless to us. If we always worship in the same way, worship will come across as monotonous and uninspiring. From time to time we need to stop, look at ourselves as a worshipping congregation, and measure our worship habits against the great principles of biblical worship. Combined with the feedback from the congregation, the biblical reference will help us to assess our situation and take measures toward improvement so we can realize a more meaningful worship service.

7. Develop Strategies of Change

Change is a meaningful procedure and must come as an answer to an established and defined need. It should never happen out of a desire for novelty only. Desire for change grows out of a necessity for change. If the congregation desires change, the members spontaneously express themselves regarding this need.

Change is essential to maintain life, and this is also true for the life of the church. Renewal and change keep the church alive; they safeguard the freshness of the worship experience. Today's congregations are looking for a more

participatory worship experience. They yearn for simplicity of message, joy
and spontaneity, and the urgency that moves and persuades hearts. Yet these
wants come with a deep need for mystery and the transcendental.

The following reflections are meant to provide help to churches and worship commissions that wrestle with change in their worship service, so that
they may find a common ground for growing and working together toward
the adventure of change.

Seek wisdom. At the beginning of every effort for change stands the need
to seek wisdom—through prayer, in Scripture, and from previous experience
(history). The learning from Scripture and history sharpens discernment and
strengthens decision making. As this is done prayerfully, we find comfort in
knowing that we are not alone in this struggle.

Be aware of the needs and languages of the congregation. A church is made
up of many different constituencies. Leaders are responsible for making it
possible for every member to enter into a real worship experience.

Promote group decisions. Worship and music matters are not the sole privilege of the pastor or music minister. These matters belong to the whole
congregation. The congregation *owns* the worship service and must be included in the plans made for change. The worship commission, representing
the various constituencies of the church, is the right place for making such
plans. The members of the worship commission function as collective "ears"
for the congregation. Constructive feedback brought in by church members
of all ages is considered and discussed within the worship commission. As a
result, a variety of needs for worship will surface and trigger the worship
commission's reflection on change. Group work, though, involves the reality
of different temperaments, preferences, and/or needs. That implies we have
to sometimes relinquish our own musical tastes and desires.

*Create awareness of the nature of the worship experience and the role of
church music.* This is fundamental to any discussion about worship and music
but does not happen naturally. Worship must be taught, modeled, and men-
tored. Music in worship is meant to serve the Word and not to replace it.
Music's purpose is not to provide an educational or entertainment opportunity, but to accompany a spiritual experience/encounter.

There is no better way to create awareness about worship than through a
series of sermons on worship. The worship commission may ask the pastor to

prepare such a series of sermons. Alternative venues for the preaching or teaching of worship are the prayer meeting or Friday night services, where available. If the pastor creates in the congregation the wish to improve worship, change comes not as a surprise or shock, but will be desired and eagerly welcomed.

Give people the opportunity to understand. Let the congregation know what is happening and why it is happening, and give them a chance to participate in the effort for greater understanding and meaningful change. Once the commission decides to implement a change, the change should be explained ahead of time to the congregation. This explanation should include the rationale behind the change: what will happen and why it will happen. People are often afraid of new things because change creates a feeling of insecurity. If the worship commission allows the church members to prepare their minds for the change, they may end up thinking that the change is a good idea after all.

Create trust. Without mutual trust we will never see the end of our discussions. The leaders must trust the congregation, that is, listen to the members' feedback and take their remarks seriously. On the other hand, the congregation must trust the leaders in their decision making. To gain and uphold this trust, it is imperative to avoid shocking the congregation. This is achieved by working with worship components that people can reasonably adopt or adapt themselves to. Most important, only those components that fit the congregation's sense of dignity should be introduced. If the church sees that the changes that are introduced show respect to the biblical principles of worship, affirm strong values, and induce the desire to grow spiritually as an individual and as a group, the church will follow more readily on the path of renewal and innovation.

Introduce change on a trial basis. If the commission informs the church ahead of time that it plans to introduce a change or modification on a trial basis—just for one time—much of the threatening character of the procedure is taken away. Many can live with "just once" because they know they will soon get back to what is familiar and customary. It is imperative to remain sensitive to people's responses, to ask questions as to why they are upset at the change that was made, and even to back off if the change offends them. Not every reason for the refusal of change is good enough, though, and the worship commission needs to continue educating the church members about the necessity of change. But if the change introduced prevents a whole group in the church from truly worshipping, the idea for change or the manner in which the change was introduced must be revisited. However, it is equally possible to come across a situation in which some individual will ask, "So when are we going to have some more of what was done a few Sabbaths ago?" This type of reaction indicates that the church is alive and moving forward toward a more meaningful worship service.

Be patient. Change never happens quickly. Dealing with issues of music and worship and change is a matter of spiritual growth. Growth does not happen overnight. People need time to deal with habits, preconceptions, biases, and/or personal preferences. They also need time to learn to grow toward one another. Time is of great help here because it prevents shock. Rather than pushing ahead too quickly, be ready to take a small step back and then a big step forward again.

Remember that there is a variety of ways to achieve renewal and change. Much emphasis is put on the *new* in our discussions about change in worship and worship music. It is true that in the same way that our forefathers broke out of their ruts and brought about renewal and revival, we need to look at our times and our future generations and provide worship avenues that speak to us and to the youth in the appropriate language. However, we also need to remember our roots. The *old* is as important as the new. Our journey as a church is built upon experiences of the past. Our spirituality is rooted in the faith of our forefathers. Not everything new survives—history has proven to be a great crucible for music and worship practices. Renewal can also take place through the old. By refreshing traditional ways and reintroducing some of the lesser-known components in both music and worship practices, renewal, and revival can also be achieved.[12]

Handle disagreement in a Christian manner. The issue of music and worship is intimately linked to church life, but many congregations do not know how to handle it gracefully. It seems as if all of our principles of behavior fly out the window when we deal with music. Because music is such a subjective and personal matter, and because we come from so many different backgrounds, we are unable to handle the topic of music adequately. This should be one more reason to *learn* how to deal with it in a Christian manner. Our devotion to beauty should not come without tenderness, affection, and tolerance. Christ, in His relationship with people, always showed openness, tenderness, and love. How often in our discussions about music or worship do we come to the point where, in the heat of the debate, we completely forget what the discussion is all about: it is about God and about worship, not about our personal opinions or convictions. It is about coming to Him in perfect humility after making peace with our fellow worshippers.

Singing and making music in church in a spirit of peace, using the Word as a guide, is exactly what Paul advises: "Let the peace of Christ rule in your hearts. . . . Let the word of Christ dwell in you richly as you teach and admonish one another with all wisdom, and as you sing psalms, hymns and spiritual songs" (Colossians 3:15, 16). In his letter to the Philippians Paul presents guidelines that can help a congregation in the journey toward mutual understanding and concerted action: "And this is my prayer: that your love may abound more and more in knowledge and depth of insight, so that you may be able to discern what is best and may be pure and blameless until the day of Christ" (Philippians 1:9, 10). The beginning words of this text, "And this is my prayer," bring out clearly that the first step is to ask God to accompany us in our study and discussions. After laying this strong foundation for the subsequent stages of the process, Paul formulates several requests. And the order in which the requests are presented seems to be of importance. The first is to love and learn. Without mutual love there is no way to gain insight into one another's experiences with music or to learn from one another. The process of learning starts with a desire to really know one another better. A relationship of love is established within the community, and people will be able to *hear* one another. But love is not enough. Truth must also find a place in this journey. The apostle encourages the church to develop discernment of what is best. Discernment in matters of music is needed in order to be able to make wise choices, because we deal with music for God and because the whole community is affected by the worship experience. The values we choose to direct our music making and our interaction as a community must be pure and blameless.

Music is a community event, so let us sit together, listen, and hear without judging and without arrogance but with an open and tolerant mind. Let us establish real dialogue, think, discuss, and find solutions together. As we discover and work out our way prayerfully, slowly, in a spirit of love and respect, our music will become an acceptable offering to the glory of God, pleasing to God, and relevant to the whole community.

As we close this reflection on the process of change, we need not fool ourselves—it is impossible to please everybody. Change is a difficult task and must be learned by everyone. It is a good thing to keep in mind Saint Augustine's principle of conduct for dealing with different practices or customs: "When they are not contrary to faith nor to good morals, but help exhort us to a better life, that wherever we see them or know of their existence, we do not criticize them, but praise and imitate them, unless this will be a hindrance to those whose faith is weak. But even on that account, if there is greater hope of gain than fear of loss, they should be performed without question, especially when they can be strongly defended from the scriptures."[13]

Finally, let us not fall prey to the illusion that changing the order or the style of our worship service brings about a renewal of the worship experience. Only the renewal of our relationship with Christ can bring about change in the worship experience, because everything done during worship, whether by the worship leader/musician or the member in the pew, flows out of hearts and minds that have been renewed by the spirit of God.

The task of the worship commission seems to be a huge one. Many responsibilities are put on the commission's shoulders. This demonstrates how important it is that these decisions be made not by one or two individuals only but by a group that represents the whole church. The wide scope of the commission's task also speaks to the importance of choosing the members of this commission wisely. The right choice of people assures that, instead of wasting hours in dispute and empty discussions to make one's point, real dialogue and discussion will happen and real progress will be made toward an appropriate and fulfilling adoration of God.

---

[1] Sources are available for such study sessions. See Robert E. Webber's, *Worship Is a Verb* (Nashville: Abbott/Martyn, 1992); Don E. Saliers, *Worship Come to Its Senses* (Nashville: Abingdon Press, 1996); Ronald Allen and Gordon Borror, *Worship: Rediscovering the Missing Jewel* (Portland, Oreg.: Multnomah, 1982); Franklin M. Segler, *Understanding, Preparing For, and Practicing Christian Worship,* 2nd edition, revised by Randall Bradley (Nashville: Broadman and Holman Publishers, 1996); and C. Raymond Holmes, *Sing a New Song: Worship Renewal for Adventists Today* (Berrien Springs, Mich.: Andrews University Press, 1984). More recent books on worship also include a discussion about music in the context of worship. See Barry

Liesch, *The New Worship: Straight Talk on Music and the Church*, expanded edition (Grand Rapids: Baker Books, 2001).

[2] Cf. also Jacques Doukhan, *Hebrew for Theologians* (New York: University Press of America, 1993), p. 194.

[3] E. G. White, *Evangelism*, p. 137.

[4] E. G. White, *Testimonies for the Church*, vol. 1, p. 497.

[5] E. G. White, *Child Guidance* (Washington, D.C.: Review and Herald Publishing Assn., 1954), p. 523.

[6] E. G. White, *Testimonies for the Church*, vol. 4, p. 71.

[7] E. G. White, "The New Heart," p. 1.

[8] The following literature references are excellent materials to use for such events: Kevin J. Navarro, *The Complete Worship Leader* (Grand Rapids: Baker Books, 2001); Terri Bocklund McLean, *New Harmonies: Choosing Contemporary Music for Worship* (Herndon, Va.: The Alban Institute, 1998); and J. Nathan Corbitt, *The Sound of the Harvest: Music's Mission in Church and Culture* (Grand Rapids: Baker Books, 1998).

[9] Worship conferences are venues that provide spiritual and technical training for worship/music leaders or music ministers. Andrews University offers a yearly Music & Worship Conference that aims to fulfill both these roles. For more information, see www.auworshipconference.org.

[10] Contrary to the belief of some Seventh-day Adventist churches, there is no order of service prescribed by the General Conference of the Seventh-day Adventist Church. There are recommendations only about elements of adoration that should be present in the worship service. See especially the chapter "The Worship Service," in *Seventh-day Adventist Minister's Handbook* (Silver Spring, Md.: The Ministerial Association. The General Conference of Seventh-day Adventists, 1997), pp. 145-166. The whole section is filled with practical, common-sense advice that can be helpful to any congregation that is discussing or evaluating its worship service.

[11] For a sample survey form, see Appendix 2.

[12] For ideas on how to renew hymn singing by incorporating historical or less familiar songs, see Lilianne Doukhan, "Twenty Centuries of Living Hymns," online article, *Notes* (Winter, 2000), The International Adventist Musicians Association, www.iamaonline.com, accessed July 15, 2008.

[13] Saint Augustine, "Letter No. 55," chap. 18, in J.-P. Migne, ed., *Patrologie Cursus Completus, Series Latina*, vol. 33, p. 220, quoted in David W. Music, p. 11.

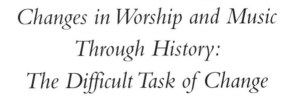

CHAPTER 23

{ *Changes in Worship and Music Through History: The Difficult Task of Change* }

T his section on music ministry closes with a reflection on the process of change; how it happened in biblical worship; and how the church in general, and the Seventh-day Adventist Church in particular, dealt with it through time. I hope these reflections help to ease the process of change as it becomes clear that our situation is not unique—that change with regard to worship and worship music is as old as the church itself—and as we try to learn from history which attitudes toward change helped and which ones didn't.

The Process of Change

Change is an essential part of life. Life *is* change. Change is in nature and in us: the seasons, the weather, our children growing up and ourselves growing old, etc. Change is not only natural but also inevitable. The new becomes standard, then traditional, then old. The innovations of one generation become the traditions of the next generation. In our attitudes toward change, we move from scorn to rejection to acceptance.

Change is also necessary. Without change we become too comfortable and don't even realize the banality and routine character of what we do. It is the same with worship: when it becomes familiar and routine, it needs to be rejuvenated with new, fresh ideas.

The process of change is not an easy one. It is painful and threatening because we like things to be stable, predictable, and familiar. We do not like to be pulled out of our comfort zones.

Besides the psychological aspect of change, there are two major forces that make change difficult: the power of tradition and the power of the past.

The Power of Tradition

In a traditional setting anything *old* is equivalent to *truth*. The old way is the way we grew up with, it has been consecrated by the past, and it has proved itself. Early reactions against the Authorized King James Version illustrate this kind of attitude. As this new version of the King James Bible was about to be published in 1611, Dr. Hugh Broughton, a seventeenth-century British scholar in Greek and Hebrew, wrote the following review: "[The Authorized Version] was sent to me to censure: which bred in me a sadness which will grieve me while I breath, it is so ill done. Tell his Majesty that I would rather be rent in pieces by wild horses, then that any such translation by my consent would be urged upon the poor churches. . . . The cockles of the seashores, and the leaves of the forest, and the grains of the poppy may as well be numbered as the gross errors of this Bible."[1]

The power of tradition is sometimes put on the same level as the authority of the Scriptures.[2] There is, however, a major difference between the authority of the Scriptures and that of tradition. Tradition is a human achievement. Scripture is of divine origin. Scripture, therefore, needs to be taken seriously. We readily refer to the Scriptures as a guide and counselor in various life situations. But does Scripture give us any indication as to a specific style of music to be used in church? We saw earlier that Scripture does not, in fact, refer to matters of style. It does, however, give us strong information about improper attitudes with regard to worship and lifestyle. If we want to use the biblical argument, we must stay within the limits of what Scripture tells us and not invent things that are not addressed by it.

Still another way tradition is misused is in the declaration that the old way is the way things have always been done in church. First, this declaration refers to man-made criteria. Second, using denominational tradition as an argument to justify the status quo in matters of worship is in direct contradiction with the historical reality of the Seventh-day Adventist Church. With respect to matters of music, James White distinguished himself as a fervent advocate of new songs and hymns. He actively encouraged people to write new hymns, especially ones related to the Seventh-day Adventist message. He even organized competitions for hymn writing. Also, from the time of the early editions, Seventh-day Adventist hymnals have contained a number of hymns based on secular songs.[3] Both James and Ellen White were fervent advocates for the use of instrumental music, especially the organ—and this in spite of the then general hostile attitude toward the use of this instrument.[4] Likewise, Ellen White encouraged the use of the guitar in church, as it was a popular instrument in those times for the accompaniment of singing.[5]

As far as worship style is concerned, Ronald D. Graybill's article "Enthusiasm in Early Adventist Worship" presents early worship practices among the Seventh-day Adventist pioneers, who "had livelier services than many of us would be comfortable with today."[6] Already, then, worship practices in the Seventh-day Adventist Church were subject to cultural context, affected by new understandings of the biblical truths and Seventh-day Adventist theology, and shaped by an ongoing concern on the part of the leaders to balance out excesses and extremes. The lesson to learn from this example is that change *did* take place within Seventh-day Adventist practices of worship, and what we are doing today is not based upon a long-standing, unique tradition of worship.

The Power of the Past

The general idea that only the past is valuable and worthy of interest is a product of the Romantic period (nineteenth century). The idea grew out of an evolutionary understanding of the world as an organic complex in which the past represented the original state when things were still pure and unspoiled. The past soon came to be seen as the "golden age," and things from times gone by quickly acquired a superior status. In many ways today, we are still the heirs of the Romantic spirit and are indebted to the same ideas.

These theories were also applied to matters of worship and music, a field in which tradition already occupies an important place. It is, then, easy to understand why the music of the past was, and still is, given such a predominant position in churches.

As we face this strong grip of the past on the music in church, why not rethink the matter with a slightly different slant? What would happen if churches adopted the *spirit* of the past rather than the products of the past? The spirit of the past in matters of music was, interestingly, marked by constant renewal and reinvention. Before the nineteenth century no church musician would ever have thought of performing music from the past. Composers such as Josquin des Prez, Giovanni Pierluigi da Palestrina, Heinrich Isaac, Claudio Monteverdi, Heinrich Schütz, Johann Sebastian Bach, Anton Bruckner, etc., would not perform someone else's music for a church service. Reference to music from the past existed, of course, but it was done either in the form of borrowing themes or entire passages from the works of earlier composers as the basis for new compositions, or through allusions to prior music. In reality, many composers toiled away at composing something new for every Sunday. Under the constraint of time they would occasionally borrow from their own repertoire and piece together a new composition. But never would it come to the mind of J. S. Bach, for example, to perform a Telemann cantata for the Sunday morning service in his church. This practice came into use in the nineteenth century, under the influence of the revival movement of "old" music, which started with Mendelssohn's discovery and performance of Bach's *Saint Matthew Passion.*

In the light of these *traditional* practices, we might today wonder where we have left the music of the twentieth and twenty-first centuries. The bulk of church music performed in today's churches belongs to the nineteenth-century tradition and before. Why aren't we listening to the great works written for the church by composers of the twentieth and twenty-first centuries? And what about the vast repertoire of twentieth-century hymns so conspicuously absent from our church hymnals?

Antiquity is not a value in itself. While tradition is often a matter of comfort and ease, it must be put to the test in the light of biblical truth. The concept of culture is very readily put to such a test, and tradition needs to be submitted to the same procedure in order to find out whether it is a repository for old habits or, on the contrary, holds deep meaning.

As we become aware of the reasons behind the power of the past by looking at the origins of this infatuation, we are more inclined to understand the significance of the present and the value of music and worship practices that grow out of our own time and concerns. An objective look at the situation helps to demystify the grip of the past and dedramatize the difficulty of the process of change.

A brief look at the history of worship practices in the Bible and the history of musical practices throughout the history of the church confirms the constant presence of change. These illustrations help us to go further on the path of conquering our fears and prejudices about change in worship and worship music.

Changes in Biblical Worship Through History

As we look at the biblical worship practices, the Scriptures reveal not only a multiplicity of worship gestures but also a series of developments and modifications. These developments took place as a result of change that happened on the levels of theology, society, and culture. As the people of Israel went through their various sociopolitical stages, from a family of nomads to a people, to a sedentary nation, their worship practices also took on different shapes.

In the Garden of Eden Adam and Eve worshipped God face-to-face (Genesis 3:8). After the Fall they came to worship at the east gates of the Paradise, where the cherubim stood with their flaming swords (Genesis 3:24). Later, in the time of the patriarchs, worship took place around altars erected in specific places (Genesis 8:20; 12:7; 28:18; Exodus 24:4). As Israel became a people and then a nation, they worshipped in the tabernacle (Exodus 40:34) and in the Temple (2 Chronicles 5:13, 14). As a result of the destruction of the first Temple, synagogue worship took the place of Temple worship.[7] After the destruction of the second Temple, the early church adopted for its own worship the practices and styles of the synagogue.[8]

The biblical account of worship practices witnesses, then, to a variety of ways to worship. It is clear that the *essence* of all these types of worship remained always the same, while the *form* of the worship was modified according to changes that had taken place in the structure of the believers' lives or society.

Similar developments may also be observed with regard to the biblical practices of music for adoration. Earlier periods showed simpler uses of music—both individual and congregational—such as singing with the harp (Genesis 31:27) and acclamations (Numbers 10:35, 36; Judges 7:18). The later sedentary period featured a full-fledged body of liturgy utilizing the psalms and a sophisticated structure of music (1 Chronicles 25). This, in turn, was to be enriched by a new repertoire of songs in New Testament times, the hymns (1 Corinthians 14:26; Colossians 3:16).

The scriptural examples of worship and the account of the musical practices during those occasions certainly confirm that change happened in matters of worship practices during biblical times. This pattern of change then continued in the church at large, especially with regard to its music.

Changes in Church Music Through History

The past struggles of the church with music confirm that our present-day situation is not new and that we are not the first ones to encounter the difficulties of change. Indeed, we were able to observe how the church encountered issues similar to those we face today—for instance, the insurgence of the popular element into the church. The recurrence of this particular problem indicates that there might be a common context to all these situations.

Interest in secular models generally occurred, in a striking manner, during times of religious revival. At those times the pattern of borrowing became very conspicuous. The early Christians, the fourth-century Arians, Francis of Assisi, the great Reformers Jan Hus and Martin Luther, and, later, the Pietists all borrowed tunes from the secular world to ensure that there were songs ready and available to express and teach the newfound truths. In subsequent periods these reformers were followed by the Wesley brothers, William Booth, the great American tradition of camp meeting and gospel songs, and the disciples and successors of the Jesus movement in the 1960s. The common desire in all these instances was to put the music back into the hands of the people, to involve them more actively in the experience of worship.

Change has, thus, been a fundamental reality in the practice of worship and music. But how did the church handle this change, and what can we learn from the past for today's situation?

Reactions of the Church Toward Change

Negative reactions toward change and the introduction of new elements in worship came not only from the leaders of the church. Some negative reactions originated right in the midst of the congregation. The following examples illustrate various fears and concerns on the part of church members in the face of upcoming change. Here again, the issues addressed were still the same. They mainly dealt with the way the singing was done in the church and with the use of instruments in worship.

In the mid-seventeenth century efforts were made by the Puritans to improve the poor state of singing in the churches. Most people at that time were illiterate, thus not able to sing from the Psalter. The practice of singing psalms had degenerated to the point at which worshippers would sing the psalms at their own paces and harmonize or decorate the tune according to their own fancies. This resulted in a kind of semiimprovised chaos. Here is an eyewitness account of the effect produced by this manner of singing, also called the Old Way: "I have observed in many places, one Man is upon this Note, while another is a Note before him, which produces something so hideous and disorderly, as is beyond Expression bad. . . . And besides, no two Men in the Congregation quaver alike, or together; which sounds in the Ears of a good Judge, like *five hundred* different Tunes roared out at the same Time."[9]

Some individuals hoped to improve this poor singing manner by introducing a new way of singing, called Lining Out or the New Way. In this new way, the minister or some other person would read or sing the psalm line by line. The congregation would echo each line, imitating the leader's singing.[10] Though the method was well-intended and efficient, it was badly received, as can be seen from a singing teacher's own words: "A mighty spirit came lately upon abundance of our people to reform their singing, which was degenerated in our assemblies to an irregularity which made a jar in the ears of the more curious and skilful singers. . . . Tho' in the polite city of Boston this design [the new way of singing] met with general acceptance, in the country, where they have more of the rustic, some numbers of elder and angry people bore zealous testimonies against these wicked innovations, and . . . not only . . . call the singing of these Christians a worshipping of the devil, but also they would run out of the meetinghouse at the beginning of the exercise."[11]

In 1712 Thomas Symmes, who had been trying to teach people to read music and to improve their singing in church, wrote a pamphlet in which he replied to the strong objections voiced against the new method. Here are some of these objections to the New Way: "1. It is a new way, an unknown tongue. 2. It is not so melodious as the usual way. 3. There are so many tunes that we shall never have done learning them. 4. The practice creates disturbances, and causes people to behave indecently and disorderly. 5. It is Quakerish and Popish and introductive of instrumental music. 6. It is a needless way since our fathers got to heaven without it. 7. They are a company of young upstarts that fall in with this way, and some of them are lewd and loose persons."[12]

This story demonstrates the difficulty of the process of change. Some congregations refused change even when the change clearly improved the worship experience. Because the method was new and not "needed" earlier to worship the Lord, change was difficult to implement. As time went by, however, the New Way found its way into other churches, and improvement finally could take place.

A similar experience happened in a North American church as it considered acquiring an organ for the worship services. Edward S. Ninde relates the following incident that happened in Boston during the nineteenth century. In those times most churches did not accept the use of instruments in worship. Organs were not allowed either since they were commonly used in theaters for entertainment. But one progressive church went against the established tradition. Here is the story: "Though the demand for better music was becoming increasingly insistent, the non-Episcopal Churches were very reluctant to admit organs. An English gentleman made an offer of 500 pounds to the first 'dissenting' church that would venture on the innovation. . . . Finally the Brattle Street Church surrendered to the inevitable and decided to have an organ, but even after the order had been sent to England and the instrument was on its way, the congregation was torn with bitter strife. One wealthy member besought with tears that the house of God be not desecrated, promising to refund the entire cost of the organ if the evil thing might be thrown to the bottom of Boston Harbor. But gradually opposition subsided."[13]

Another incident, in Germany, demonstrates how churches in the time of Johann Sebastian Bach reacted when new instruments were introduced in their worship services. Here again, the fear was one of syncretism of the secular with the sacred. Surprisingly, this incident had nothing to do with the use of popular music in church, but happened within the sphere of classical music in a church setting: "When in a large town [Bach's] Passion Music was done for the first time, with 12 violins, many oboes, bassoons, and other instruments, many people were astonished and did not know what to make of it. In the pew of a noble family in church, many Ministers and Noble Ladies were present, who sang the first Passion Chorale out of their books with great devotion. But when this theatrical music began, all these people were thrown into the greatest bewilderment, looked at each other and said: 'What will come of this?' An old widow of the nobility said: 'God save us, my children! It's just as if one were at an Opera Comedy.' But everyone was genuinely displeased by it and voiced just complaints against it."[14]

We certainly are able to recognize ourselves in the reactions to the introduction of new elements in the worship service, as encountered in these stories. The stories make us aware that it is not necessarily *what* is introduced that causes a problem, but rather the fact *that* something new is introduced. What are some possible reasons for our vulnerability in these situations of change?

Tension and Uneasiness in the Face of Worship Practices

In matters of worship there has always been tension. Tension is brought about by the particular nature of the partners who meet in worship: the Holy God and the human individual. Those who, in their dealing with change and renewal in worship, opt to rule out the voice of the people refuse to live and work within this tension. They are unable to reconcile the participation factor with the lofty ideal of worship. To acknowledge this tension, to accept to live with it, and to struggle through it are the first steps toward a balanced worship service, one that includes both the vertical and the horizontal dimensions.

Three subject areas in regard to church music have greatly contributed to the uneasiness, opposition, and misunderstanding that characterize today's discussions about music: (1) the purpose of church music, (2) the perennial and exclusive status of high church music, and (3) the relationship between sacred and secular music in matters of worship. The resolution of these issues—as they are put into perspective and a better understanding of their nature is reached—help to reconcile the tension between the lofty ideal and the reality of human participation in worship.

Conflicting Views on the Purpose of Church Music

For some, the purpose of church music lies primarily in its capacity to elevate thoughts and respond to the transcendental aspect of religion. Church music, according to this view, belongs to the domain of the aesthetic and the abstract. Emphasis is put on the intellectual depth and symbolic content of the music. These characteristics are predominantly found in classical music. The overlap of secular and sacred is not perceived, here, as an issue, even though both the sacred pieces and their secular counterparts use the same style characteristics.

For others, music functions essentially as a means of expression for the believer. It is situated at the emotional and experiential levels and represents the human aspect of religion. Here, interest is focused on simple, direct style, enabling the people to understand easily and to join in naturally. While the dichotomy between secular and sacred is often perceived as a threat, it also has been understood as a surmountable obstacle, in the sense that new meaning can be given to a secular model: the world can be transformed by Christ.

Both views of the purpose of church music have been proved right, even though they seem to be at opposite ends of the spectrum. When defenders of one or the other become antagonists, it is because they forget about the tension that should come with authentic worship. The contenders believe each view should be implemented exclusively, not in combination with the other. In reality, the two positions are not that far removed from each other, and this fact should already be helpful in reconciling them.

The Exclusive Status of High Church Music

The term *high church music* generally refers to a style that predominantly relies on classical works from the past and present, performed with the traditional resources of that style—organ, piano, choir, and the instruments of the orchestra. High church music is typically produced by professional leaders who work either with other professional or semiprofessional musicians. The music is mainly presented for the congregation to listen to, not participate in.

As one looks at the development of church music, one finds out that the high church style was not an exclusive norm, as many would like to believe. High church traditions always ran parallel to a popular *low church* strain that consisted typically of congregational song. Within the context of the Catholic Church the popular component flourished outside the official liturgical rituals. Within the Protestant churches it was an integral part of the services. In the latter case the congregational participation was generally incorporated into the music performed by the choir or organ in the form of singing chorales. Both the high church and low church styles fulfilled their respective roles and coexisted side by side.[15]

The split between the high church and low church styles came about during the nineteenth century. The quality standards of church music had, by then, greatly declined, partly because of a waning interest in traditional religion on the part of musicians, and partly because of an ongoing process of secularization. Moreover, these were times filled with nostalgia for the past, and the great masterworks of church music from earlier centuries were elevated to a higher rank. Also, the division of the religious institutions into established churches and evangelical movements played a determining role in creating the ever-widening gap between high church music and low church music. Established churches favored the symbolic element of high church music over the rhetorical/emotional approach that characterized the music of the evangelical trend.

The issue of high versus low church music styles resulted from the collision of two different outlooks on worship music: one outlook was informed by the lofty ideal for sacred worship, while the other outlook was concerned with the human experience of worship. Rather than working toward a well-balanced blend of the two outlooks on worship, supporters of one or the other sharply disagreed over which outlook was superior.

The Relationship Between Sacred and Secular Music

Our presentation about the music of the Reformation provided an extensive discussion on the interrelationship between the secular and the sacred in matters of music. I refer the reader to that section for a refresher.[16] It is appropriate at this point to remind the reader of the dramatic changes that have occurred in the relationship between sacred music and secular music since the time of the Reformation. In an age of increasing secularism and a growing influence of popular culture on every aspect of life, it is imperative to raise the questions of appropriateness and quality. Today's lack of understanding of worship and the scarcity of appreciation of excellence have made it more difficult, though not impossible, to tackle the relationship between the sacred and the secular. Addressing this relationship is, indeed, a valid pursuit, and we should not deceive ourselves into dismissing the whole problem in a quick, unconsidered manner. We still live, speak, sing, and act in this world and cannot avoid carrying our everyday language, both verbal and musical, into our worship experiences. The tension between the vertical and the horizontal will always be present—it will always challenge us to be resolved. Our times call for more awareness, more discernment, and more commitment as we try to bring together the two poles.

We have observed how those in the past wrestled and dealt with the problem of change in church music, and we have been reassured that today's issues in worship and music are certainly not new. They are representative of the same desire for revival on the part of the church that has been in existence through-out history. History has shown that there are two ways to respond to this desire: resistance or embracement. Resistance created rupture and division. Embracement, when done rightly, became a powerful tool for renewal.

Here is my invitation to all those who deal with the issue of change in music in worship and who have a say in the discussion: rather than resist change, embrace it, utilize it, and make it meaningful by actively participating in the process of shaping the new elements while refreshing the old ones.

---

[1] Quoted in F. F. Bruce, The English Bible (Oxford, U.K.: Oxford University Press, 1961), p. 107.

[2] See, for instance, the way in which the church hymnal is considered, by a number of churchgoers, as being on the same level of sacredness as the Bible.

[3] Cf. Wayne Hooper's extensive report on SDA hymnody, "Seventh-day Adventist Hymnody," in Companion to the Seventh-day Adventist Hymnal, Wayne Hooper and Edward E. White, eds. (Washington, D.C.: Review and Herald Publishing Assn., 1988), pp. 11-43. See also James R. Nix, Early Advent Singing (Hagerstown, Md.: Review and Herald Publishing Assn., 1994), pp. 11-13.

[4] One of the last wishes of Henry N. White, the eldest son of James and Ellen White, before his death was to have his brother Edson play to him on the melodeon (a small parlor organ). See Adelia P. Patten, "Brief Narrative of the Life, Experience, and Last Sickness of Henry N. White," in Appeal to the Youth (Battle Creek, Mich.: Steam Press of the Seventh-day Adventist Publishing Assn, 1864), p. 23, quoted by Ronald J. Graybill, "Enthusiasm in Early Adventist Worship," Ministry, October 1991, p. 12.

[5] Ellen G. White, in Historical Sketches of the Foreign Missions of the Seventh-day Adventists (Basle, Switzerland: Imprimerie Polyglotte, 1886), p. 195; quoted by Ronald D. Graybill, "Enthusiasm in Early Adventist Worship," Ministry, October 1991, p. 12.

[6] Graybill, "Enthusiasm in Early Adventist Worship," pp. 10-12.

[7] A. Z. Idelsohn, Jewish Liturgy and Its Development, pp. 16, 17.

[8] See Paul F. Bradshaw, Daily Prayer in the Early Church: A Study of the Origin and Early Development of the Divine Office (New York: Oxford University Press, 1982), p. 25.

[9] Thomas Walter, The Grounds and Rules of Musick Explained: Or, An Introduction to the Art of Singing by Note, Fitted to the Meanest Capacities (Boston: Printed by Benjamin Mecom, 1721), p. 5.

[10] This method of singing is still practiced today in a number of Baptist churches in the southern United States.

[11] Cotton Mather, "Letter to Thomas Hollis, Jr., November 5, 1723," in Kenneth Silverman, comp., Selected Letters of Cotton Mather (Baton Rouge, La.: Louisiana State University Press, 1971), p. 376.

[12] Thomas Symmes, Utile dulci, or a Joco-Serious Dialogue Concerning Regular Singing (Boston: B. Green for Samuel Gerrish, 1723), 56 pages.

[13] Edward S. Ninde, The Story of the American Hymn (New York: Abingdon Press, 1921), pp. 96, 97.

[14] Christian Gerber, 1732, in The Bach Reader: A Life of Johann Sebastian Bach in Letters

and *Documents*, H. David and A. Mendel, eds., rev. ed. (New York: W. W. Norton, 1966), pp. 229, 230.

[15] An illustration of the coexistence of the two trends can be seen, for example, in the simultaneous occurrence, in England, of the Tractarian (Oxford) Movement and the various revival movements, such as by D. L. Moody and Ira Sankey, and the Salvation Army.

[16] See "Sacred Versus Secular in Luther's Time," pp. 179-182 of this book.

{ *In Tune With God* }

We have come to the end of our journey together. We have traveled through many places, moored our boat on several shores, and perceived and dreamed of distant horizons still to be reached. Along the way we might have touched sensitive points and raised questions and perhaps passionate reactions. Indeed, in this discussion on music in worship, disagreement should be expected. For although we all worship the same God, we have all been created different. Not only our personalities are different but also our cultures and our personal experiences with God. But what is important, ultimately, is to find ourselves in tune with God. That was the purpose of the whole journey. It is, therefore, important that we pause and reflect on what it means to be in tune with God.

To be in tune with God means first of all to play in tune. Musicians, who play instruments with variable intonation, such as string instruments or some woodwind instruments, know how much work and effort go into achieving good intonation. To play in tune means not only to play without wrong notes but also to play the notes just right. Even the subtlest nuances of sound are worked out to the utmost to bring the right color or shade of sound, the right articulation, and the right emphasis. To play in tune is a lifelong task for the musician, who constantly needs to check the sound that is produced against the highest standards. To play in tune requires long and fastidious preparation until every note is well thought through and worked out, and falls in its right place. The first lesson, then, is an invitation to play in tune with the music.

To be in tune with God also means to play in harmony with a group. Playing in tune in a band or in an orchestra implies listening to the other players.

The ability to listen to the others is of primary importance—not only to listen to them but also to adjust one's own sound to theirs. The process starts right at the beginning of the performance, as all the players tune their instruments to the pitch given by the oboe. This is a process that takes time and constant readjustment. Everyone waits until the last player finishes tuning his or her instrument. Then, during the performance, players continue to listen to their fellow musicians so as to be able to blend their sound with that of the rest of the group and to create harmonious music. This is an important discipline because it trains us in humility. This exercise increases our capacity to receive and respect the contribution of the other players, and teaches us that our own performance has no value by itself, but makes sense only in connection with the other performances.

To be in tune with God is also to be fully aware of the *listener*, for whom the music is played. Every musician desires to offer the audience an experience into which they can enter, and of which they can partake, a performance that is pleasing to them. To play in tune goes beyond playing the right notes; it is more than being in tune with the music and the musicians. Ultimately, it means to be in tune with the hearts and the singing voices of those for whom and with whom the music is performed. This lesson obliges us to go outside of ourselves to meet the people where they are—musicians as well as nonmusicians, people like us as well as people of another culture, age, or education. It obliges us to communicate with them and touch them and share with them the musical message we have ourselves received. This exercise calls us to both responsibility and service. Responsibility, for we have the duty to educate and help other people reach that level of enjoyment and understanding. Service, for we have the obligation to respond to the needs and the various sensitivities of the listeners and worshippers. This music is not only our music; it should also resonate in their hearts and in their voices as *their* music.

Most important, in tune with God means that we bring our music not only to express and enhance our worship experiences but also to place ourselves in accord with the great God, Creator of heaven and earth. Music in worship is, then, not just a mere aesthetic work or a social event. Music speaks the word of God. This means that it brings more than our own particular touch or our brilliant performance. The Spirit finds its way through the sounds and the emotions that are generated in that sacred moment and surprises us, fills us, and elevates us to the absolute that is beyond our words and ordinary thoughts. Therefore, music in worship is a task that should unite us under the great God, who transcends and harmonizes all the voices and all the songs. *To be in tune with God* contains all the other lessons of what it means to be in tune. It appeals to us to work in tune with the sublime music, in tune with the other artists, and also in tune with the diverse members of our worshipping congregations. Instead of producing tensions and disputes, music in worship should therefore bring to us love and harmony, for "all things were created by Him and for Him. He is before all things and in Him all things hold together" (Colossians 1:16, 17).

Sanctuary
Worship-leading Guidelines

Our goal is to provide an atmosphere in which a worship experience can take place.

Excellence honors God. We seek to bring our best before Him, including our talents and hearts.

Prepare yourself through prayer. Such a ministry can be properly performed only by members whose lives are sustained by prayer and the anointing of the Holy Spirit for their appointed roles.

Prepare yourself through practice. Know your parts as well as possible; have more than simply a general familiarity with the material.

Show by your own example the appropriate attitude of reverence for the worship service: bow your head during prayer, etc., remembering that we are in the service of God.

Fully participate in the worship experience: join in the singing when not playing; engage with the worshippers through eye contact, facial expression, etc.

Dress appropriately, which includes no jewelry except wedding bands. Men, please wear nice shirts, dress slacks or suit, dress shoes. Ladies, please wear knee length skirts, a modest neckline, and covered shoulders. Please check with the worship director and/or media director regarding colors and patterns.

Thank you for your willingness to participate and offer your talents in service to the Lord!

Worship Survey

1. I would like:

Less	Just Right	More	
☐	☐	☐	Contemporary Praise
☐	☐	☐	Hymns
☐	☐	☐	Responsive Readings
☐	☐	☐	Interviews/Testimonies
☐	☐	☐	Video Clips
☐	☐	☐	Variety in Prayer
☐	☐	☐	Organ Music
☐	☐	☐	Choir Music
☐	☐	☐	Band/Orchestra Music
☐	☐	☐	Solos
☐	☐	☐	Congregational Participation
☐	☐	☐	Children's Story
☐	☐	☐	Special Features (art, poetry, drama, etc.)

2. Here are some suggestions I have for next year's worship:

3. Here are some suggestions I have for next year's preaching:

Age_____

☐ Male   ☐ Female
☐ Student   ☐ Faculty/Staff   ☐ Community

Learn From the
Master Teacher

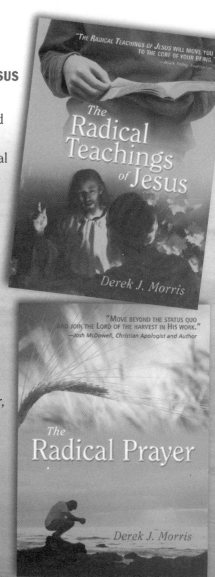

THE RADICAL TEACHINGS OF JESUS
Derek Morris

Jesus ignored human traditions and presented His listeners with God's truth. Encounter some of the radical ideas He taught that defied conventional wisdom and customs then— and that continue to do so today. Hardcover, 978-0-8127-0498-3.

THE RADICAL PRAYER
Derek Morris

Are you ready to pray a prayer that God will answer with a definite yes? Discover an incredibly powerful prayer that enables God to change the world—through you. Hardcover, 978-0-8127-0486-0.

"THE RADICAL TEACHINGS OF JESUS WILL MOVE YOU TO THE CORE OF YOUR BEING."
—Mark Finley, Evangelist

The Radical Teachings *of* Jesus

Derek J. Morris

"MOVE BEYOND THE STATUS QUO AND JOIN THE LORD OF THE HARVEST IN HIS WORK."
—Josh McDowell, Christian Apologist and Author

The Radical Prayer

Derek J. Morris

Experience . . .
Vibrant,
Authentic
WORSHIP

Majesty

Worship is a vibrant, ongoing, authentic encounter with God— a life-changing experience! In these pages Joseph Kidder shares scriptural principles to guide you into a genuine worship experience that will transform your soul and leave you hungry for God's presence. 978-0-8280-2423-5.